OVER AND OUT

John Gascoigne, New Zealand-born and raised, has worked in Melbourne-based media, including the former *Herald*, for which he was a court reporter and political correspondent in Canberra; the ABC, in its radio and television news departments; and Pacific Publications, for which he wrote and edited on the national magazines *TV Week* and *Australasian Post*. Before working in Canberra, John played two seasons with the St Kilda Cricket Club, and from 1983 until 1998 he umpired around the parks of Melbourne. When *Post* relocated to Sydney, John joined the staff of the regional daily, the *Bendigo Advertiser*, and became its feature writer. In 2001, *Nuggets: Golden and Human*, a book of his stories about 'characters and icons' of central Victoria, was published.

OVER AND OUT

Cricket umpires tell their stories

Compiled by John Gascoigne

Foreword by Doug Walters

Penguin Books

Penguin Books

Published by the Penguin Group
Penguin Books Australia Ltd
250 Camberwell Road, Camberwell, Victoria 3124, Australia
Penguin Books Ltd
80 Strand, London WC2R 0RL, England
Penguin Putnam Inc.
375 Hudson Street, New York, New York 10014, USA
Penguin Books, a division of Pearson Canada
10 Alcorn Avenue, Toronto, Ontario, Canada M4V 3B2
Penguin Books (NZ) Ltd
Cnr Rosedale and Airborne Roads, Albany, Auckland, New Zealand
Penguin Books (South Africa) (Pty) Ltd
24 Sturdee Avenue, Rosebank, Johannesburg 2196, South Africa
Penguin Books India (P) Ltd
11, Community Centre, Panchsheel Park, New Delhi 110 017, India

First published by Penguin Books Australia 2002

10 9 8 7 6 5 4 3 2 1

Design by Brad Maxwell, Penguin Design Studio
Cover image © Getty Images
Typeset in 10.5/15 pt Giovanni Book by Midland Typesetters, Maryborough, Victoria
Printed and bound in Australia by McPherson's Printing Group, Maryborough, Victoria

National Library of Australia
Cataloguing-in-Publication data:

Over and out : Cricket umpires tell their stories.

ISBN 0 14 300041 1.

1. Cricket – Umpiring – Anecdotes. 2. Test matches (Cricket) – Anecdotes.
I. Gascoigne, John.

796.3583092

www.penguin.com.au

To Jocelyn

Contents

Foreword

One of the first statements I ever heard from an umpire, that turned out to be absolutely true, was 'I've never made a mistake in my entire umpiring career.' I thought about it for a while and came to the conclusion that the ego of this chap was a little over the top. However, I didn't forget his statement during the match, and while we were sharing a beer together afterwards, I queried a couple of the decisions he had given and asked whether he still stood by his earlier claim. He replied, 'You check the scorebook and have a look in the paper tomorrow morning. That will give you the proof my rulings must have been correct.' Eventually, I acknowledged that he was right and that his words represented good advice for any cricketer who feels like questioning the decisions of the umpire. In other words, accept the decision (he's doing his best) and don't argue.

I never had any intention of becoming an umpire and feel fortunate that I haven't. I simply don't fancy the umpire's difficult role. Thus I have the utmost respect for anyone prepared to stand in that position and am pleased to see that a couple of our ex-players have been brave enough to take it on. I'm sure they will learn that it is not as easy as they may have first thought, but I do wish them every success.

Fortunately, cricket's Laws have changed very little over the years. However, the advent of video replays has given birth to the use of a third umpire. I am a little concerned about how far this modern innovation will go because, just recently, I have heard some discussions about whether to use the third umpire to adjudicate on lbw decisions, and I think this particular Law should be the last one to be interfered with. I guess only time will tell whether my worries are well-founded. I do think that making an umpire's job easier is very worthwhile, so apart from the lbw decision, I'm all for using the third umpire. I'm also in favour of the presence, since 1994, of neutral umpires, as that helps diminish allegations of bias, and I approve of anything that reduces arguments in the cricket world.

People seem to forget that umpires are human and live normal lives outside the cricket grounds. I have had some great times with their brigade, both while I was playing cricket and since my retirement. In fact, I still enjoy reflecting on some of the umpiring decisions I've witnessed. I'm sure all umpires, along with players and spectators, have favourite players. I can't remember the name of one Indian umpire we came across during the 1969 Australian tour of India, but he made no secret of which player was his favourite. He was waiting to greet everyone as we hopped off the team bus on the first morning of a tour match, and his first words were, 'Where is Mr Mallett?' Ashley Mallett was our off-spin bowler on that tour and this umpire was obviously impressed by his skill. Once he found Ashley, he took hold of his hands and informed him that he was his favourite cricketer. His words weren't wasted on our captain, Bill Lawry.

The wickets deteriorated very quickly in India and not too many sides would be sent in to bat first – the trick being to avoid batting on a spin-friendly, fourth innings pitch of the crumbling, dusty kind notorious in that nation. So spinners are of prime importance, sometimes even from the start of a match. Bill lost the toss that day and we, of course, knew we'd be required to take the field. The two opening bowlers had delivered their mandatory two overs each to take the shine off the ball when Bill tossed it to Ashley so he could bowl from the end where 'his mate' stood. This particular wicket began turning at right angles from the very first ball Ashley bowled, so it didn't take long for him to put his new-found friend's admiration to the test. His second delivery to the opening batsman spun so far that the poor man decided his best form of defence was attack and that he should get down the wicket to Ashley's bowling to negate the spin by hitting the ball on the full or half volley. Ashley's third delivery brought the batsman charging several paces down the wicket. But 'Rowdy', as he was known, had seen him coming and, with the great skill he had, bowled this ball a little higher and a little wider than the previous two. The batsman never quite covered the pitch of the ball, which spun back at him, hitting his pads

We always said Ashley would never die wondering whether a batsman would have been given out, and he frequently appealed to the umpire if he thought there was even the remotest chance. He didn't let us down on this occasion either, and quickly turned to his mate to ask the question. Instantly the umpire's finger was raised. The batsman wasn't at all impressed with the decision and stood his ground for some considerable time, with Ashley's friend's finger giving him out repeatedly. I was fielding close by at mid-off at the time and the umpire walked over to me, saying, 'Mr Mallett is a really great bowler.' Because the No. 3 batsman had arrived at the crease, the opener was left with no option but to pick up his bat and depart. It was soon obvious the new batsman had watched Ashley's first three deliveries with interest, and his actions indicated he thought the only mistake the opener had made was in not getting down the wicket far enough to hit the ball on the full. As Ashley began his run-up for his fourth delivery, the No. 3 commenced his strides down the wicket. The batsman took a couple more paces than the opener before him, but Ashley had another trick up his sleeve – tossing this ball up higher, shorter and wider. As you might guess, this ball also spun back and rapped the batsman on the pads. Ashley's confidence was now higher than the ball's trajectory, and his lone appeal to his mate was deafening. Again, without delay, the finger was raised and once more the umpire made his way over to me, saying, 'I told you Mr Mallett was a great bowler, didn't I?' I'm not sure how Ashley missed his hat-trick as I'm certain he never had a better chance to achieve one than on that day.

I imagine most cricketers have their favourite umpires. Dickie Bird was my favourite and, I think, the favourite of many others. Some umpires like to talk to the players, and some don't. It's their prerogative, but Dickie was one of the first in my experience to often do so; he loved a chat. I believe the players appreciated this, and it seemed to result in fewer on-field incidents of disagreement. We all had the utmost respect for Dickie, and I believe that's the way players should treat all umpires.

I heartily commend John Gascoigne and his umpiring colleagues for writing *Over and Out* and shedding some light on this multi-faceted vocation. It's a great read, and players and cricket fans alike will get many laughs as part of their enjoyment. I also hope the book gives readers a better understanding of the challenging and difficult role of the two people who stand in the middle of our cricket grounds and have to concentrate on every single ball bowled during a match.

Doug Walters

Part 1

Around the Parks
by John Gascoigne

Hard Lessons at Coburg College

A cartoon in the English magazine *Punch* in the 1950s showed a gentleman of military bearing coming in to bat. With his chest puffed out, he takes guard, puts on his gloves, twirls his bat, and inspects the field as though its members were on parade and he the regimental sergeant major. In its evocation of the English class system, the cartoon batsman represents the 'Gentlemen' of upper-class gentility in a match against the 'Players' (general riff-raff). After taking an age to wordlessly stamp his authority, the puffed-up squire is skittled by the first ball. With stumps askew behind him and cheeks glowing, he trudges back to the pavilion, now barely taller than the dandelions in the outfield.

I'd have thought it a tableau long-forgotten, but the image flashes to mind after a match in Coburg in 1996, a hook shot away from Melbourne's Pentridge Prison. That establishment closed as a slammer in 1999 and has been partly preserved with a heritage listing while being converted to commercial premises and residential housing. The language in this A-grade match is as blue as the stone in the jail walls, and the testosterone is flying. This contest is as hairy-chested as they get.

One of the opening bowlers is a genuine quick, and a red-blooded opener stands two feet out of his crease to get at him all the quicker. Thump! A straight drive lands in a clump of agapanthus beyond the boundary.

Harsh, monosyllabic words are exchanged and, as often

happens in these situations, a visceral tension of clashing egos and talents builds uncomfortably. Those not immediately involved in the heat of battle tense in readiness for a possible punch-up.

The nearby prison walls, which had regularly overseen the resolution of such tensions, now seem domestically benign, because the majority of players won't allow any nonsense. They have jousted before, shared confidences and joked over a beer or ten after many such battles. And there are just enough wise heads to prevail now, their ribald gagging defusing the detonator of atavistic male rivalry that transcends the innocence of bat and ball.

Ted, the belter of that six, is about to become the victim of his own self-belief, elevated to what the Greeks called hubris. Just as it appears he's going to run down the opposition total off his own bat, he bunts the ball a few metres distant, and – as though any sudden movement would suggest he was beholden to anyone but himself – neglects to manoeuvre back into his crease. Ever so gently, his wicket is thrown down.

Umpiring at square leg, I'm invited to give him out. Ted is clearly affronted by the appeal – as though he's left his crease merely to pat down a piece of turf. No such luck, Sunshine. You're playing on matting atop a concrete slab.

In the tactful form prescribed for this occasion, I ask the fielding captain whether he is proceeding with his appeal. He says he is; my finger goes up, and this unleashes words about propagation from the departing Ted. I've no doubt the words are directed at me, but officious reaction, I've learnt from experience, will elicit strenuous denials at a subsequent tribunal where rules of the courts of common law, such as giving evidence on oath, don't apply. By taking the route of official umbrage all the way to a tribunal, I will probably hear: 'I don't remember saying any such thing, sir, but if I did say it, I'd have been talking to me. I remember I was very disappointed and angry with myself . . .' etc.

In truth, in his abuse of language, Ted had been acting entirely within the context of the occasion. Amid the dust, heat and flies of the summer's day, the cricket had been skilful; played hard – almost brutally. Being run out in such foolish and timid fashion represented serious loss of face, and that is what this contest was about: tribalism and excessive male pride taken to the level of non-contact warfare, all conducted within the laws of this paradoxically gentle game. And Ted's demise was so jarringly effete and out of place that he could only cope with it, and preserve some pride, by emitting a string of oaths as he walked across the battle zone to the anonymity of the boundary.

The next day, I umpire a match involving teams consisting almost entirely of players from the subcontinent. As with several such elevens in this Sunday competition, one of the sides contains a single Anglo-Saxon, and there's a fascination in watching this bloke being ordered to bowl into the wind, his workhorse duty invoking, to my amusement, a reversal of the stone-cast racial roles. This contest is much less intense, much more fun, and at the end, when the Indian batsmen successfully complete a run chase, the vanquished Sri Lankans stand aside to applaud them off the field.

It crosses my mind to write to the club congratulating it on its sportsmanship. In the end, I decide against it – perhaps that would compromise an umpire's presumed neutrality, or maybe I'm just lazy. In any case, such sportsmanship is commonplace among the Sri Lankans. The first time I umpired one of their teams, to my amazement a bowler apologised to the batsman and then to me after I'd turned down an appeal for lbw. It's happened numerous times since.

Cricket, I've come to believe, is a game not just of glorious uncertainty, but of striking contrasts.

No Teamwork, No 'Ton'

Umpires, by the nature of things, are spectators, too. The point was reinforced by our umpires' adviser before the usual sodden start to this season. 'Get out there and enjoy your cricket!,' orders the adviser, an affable man who explains to us his reluctance to include his phone number in the reams of written paraphernalia that clutter every umpire's season. He used to be a prison officer at Pentridge, and he's not everyone's best friend.

I think of his happy view of our role even as I bear the misery I bring upon myself by committing one of the unpardonables in a Sunday match between a Pakistan XI and a predominantly Sri Lankan XI of the Raiders club. The friendliness of the encounter is strained only by my glitch. I've influenced an outcome for the very reason that I'm enjoying my cricket too much. More accurately, I'm playing it vicariously; spectating rather than umpiring.

On their way to 0/191 in their one-day match, the Raiders' openers have each been dropped five or six times. Nothing goes right for the Pakistanis, who are sensitive New-Age types, their butter-handed virus becoming so rampant that they urge only encouragement of one another lest they be the next to catch it. So that raising a finger and relieving their bitter disappointment is a pleasurable response to their run-out appeal while I'm at square leg. The return from the field is stump height. The keeper has his rump to me, hiding the stumps, as his arm rips into them to send the bails flying. The batsman's at least a metre short. My finger's up, and I walk in confidently to reset the wicket.

Hang on – the batsman's standing his ground, and there's a muttering from him and his partner. Surreptitiously, I ask the keeper, 'Did the ball hit?' An affirmative is the reply. My decision stands, though I'm now harbouring uncomfortable doubts.

At tea, my fears are confirmed. The comments from the Raiders are unanimous – their mate has been dudded. I've ruined his day, and haven't done a lot for theirs. My wretchedness isn't helped when my umpiring partner, a rookie who I'm supposedly guiding through the afternoon, says to me as we walk out to start the Pakistan XI's response to 3/231 cc (compulsory closure): 'I know this isn't tennis, but could I have done anything to override your decision? I could see the 'keeper didn't take the ball, and it missed the stumps on the way through.'

'Bloody oath you could have,' I reply, while recognising that in the wretchedness of self-doubt, and eventual recognition of the truth, my body language has probably closed me off to a healthy and frank exchange between equal partners.

As the Pakistanis quickly fold for fewer than 100 and play out the match as batting practice, I think of the Law that could have brought the Raider his 100 (to match his partner's) and saved me, presumably, a very modest grading on the captain's assessment-of-umpire form. (There's a mutual assessment of captains and umpires, and, like the AFL umps in Australian rules, we spend a few minutes after stumps awarding 1–2–3 players' votes, in this case for the clubs' award nights and end-of-season booze-ups.)

All games have their 'if onlys'. Mine revolved around

Law 27, clauses 4 and 6. Clause 4 reads: 'An umpire may consult with the other umpire on a point of fact which the latter may have been in a position to see and shall then give his decision. If, after consultation, there is still doubt remaining the decision shall be in favour of the batsman.' And clause 6 states I can alter my decision, 'provided that such alteration is made promptly'.

Oh, dear. *Mea culpa,* as former US vice-president Spiro Agnew said when sprung for tax evasion. I won't go to jail, like Spiro, but I won't let myself off, either, until I've umpired my next game, fault free.

The Raiders were decent to the end. As I shook hands with their captain, he graciously rubbed in the salt: 'I wouldn't normally have minded, but he was on 97 . . .'

Coaching or Learning?

I'd thought the blow from Phillip, if and when it came, might be behind my ear, struck in my old age when I was too old to retaliate. 'An eye for an eye'. I hoped not to complain; rather to be grateful for a settling of scores and a clearer conscience.

Let's flash back to the 1980s. Armed with a Victorian Cricket Association-approved 'Frank Tyson coaching certificate', I was ostensibly coaching a Prahran under-16 team, while actually taking a crash course in the subtleties, and impossibility, of dealing with the fragile egos and hormone-charged identity crises of adolescence.

The main conflict to be resolved was, ultimately, unresolvable. After early practice and a single match, it was clear I had three players of talent; a hard talent to match their lives as kids of battling single parents. The others were keen to learn the game, but soft and pliable (especially to opposition teams), and sons of mostly well-to-do eastern suburbanites; a fact I gleaned from house-to-house meetings with the parents to obtain signatures for registration.

The question was: who to appoint as captain? James would do; the son of a lawyer in a sylvan Toorak street, who batted and spoke with the style of a chum from Eton, but who instantly raised the hackles of young Phillip, George and Walter. By round two, I was supervising two matches each Saturday morning – the official one, and the internecine rebellion waged by three against eight, by picking off their leader, James, and constantly challenging his instructions on when and where to bat, bowl and field.

Six matches in, I'd become that unspeakable coach/parent type whose vicarious involvement in the game colours its outcome and enjoyment. In my defence (a stance that already underlies this reminiscence), the club provided minimal support in the two midweek practice sessions or, more significantly, on Saturdays when other teams invariably had half-a-dozen outriding dads helping to lay out mats, umpire, and keep in check the ebullience and skylarking of their sons.

Prahran's boss that year was doubling as chairman of the Australian Cricket Board, and a leadership vacuum seemed to flow down the ranks. Two of the club's Test players, Dav Whatmore and Julien Wiener, occasionally joined the boys at practice, but English professional Derek Randall – at odds with his on-field hyperactivity – never came near, preferring to bury himself in a book when not actually holding a bat.

When the gentle but nervous club secretary of some thirty years reminded me that my team was facing relegation – a status with which the club was happy to remain unacquainted – I made my move. James was out as captain; Phillip in.

Within a fortnight, we'd made headlines. On the morning of match day, the city dailies detailed the disappearance of a valuable eighteenth-century cricket bat from the club. The same day, as he buckled his pads, Phillip was approached by two policemen, who spoke to him at length. Three nights later the bat was found – slipped under a fence into long grass near the practice nets.

More than ever, I needed Saturday assistance. Post-match, when adult help was most needed for rolling up mats, returning them and cricket gear to the club, checking and signing scorebooks, etc., I was instead doing the diplomatic rounds, apologising to parents of the opposition for my champion trio's obscene sledging, which omitted none of the 'isms' – from racism and sexism, to classism and ability-ism.

In the final match, which we had to win to avoid the dreaded demotion, I performed my 1000th forfeit of umpiring neutrality by telling Phillip, by far our most potent bowler and batsman, to bring himself on for a bowling stint at the toilet-block end. Complaining of heat exhaustion, Phillip took himself *off* to the toilet block, to drink like a camel. Only when the match was lost did he feel able to return.

I walked to my car after a typically angst-ridden apology session and found Phillip spread across the front seats, yanking at – so he later said – the seat-angle-adjustment lever. In my exhausted and furious state of mind, I interpreted his twisting action as an attempt to dismantle the seat. As he'd already dismantled our cricket team, I snapped. It took the form of a fist to his chin. His 16-year-old chin – the chin of a child, as I told myself as I sat down to write my resignation letter, having weathered a punch to the gut and hurled drink bottles as acts of solidarity by Phillip's friends, George and Walter.

Flash forward to a hot Sunday seventeen years later. A robust man, new to our umpiring ranks, approaches me as I walk to the wicket. 'You probably don't remember me,' he says. Oh, but I do. We exchange a formal greeting and a long silence. Then, almost together, we blurt out many words: me, an apology; he, a confused, even hurt, 'Why did you hit me? You said I could rest in your car – I was only adjusting the seat.'

Was he? I'd carried no memory of the incident as he related it; only regret.

For the rest of the afternoon, as sultry and unpleasant as that day long ago, I keep a wary eye on him and a safe, physical distance. But umpiring is a combined effort, and we team well. By 6 p.m. there's an unspoken mutual forgiveness; a solidarity such as I'd hoped for when I granted him the captaincy all those years ago, hoping responsibility would bring maturity. That, I see, was a faulty assumption based on amateur psychology, or on some *Boy's Own* yarn, read and misunderstood in my own adolescence.

And there it should have ended. But Phillip preferred the combat of playing. A month later he was back, in cream trousers, ball in hand, with me and my partner as umpiring bookends. And here, within the hour, was the immutability of human nature being played out by Phillip – scattering the stumps of a batsman from the subcontinent, directing him back to the pavilion with four-letter words.

As I braced myself for the old racial taunts, my colleague stepped between the players. I'd already explained to him my history with Phillip and now asked him to administer his own justice. 'Give me this over to think about it, and I'll tell you what I'm going to do,' said this schoolteacher and hardened guerrilla of the blackboard jungle as he headed to square leg to ponder.

Solomon couldn't have been wiser. The tea break ended with Phillip apologising and shaking hands with the offended batsman. It was that or face the tribunal.

It was an ideal invocation of Law 43, which is a bit like the 19th hole, where the best golf is played. Cricket's Laws expire with Law 42, but umpires' advisers equate the notional 43 with using commonsense – a commodity that deals with the regular blips and hiccups that, happening every second week, remain unprescribed by the mandarins of Marylebone.

Phillip and I were polar opposites, or so I thought for seventeen years. Yet subsequent events caused me to question that; clearly, we both had short fuses. I hope Phillip found his niche in the game, and in the larger game of life.

Politburo Nights

I never attended a meeting of the old Soviet Union's politburo, so I can't swear that my umpire association's meetings are exactly like the former grey assemblies of old Reds in Moscow. But dammit, they can be boring! Thirty minutes, max, of genuine business is drawn out to two hours by codgers of the down-under gerontocracy spinning ancient yarns and dishing out saccharine bonhomie like monarchical Rotarians.

So it follows that as chairman Max droned on about a newly deceased umpire who'd put in forty-eight years' service with the mob my association amalgamated with a year earlier, I wasn't paying strict attention. Didn't even catch his name.

Most of my senses were switched off after a hard day at the office, but my eyes were still on active duty, scanning the football photos around the walls and the cardboard advertisements stapled to the sloped ceiling. 'Stan's Auto Service – We'll Get You Going', with the 'we' being a blonde draped over a bonnet.

' . . . so I'd ask that before you start on Saturday you get the teams to observe a minute's silence,' Max finally concludes.

The umps on either side of me belong to the deceased's mob, pre-amalgamation. They look about his vintage. Better not ask who it is we're mourning – I'll only be displaying my lack of attention. No, I'll wait until Saturday and play it by ear . . .

Saturday's here. However, my alert ear picks up nothing, and it's time to call the captains together for the toss. I could, of course, avoid the pitch-side ritual. But, it occurs, the captains may have been briefed on the obsequies and would regard any deliberate oversight as blasphemous.

So, with the toss done, I mumble, 'You know one of our members has died – nearly fifty years' service – so if you wouldn't mind each calling your players together in the centre, we'll have a minute's silence at three-minutes to one o'clock'.

At 12.57 p.m., having made a final adjustment to the stumps, I look up to find myself surrounded by twenty-two white-clad cricketers, ready to mourn.

Quickly, surreptitiously – desperately – I ask two non-captains who it is we're honouring. Shrugs of shoulders. So I draw myself up in priestly fashion and say, 'Thank you, fellas, we're honouring one of our long-term umpires – let's have a minute's silence.'

I glance at my watch at twenty, then at forty seconds. The time drags painfully. I am tense. Braced. Waiting for a titter; worse, a question – the one that goes, 'Who are we standing here for, ump?'

Blessedly, no one asks. No one titters.

'Thank you, guys,' I say, and thirteen players walk to their positions to start the match.

Later, with the game under way, I tell myself we've stood respectfully at the tomb of the Unknown Cricketer – assorted old umps whose personal counters clicked over to seven and the many pre- and un-helmeted players who, over the decades, wore a shiny red Kookaburra or Platypus projectile around about the temple and never woke up.

It Doesn't Rain, But . . .

It's the stuff-ups that engage the memory, and the disasters you drive home with, which add another layer to your psychological scar tissue. There are rare days so bad that months and years later, you look back and still see yourself standing alone in the vortex, watching a career going down the gurgler . . . Days so bad that writing your pre-emptive letter to the umpires' boss, knowing he'll be getting a poisoned-pen prosecution from one or both captains, is a therapeutic launch to the task of mustering enough confidence to front up for another match in seven days.

This sad tale I posted to our umpires' adviser early the next week demonstrates the good sense of the fundamental rule: don't deal directly with individual players in a fielding side; talk to their captain, and let him convey the message. Then, if the player doesn't accede to an instruction enforcing the rules or Laws, knock off the captain on the report form (for a tribunal hearing) or mention him disapprovingly on the match report form (establishing 'form' to be considered in sentencing should he offend more egregiously later). The captain, after all, is responsible for his team's actions on the field of play.

Co-umpire Terry Bennett stood by, sympathetic but helpless, that afternoon as I tripped up in a finals series elimination match between Kensington, a suburb neighbouring Flemington Racecourse (home of the Melbourne Cup), and an outfit called Pascoe Vale Uniting from near Essendon, home of the Australian Football League's powerhouse Bombers.

Unedited and unembellished, these are the notes I attached to the report Terry and I sent to the association's record keeper:

During Pascoe Vale Uniting's innings, which was the first of the match, I incorrectly called a 'no-ball' to a full toss that was a couple of feet wide of the matting, above the grass. However, it was struck on the full by a batsman, for a single. I realised at the time I had acted in error, but I am aware that I was at this point 'rattled' by a series of incidents concerning Kensington's wicket-keeper, Jerry Anderson.

About an hour after the no-ball incident, at the end of the innings, I decided to approach the scorers and ask them to strike the no-ball from the score. I informed Terry of this, then the Kensington captain, Eddie Pinter. Mr Pinter pointed out to me that, in fact, a run had been scored off the bat from the incorrect no-ball, and I let my error stand.

At 2.55 p.m., before this incident happened, Anderson, standing back some five yards, complained that a batsman had turned in running without grounding his bat. I had been watching closely and saw the bat touch the concrete comfortably past the batting crease. I told Anderson this, and said I was in a better position to judge it than he. He muttered several things that I could not hear.

An over later, Eddie Pinter approached me and told me Anderson was saying that, when I was at the bowler's end, I was not standing directly behind the wicket, so would not be able to properly judge an lbw. I was amazed and offended by this remark. Mr Pinter told me Anderson was 'very competitive' and that he, himself, had trouble keeping him quiet.

My response on being told I was not standing directly behind the stumps (by a keeper who, typically, was standing well to the off because of an offside bowling attack) was something like: 'Fifteen years of umpiring, and today I learn I've been standing in the wrong position all this time.' A few balls later, Anderson stayed behind the stumps to demonstrate where he thought I was standing. His right foot was in line with middle and leg. I said, 'You're just not telling the truth.' He replied, 'Are you calling me a liar?' I made no answer.

I then turned down a run-out appeal from square leg, and Anderson said, 'You've got to be kidding.'

When I then rejected a loud appeal for caught behind (the ball cut away on pitching, but clearly missed a left-hander's bat), Anderson said loudly, 'Totally incompetent.' I then told him and his captain I was giving him a final warning and would report any further dissent.

Within minutes, while standing at square leg, I again turned down an appeal. Anderson then said, quietly but clearly enough for me to hear it, 'Don't bother, it won't make any difference anyway.' I reported this to Eddie Pinter, who was the nearest fieldsman to me. Mr Pinter said he had heard nothing, and believed Anderson had said nothing.

I then spoke directly to Anderson who said he had been speaking to one of his team mates – not to me. At the end of the over, I told Mr Pinter that Anderson had, with this remark, at least admitted to speaking out. Mr Pinter waved me away and said he didn't want to talk about it any further. (Neither did I at this stage.)

I then made the no-ball error. I am certain it was the first error I had made, yet Anderson by his constant talk and undermining had created the impression on the ground that I was incompetent. The 'incompetence' I would admit to was in not taking a firmer hand, and reporting him.

In Kensington's run-chasing innings, Anderson was involved in a verbal altercation with a Pascoe Vale fieldsman. He was, from my point of view, the only player to introduce a hostile element into an otherwise hard-fought, but friendly match.

Yours sincerely, etc.

Of course, it doesn't rain but it pours. Next week, deservedly umpiring a much lower grade, I run into a spot more bother. Again I get drawn into the drama, but the rule about engaging players through their captain no longer applies. This time the chief offender *is* the captain.

Again, down go the details that night, directly after my headache tablets kick in:

Today's D-grade match between Rowville Rangers and ASWG became a shambles in the second half of its course after ASWG, having made 132 all out, began defending its total. A sequence of events that will result in the ASWG captain, Raul Nandi, giving me a poor report, went as follows:

Mr Nandi alerted me to a problem when he began muttering the word 'F—' regularly whenever his own bowling was scored from. I ignored this, as few people, apart from the non-striker, close fielders and me, could have heard it. The problem became more pronounced when, in one over, Mr Nandi said twice, still relatively quietly, 'F— c—', after being scored from. Again, I gave him the benefit. It was either at the end of that over, or the following one, that on my calling 'Over', he shouted the word, 'F—'. I walked to his side and said that I was officially warning him.

He challenged me, and, as words were exchanged between us, some of his team-mates surrounded us and play was held up for perhaps two minutes. Leading up to this incident, he had shown subtle dissent against my turning down a run-out appeal from square leg. He said, 'That's three lives, fellas' (two catches had been dropped – but I had also given an extremely close run-out appeal by his fieldsmen in his team's favour).

Mr Nandi then appealed for a front-pad lbw off his own bowling. When I turned it down, he asked me why. I gave a noncommittal answer, and he objected, saying he had a right to know. I then said something like: 'I've been umpiring fifteen years and every year I've been told by our advisers not to give reasons for questions like yours – it's either out or not out. That's all there is to it.' Then I added, no doubt unnecessarily: 'If I gave you out on the front pad six feet down the wicket, you'd moan all the way back to the pavilion.'

In saying this I'd formed the impression Mr Nandi would argue any decision not going in his favour, and that bullying and insults were now part of his captaincy tactics.

Certainly his team's talk to Rowville's batsmen was often insulting of their technique and temperament – in a way that Rowville had not applied in the ASWG innings. On four occasions I called 'no-ball' to waist-high (or higher) full tosses. On all except the last occasion, Mr Nandi and some of his team-mates argued against my call. Long before this match I had decided to err in the bowler's favour in the case of borderline deliveries, so I was very confident my calls were correct. The third such call I made, to a waist-high quickish full toss, was challenged strenuously by Mr Nandi who crossed the wicket to confront me.

I got into quite a heated argument with him. He said something derogatory about my umpiring – I'd also turned down two of his lbw shouts, again attracting moans and expressions of incredulity – and in response to this latest comment I pointed at him and said something like 'And maybe it's time for your club to get a new captain'. I think, in the heat of the moment, I also called him a 'bonehead' or something similar.

My colleague Vernon stepped in and, I believe, in wanting to defuse the situation, he called 'Over'. The worst thing now happened because in explaining to Vernon that a 'no-ball' had to be followed by a further ball to complete the over, we became surrounded by ASWG players, and an all-in verbal barney ensued. Vernon insisted on sticking to his decision, while I said, 'This isn't tennis; you're not the central umpire who can overrule.'

I had already let Mr Nandi get too far under my skin and as my decisions now seemed to carry no weight, even with my co-umpire, I decided it was time to quit, and as I walked to the boundary I had it in mind to resign. I explained briefly to the scorers what had happened in the centre, and they appeared to approve my interpretation, then, on being asked what was happening to the match, I remembered I had already been paid, and so returned quickly to the middle where a final ball was bowled to complete the over. Perhaps between five and seven minutes was lost over this incident.

A few overs later, because of an element of doubt, I had to give the benefit of it on a stumping appeal to the batsman. On reflection, this is the only decision of the day I might now change; I'm totally confident that all the UMPIRING DECISIONS, apart from this one, were correct; I wouldn't change one of them – as distinct from my over-reactions to the foul-language and unsportsmanlike verbal put-downs to opponents from Mr Nandi. He is the captain, and his lead was followed frequently by several of his team-mates. After my stumping denial, he accused me of being 'a racist'. I took fairly strong verbal exception to this too.

At stumps when I'd expressed regret to Vernon that his

> well-meant intervention had made a difficult situation worse, he told me of a pre-existing knowledge of ASWG's – or this particular team's – practice of using bad language.
>
> I regret the rapid and dramatic deterioration in the standards of this match, and accept responsibility for it, in as much as I was sucked in and engaged Mr Nandi in inappropriate dialogue on his own terms.

Some days – the ones when at least one of the teams reckon you should forfeit your match fee – you really earn your keep.

By now I figure I've learned my lesson – thicken your skin, stick your fingers in your ears, and talk of serious, cricketing matters only to the skipper. And if the skipper's a wild man bent on breaking the Laws and spoiling the game, give him the mandatory two warnings, then book him. (If he still carries on, award the match to his opponents and draw stumps.)

Not Tonight, Napoleon

For me, umpiring started at a place where a seasoned cricket umpire might very well decide to finish – provided the experience didn't produce rapid burnout, removing the luxury of choice.

The Ferntree Gully Cricket Association, in the foothills of the Dandenong Ranges, east of Melbourne, reflected its working-class surrounds in 1983. Devoid of public transport (save a branch rail line extending like a single vein serving a blood-starved limb), it was a region of too many people and too little employment.

The cricket was played on unevenly turfed sand and clay heaps surrounding concrete slabs on which coir mats were laid. Mouth guards would have been appropriate apparel for outfield duty, but charges of wussiness would, of course, have forbade them. The cauldron of Ferntree Gully cricket at least provided a release of frustration for the young men who played in it.

The season's opener brought me quickly up to speed. Like Wounded Knee the day after the battle, the Dandenong Ranges was still abuzz over a grand final six months earlier when fights broke out among spectators, and the umpires locked themselves in the toilet while milling throngs clamoured for their blood.

A loyalty to my new Saturday afternoon employers (the players, who paid $2 a head for my attendance) settled a fleeting journalistic urge to dig deeper into this scandal that had excited the local police but was missed by the papers.

'This year we stand for no bullshit,' demands our umpires' adviser, Ron Nevill. 'We book 'em and the association will back us up. If they repeat the offence, they're thrown out. No comebacks.' There was more of this drilling before we Dirty Harrys in white took the field to start the new season.

It had been a wet footy season, and the groundsmen from Menzies Creek to Ferntree Gully and across the foothills had settled the mud by burying it under deserts of sand. It would take at least five summers, I figured, before my uncanny eye, ear and judgement reached the attention of the Victorian Cricket Association umpiring hierarchy. First, I decided I would stamp on local minds my certainty of conviction, expressed by arm movements of majestic sweep and brio.

In the midafternoon an amiable meat processor belts one skyward. Four all over it. I'll not only be confident, I'll be quick, I decide, signalling four even as the ball descends. With my back to it, I imitate a Grand Prix flag marshal for the scorers. Hang on. Last season's riff-raff are still here, for the words ring out, 'Bloody idiot!' Instinctively I know they are for me. I spin around. The ball has buried itself in sand a metre from the boundary – a fieldsman is searching for it – and the batsmen are running.

There is laughter. Jeering. 'Hell,' I'm thinking, 'how many have they run?' My brain is boggled. The ball is eventually found and hurled back to the 'keeper. I jog to the scorers, reckoning that in the time it takes to reach them, I'll have decided what to do.

'Cancel the four,' I tell them, 'they've run three.'

'Bloody bullshit – we ran five!' correct the batsmen after

I've returned to the wicket and satisfied their natural curiosity. Five years to the top might be a bit premature, I decide.

The following season the personal game-plan stretches further, to infinity in fact, after a particularly high-stress match between the combative Upper Ferntree Gully XI and a team of comparatively bland civility.

I had been warned about the UFGCC captain, a fellow the size and shape of Napoleon Bonaparte, but possessed of much more than the General's arrogance. The warning proves inadequate to the reality of Bonie the Bowler, whose standard practice is to mutter obscenities even as he shoulder-charges batsmen with the temerity to push him for singles.

I umpire two of his matches in my second season; by the end of each day I'm suffering lockjaw from the tension generated by Bonie. He is, after all, the UFG captain; there to set a good example, one presumes. His example *is* followed; the atmosphere is poison. By the fourth day, I've booked him for throwing his bat and cursing me for my decision to despatch him lbw.

At the tribunal three nights later, I sit relaxed with the hearty Ron Nevill, who is famous in the district for his parsimonious approach to lbw appeals. 'I'll give one [lbw] before Christmas, and maybe one after,' is Ron's personal credo, and though he leaves it up to us as to what philosophical stance we take to leg-before shouts, I feel poorly that he's been called out on a weeknight to back me up on my lbw decision and enforce the new 'get tough with hoons' policy.

In evidence counter to my own, the subdued Napoleon now demonstrates with his hand how the offending ball – the one that dismissed him – thundered into his groin. I'd thought, naively, that it would be absolutely not cricket –

unheard of – for fibs to be told in the noble game's tribunals, and in nominating to the tribunal chairman the knee-roll of Napoleon's pad as point of contact, I thought I'd erred generously in the batsman's favour. I was sure the ball had struck him lower.

On hearing the bare-faced lie as Napoleon points to his crotch (above bale height, even in this stunted individual) as point of contact, something snaps. I stand up. 'Sorry, Mr Chairman,' I say, half choking with anger, 'but I don't have the constitution to listen to this bullshit.'

Twenty minutes later, justice is still being done behind a door that emits a shaft of light on to the oval that I pace in agitation and annoyance at my short-fuse temper. It dawns on me: I've been viewing each match as a player (which I'd been before starting this caper), not at all dispassionately or with disinterest. Within a few hours of the start of each contest I have been seduced by the flair or pluck of player 'A', whose clout through the covers draws expletives from opposing fieldsmen 'B' through 'L', whose on-field courtesies are as absent as the tea and scones whenever I do duty on their home ground. Who will not own up to taking a hard line on lbw and associated matters when these flannelled hoods – so different to their opponents – take the new ball and appeal like bovver boys?

Then there's Chris, the Menzies Creek captain, ex-Vietnam war veteran, who plays like Botham, bowls unchanged all afternoon, injects himself with pain-killers for a bad back before start of play, lies flat on the same damaged spine for half an hour after stumps before limping to his car, and is so unstinting in his encouragement of the callow youths under his charge that my heart bleeds for, and warms to, him. Each season this disarming coaxer raises money to keep his club afloat and pleads (successfully) with the association executive not to relegate its ever-losing first XI to a lower grade. He's a stout, first-out-of-the-trenches type who wins me over at our first meeting by offering me a spot in the first XI should I come out of retirement. Who again, at some subliminal level, won't exercise a sympathetic bias towards these bucolic under-achievers whose picturesque home ground is a lopped hillside on which the grass is never less than ankle-height?

Well, I tell myself, I won't fall into that trap. But I'd bet I have, at times, in most of the ensuing summers. The tendency, though, has become greatly reduced with experience over time. Becoming aware of these hidden battles of the subconscious constitutes the first stage of winning them. The business of resisting temptation towards bestowing favouritism becomes easier with the passing of the seasons, as the instinct of the former player to vicariously 'feel' the contest ebbs away. The tests of eye, ear and judgement can be contained in the shouted appeal of a spinner when a confusing confluence of bat, pad and turf propels the ball into silly mid-on's hands, or in the guttural demand of a quick when bat, pad, gloves and thigh guard move towards the ball, leaving no discernible deflection or sound of contact if the wind is at the umpire's back. The battles of the mind in preserving concentration and bringing harmony to a vigourous contest need to be understood and won early because the frequent calls to judgement of the senses are more than enough to separate the good umpires from the ordinary, and the ordinary from the bad.

OK, let's get back to business. I summon my nerve, swallow my pride and re-enter the pavilion, just in time to hear the tribunal's verdict. Napoleon is suspended for five playing days, and I later hear that Ron's summing up has left it little choice other than a harsh sentence. Disappointment and embarrassment at walking out on the proceedings are my immediate preoccupation; certainly I feel no pleasure in the sentencing. Accused and accuser leave the pavilion at about the same time, saying nothing to each other. The atmosphere between us hints at summer's end, at cooler days just around the corner. I hang back to let Napoleon leave first, deciding it wouldn't take much to run my ageing Mini Minor off the road.

The Torture Box

Moving house means moving to a new Cricket Association, and this one, based in the outer Melbourne suburb of Dandenong, is dramatically undermanned. All umpires officiate end to end – no slumbering at square leg with alternate overs – and each team has been asked to provide an honorary umpire, an altruistic bloke prepared to give up weeknights to learn, and practise administering, the MCC's Laws and the local rules.

Our umpires' adviser implores us to talk to, encourage and be nice to these honorary, sporting philanthropists. My dreams of high honours; of handing Curtly Ambrose his sweater, are about to flicker and die.

It is a brutally hot day . . . willy-willies hurl pebbles into the air at long-on. Angry wasps scud about my legs and the battered stumps before me. Dust coats the roof of my mouth. My head aches. My eyes are burning slits.

On such days the psyches of fielding teams go through cycles, as fixed and unchanging as the seasons. There is the midafternoon torpor . . . the pre-Liptons or Robur euphoria, often accompanied by a wicket . . . then the post-tea babble when fieldsmen blabber and gambol and expectations of a quick wrap-up are high. Next is the precursive calm as batsmen dig in . . . the surly reaction when hopes are dashed and a single voice attempts to raise spirits ('Come on, guys, talk it up!' followed by weary mumbles) . . . then prolonged doldrums when the game becomes work . . . and an unnatural, second-wind vigour as stumps looms.

We have entered this final phase, when combat is often at its sharpest and the vitriol flows most freely. More involved in the fray than I realise, something snaps in me. (Familiar territory!) Afterwards, in my car's mirror, I see myself: a portrait of Alec Guinness emerging from his torture box on the searing parade ground in *The Bridge on the River Kwai.*

The catalyst is a modestly performing, sandy-haired batsman who, after I have raised my finger to a leg-before shout against him, hurls his bat over the head of square leg, tells me he 'effing nicked it', and walks off. In an instant, I am at his side. For the next minute or two I busily engage myself in becoming the first umpire ever to sledge a batsman all the way back to the pavilion.

The massively disappointed lad, having bowled for much of the afternoon before taking his turn to bat, is white around the eyes, which are glazed. Flecks of dried foam score the corners of his mouth. Even as I defame his parents, I can tell he is unwell. I know we both are. I am grateful when he declines my invitation to step outside the ground.

Later, as we apologise to each other over a medicinal beer, he tells me how much he loves cricket, so much so that he's taken on the job of honorary umpire. I die a little more.

No, I am not cut out for higher honours, I tell myself after this encounter. Though my eye, ear and judgement are sound enough, my temperament will keep me among the lower orders. And I know my command of the copious Laws of Cricket is inadequate when, on the day Dean Jones is so cruelly run out in Guyana – not in the least part due to an umpire's ignorance of the relevant Law in 1991, No. 27(5) – I experience a surge of fellow feeling for the benighted man in the white coat.

A Son of Yorkshire

I've been thinking about a great character of Yorkshire, George Yelland. The name even sounds Yorkish, and George was christened with a white rose pinned to his swaddlings.

When I last co-umpired with him, about five years ago on a scorching Melbourne Sunday afternoon, George remained striking for his northern burr, general sharpness, astuteness of umpiring judgement, and his stamina. (In the tea break, with only tap water available in the pavilion, he declined a refrigerated drink when I said I'd fetch one from the milkbar down the road. 'Trying to watch my weight', he explained, to my amazement.) And he was getting on a bit.

For more than five decades, George had been a dyer of woollen and cotton yarns, at first in his native Bradford, then, from 1960, for various top-makers and mills around Melbourne. Thread-sense doesn't necessarily equate with dress sense, however, and in the latter, George was, perhaps . . . different. He appeared to be unaware of his over-large underpants whose waistband protruded an inch or more above his belt buckle; or, accounting for the white elastic between the twain of pants and shirt, were those dacks vertically challenged? The players of the match we were assigned to seemed not to notice or care because, like another Yorkshire umpire, Dickie Bird, George was so likeable and obviously skilled at his job, that respect and affection were won as of right.

After umpiring a couple of matches with him, I would seek George out at YCW umpires' meetings, which were held in the

Victorian Cricket Association boardroom at Jolimont, a Viv Richards drive from the Melbourne Cricket Ground. As an ABC news reporter, I once stood on the steps of that VCA building so that I could accidentally brush the coat sleeve of Sir Donald Bradman as he left a meeting.

Like me, George Yelland was impatient with the tedious form of the YCW meetings, despite the joviality of their chairman, Adrian Crawley who, thankfully, didn't suffer fogeys jumping to their feet to reminisce (unless they were entertaining). But if we wanted to umpire finals matches, attend we must. While not denying the meetings had an important function (briefings on the Laws and local rules were vital, as long as they were understood and applied), the motive prompting George and me to actually turn up lay in ticking off our names on the attendance sheet, absorbing rule changes and advice from the aptly-titled umpires' adviser, and escaping into the night as early as possible. (The YCW, incidentally, stood for Young Christian Workers, which seemed paradoxical: they played only on Sundays and, in the case of the Caucasian brethren, swore like merchant mariners.)

By the time the appointment secretary had paired George and me for a third time, I was looking forward to his company. At the end of day one, when cold drinks in the clubrooms had stabilised us against the dizziness of prolonged exposure to 33-degree heat, George's love of life and cricket made him shine, and I, as much as the players, stepped back to listen and learn from him. In Yorkshire, he had played cricket and umpired soccer, and his stories embraced, respectively, a teenage tearaway, Fred Trueman, and the sublimely skilled winger Stanley Matthews.

Later, I visit him at his home for a magazine story I am

planning. George shows me photos of his special woman friend, Frances, a schoolteacher in Seattle, USA. They met as tourists at Varanasi in northern India, on the banks of the Ganges in 1985, maintained their friendship by pen and phone, and in recent years have met up in Frances's home city, again at Agra (India), and in London, just north of which lives John Yelland, one of George's three sons.

Since his wife, Doreen, died in 1968, ending a happy, twenty-five-year marriage, George has managed an overseas trip, on average, every third year. Those journeys have taken him to every continent, bar Greenland and Antarctica ('I hate the cold,' he says).

The lad from White Abbey, the toughest part of working-class Bradford, carries that toughness in every fibre of his being. The mettle has been sorely tested, and has always triumphed.

As politely as I can, I inquire as to the two dents at the top of George's skull. 'Oh, they're from my fall just after I'd retired [in 1978]. I fell over, you see, and hit my head. I was booked to go to England and when I got there John took me to a hospital at Oxford that specialises in head injuries.'

Now, George is no hypochondriac and, like the Oxford surgeon, you have to dig to extract his medical history. The dual probes into his skull go by the name of subdural haematomas, and their purpose – to release a collection of blood clots and relieve pressure on the brain – worked so well on George that within a few weeks he was pursuing the itinerary planned before his setback: travelling in Mexico and Peru, and hauling himself up ropes to the 9000-foot pinnacle of Huayna Picchu, the 'Little Mountain' and Lost City of the Incas. 'Like climbing up a needle,' he says, and it's true.

Mountaineers compare Huayna Picchu with the famously challenging north wall of Switzerland's Eiger (13,042 feet). Only a masochist will prefer it to the higher, comparative stroll up Machu Picchu ('Big Mountain'). George was seventy-four when he scaled Huayna Picchu.

Life's vicissitudes hadn't finished with the Yelland skull. Shortly before I met him, he'd been mugged while on his new daily job, selling newspapers at Melbourne's Rosanna railway station. 'Got any more?' asked a hefty chap on a red bike who pulled up alongside George's paper stack one morning. As he turned to get him the *Herald Sun*, the man drove his fist into the back of George's head, knocked him over and robbed him. A witness dashed to his car to call the police, who arrived within a minute, but the thief got away, preserving his anonymity. George wasn't so lucky. That night he was on all the TV news bulletins. The hospital checked him out, and he was back selling his papers the next day.

I surmise that, as a young man, George might have been a bit of a peacock; a ladies' man. Certainly, most of his friends are women. But that, he says, is because 'I don't drink, smoke, go to the pub or have a bet, and my interest in winter is soccer, not the rugby codes or Aussie rules. So I don't click with a lot of males; our conversations tend to be a bit limited.' And I mustn't be fooled by the photo album and mantlepiece pictures that feature more women than blokes. 'They're just friends who I look forward to seeing on my travels,' he explains. 'I was never one to play the field. In fact, as a young man, I was probably more interested in steam engines. They're the great love of my life. I've taken a steam train from China to Moscow, and driven or been a passenger in them in most of the countries I've been to.'

George lives in the present, and for the future. He's always saving for, and looking forward to, his next overseas trip to meet up with his friends and extended family. A forward focus and an engagement with life infuse his anecdotes, lifting them beyond the merely nostalgic.

I dig gently. 'How special is Frances?' (It's a women's magazine I have in mind for my story about George.) 'Well, a lot of people have asked me that,' he offers. 'Frances is twenty-five or thirty years younger than me, you know, but she is such a terrific person . . .' Drop it!

It's a most pleasant afternoon spent in his lounge room, and in his company, but at some point in the conversation my host frowns and becomes quiet. A thought has occurred to him, and what I've been imagining as his metaphoric peacock's tail – the one that drew the ladies – suddenly flaps to give George flight. The anthropomorphic flashing red eye of my tape-recorder says 'Flee!' The damn technology has betrayed the ostensible chat between new-found friends, and the interview, exposed for itself, alarms him. The Social Security, which pays his pension, will read this story and be on to him, he says. I offer to change his name. No, sorry, an invented name won't do; the bureaucrats will see through that ruse. And he takes flight, seeking the oxygen that publicity might deny him.

The last time I umpired with George Yelland he was eighty-three years old. In the five subsequent years, I often wonder about him. And when, at last, I decide to make my inquiry, I initially phone Adrian Crawley. But Adrian's not answering, and his recorded message makes me wonder why I haven't simply phoned George directly. Face it: it's who might not be there that worries me.

When he answers my call in the house he's lived in since 1962, George is three months from his eighty-eighth birthday and the voice is the same Yorkshire burr, as firm in timbre as Pavarotti's, and there's not a moment's delay in remembering our association.

With cricket in Melbourne, some things never change, and one of them is early-season rain. George copped a drenching just before Christmas 2000, caught a cold, then pneumonia, and spent five days in the intensive care unit of a repatriation hospital.

Between our last meeting and that setback he's taken two overseas trips: the first to Africa (to Victoria Falls; to the Kenyan capital, Nairobi; and a four-wheel-drive safari in Tanzania's Serengeti National Park where he watched, fascinated, as a lion ran down a zebra and dined on it with its family). Then, in 2000, he journeyed through Chile and the USA and, 'just outside' Detroit, met up with Frances and her boyfriend. That couple plan to marry, which disappointed me (I'm a romantic) but apparently pleased George – for his special friend's sake.

We're well into the second half of the 2000–01 cricket season and George, just twelve years away from his century, is talking about his 'itchy feet'. Next, they will take him to Bengal ('I want to see a tiger there before they disappear completely').

As a player of his favourite game, George had a fair innings. He was a medium pacer who swung the ball either way, who 'didn't know one end of the bat from the other', and played competitive, club cricket from the ages of sixteen to sixty-four. And his umpiring days may not yet be over. 'I'd love to do another season,' says the great disdainer of Father Time.

The Drill Sergeant

Alf wasn't quite the same after his stroke. His speech and general movement didn't appear altered. But the umpires who had borne the brunt of his withering, sergeant-major's eye and understated, sometimes sarcastic, criticism were certainly altered. We started to relax a little.

For the myriad watchers of the game who insist its standards have slipped – they tend to be into their retirement years or counting down – Alf would have been their man. Had the International Cricket Council chosen him to clean up the world game and granted him the necessary budget and sweeping powers, we'd have had none of this malarky of relaxed dress codes and manners, surly send-offs by bowlers, none of the gimmickry of stump cams and cameras at square leg to usurp the traditional role of the umpire. There'd have been no bribery, no 'Johns' offering cash or sex to swing matches for the bookies. Corruption would have gone no further than a quick draw on a Craven A in the tea break. Or whatever brand it was that Alf used to clog his lungs.

When afforded the luxury of a partner in matches, and that was rare in the association for which Alf was umpires' adviser, I'd use the alternate overs spent at square leg relaxing. The two-to-three minutes' duration of delivering these six balls before my gaze at 90 degrees to their linear path was a time for studying cloud formations, their wonderful woolly forms, reshapings and mergings, expansions, contractions and colour changes. All the while, the week's toil and stress ebbed and flowed away.

And the tree tops, remembered from previous years standing in the same park; I saw how they had altered, enjoyed the way the English deciduous types, swaying metronomically for the steady march of white cumuli, would transport me to the lands of their provenance and into the literary settings of Thomas Hardy, the Brontës, Jane Austen and E. M. Forster. A church steeple in the vicinity would invoke reveries almost of rapid-eye-movement depth. Then, alas, my ball-counting responsibilities would be abandoned, presumably to the annoyance of my partner behind the stumps. Transfixed in concentration by his position central to the action, he would be counting dutifully the balls bowled, awaiting in vain the returned signal that just one was left, when it would be my turn to officiate on the core of the action, that twenty-two yards between stumps.

Such reveries were out of the question if Alf had announced at the previous meeting that he would be scouting the parks, checking on all he had told/warned us about: neatness of dress, general bearing, clearness of signals, stillness behind the stumps, clean shoes, possession of all the paraphernalia that goes with starting and sustaining a match, even to checking that the stumps were correctly aligned and the creases clearly marked to the correct spacings and lengths.

Alf had bought himself a big, shiny Landcruiser with bull-bar, and he would drive it quietly into the park, stop it and watch. I would see the vehicle crawling along a roadway or parked beyond the boundary and my stomach muscles would tighten. I'd check myself out in the imagined mirror of Alf's gaze. Like Papa Doc Duvalier's Tonton Macoute, the deadly civilian militia described in Graham Greene's *The Comedians*, whose members hid behind their dark shades, Alf would watch us, for over after suspenseful over, behind the slightly tinted glass of his Black Maria. Then, at the next drinks or tea break, would walk on to the field to confront his victim.

And he would hedge. 'Lovely day, John,' he'd say as an en garde. 'Warm. Not over 30 degrees, though, I'd say.' Then the thrusts began. 'So, the tie. It's not done up; in fact I thought I saw you loosening the top button. The rule is, if it's really hot – over 30 – you don't have to wear a tie. You know that – I say it often enough at the meetings. But it's nowhere near 30, you know that too, and have a look at yourself – your tie's half-mast and crooked. And look at your shoes. When was the last time you put a whitener on them? Not this year, I'd say. I won't hold you up, but when you get in there for your break, check yourself out if they've got a mirror. It's not a good sight. The other thing, try and keep still when you're at square leg, 'specially when the bowler's actually delivering; you're like a bloody cat on a hot tin roof. I'd better have a chat to Jimmy. Anyway, have a good match.' And he'd stroll off for a friendly word with my colleague, Jim, who has headed to the pavilion, fumbling as he goes at his tie, shirt buttons, fly, and pausing to rub his uppers on the backs of alternate trouser legs.

Alf is what they call a stickler. I try to please him, but if I ever succeed, it's to be gleaned only by an absence of his overt displeasure.

A few seasons of this go by. I enjoy umpiring in this particular association. Its purview takes in my home suburb of Brunswick, an ethnically diverse proletariat of colourful, complementary cultures and cuisines (pity about the KFC on the corner of my street and Sydney Road though). The matches assigned me often steer me west, to cross the Maribyrnong

River to parks whose features I remember years after I've departed, and to teams whose company I mostly enjoy.

However, the disquieting feature is an awareness that each year our umpire numbers are declining. A bigger umpires' association to our north has been making overtures. They are to be our saviour by act of takeover. Or, as some of the leaders of our association insist it will be, a merger of equal partners. The meeting at which the permanent get-together is mooted is protracted, acrimonious and, at times, bigoted. The season is nearing its end and the takeover/merger question has to be resolved. We are in no bargaining position. The steering committee, representatives of each body, will make its recommendation, and we all know it will be a takeover with the Darwinian inevitability that the victor – the bigger – will retain its gene pool, untainted by our own motley molecules, and keep its name, insignia, colours, etc.

But will Alf retain his status as umpires' adviser?

Given that the northern lads have their own, and a universally popular chap whose reputation reaches frontiers beyond Alf's range, this question, too, will surely be settled in the northerners' favour. Alf is one of the fierier of our members advocating a 'No' vote to the act of takeover. For that's what it will be, insist Alf and ten of his mates who have been propping up this outfit for decades, first as players, then as umpires. And damned Alf will be if he'll shake hands with, and make concessions to, one of their leaders who's a queer; a poof. And, by all he implies in an ugly tirade, *ipso facto* not to be trusted.

I hear on the winter grapevine that the takeover has gone through, approved by the Victorian Cricket Association, and we'll begin the new season with a new name (our saviour's), new insignia (theirs) and a new umpires' adviser. It isn't Alf.

Months of not seeing him pass by, then I hear of Alf's stroke. He's come through it well, though, and is about to make his return to umpiring just as soon as he's strong enough.

Then I hear Alf has been appointed to the expanded association's tribunal, which hears and rules on cases of misbehaviour. An appropriate role, I figure, imposing standards and meting out discipline, all while sitting down.

But I hadn't planned on standing, even as leading prosecution witness, before Alf and his two colleagues, quite so soon. If at all.

Bustling, bad-mouthed trundler Robert is the medium that takes me there. It is a calm, still day when voices carry as though on a mountain top where the beating of an eagle's wings moves the air and is audible. Robert uses the 'f' word at regular intervals when his labours bear no fruit and the runs mount up, and I am sure the expletives can be heard beyond the boundary – the auditory standard summoning an umpire to issue warnings. I issue one, then a second, reasoning that like excessive bumpers hurled at a tail-end, bare-headed (helmetless) batsman, two warnings will be sufficient before taking decisive action.

And when Robert tacks a 'c' word to his favourite 'f' upon my turning down another of his appeals for lbw, the warnings and their number become irrelevant. Particularly as this time he's locked eyes with me as he invokes the ruddy, Anglo-Saxon couple, or coupling.

It's usually been the case with me that as I unhook the writing papers and stub-pencil from the shirt pocket and begin my walk to the captain to tell him of my intentions, I feel a rush of blood to my face and my heart pounding; and always in the aftermath there's a regret that my involuntary response is an immediate leap to anger – personalising the particular, when all I am in reality is a random, at-hand pressure valve for a bowler's frustration. My father was a part-time sign-writer and an expert marksman with a rifle, but none of this steadiness was inherited and, as I make my notes (time of offence, circumstances and quotations), the game is held up longer than it should be because an overheated mind, my anger, is making the task of wielding wood-encased graphite as difficult as though I were chilled to the bone and clasping it in Sir Edmund Hillary's gloves.

On Wednesday night, as I pull into the car park, there are too-few people. Alf is there with a tribunal mate, but we're short of their chairman. He's late, and no one else has thought to bring a key to the clubrooms. An association chap knows someone who will have one, and takes off in his car.

For me, reminiscence has started to kick in. Robert is standing next to a club official and his own three-year-old daughter. He's where I should have been, I tell myself, but I was never comfortable as a player, mouthing 'f's and 'c's. That was a habit I was to pick up a little later in life, somewhere in my thirties, I believe, and nowadays I give way to it too often.

What I remember is that, at Robert's age, my swearing was done internally, silently, and that the most satisfying wicket I took as an opening bowler in my teens and early twenties was with a ball that reared at a batsman's throat, driving him back and into his stumps. The fact is, that as a bowler who tried to bowl fast and never realised that of which he dreamed (deliveries at the pace of Lillee and Thommo, who came along a few years later), I converted this frustration over lack of anatomical wherewithal to frighten batsmen into an intense dislike of them.

Later, a sports commentator coined the term 'white line fever' for even-tempered men who become potential killing machines when they cross the line and run on to the field of football battle. Well, I had a strain of that disease, because for five years I experienced the maddening imbalance of running fifteen to twenty yards to the wicket in order to have my energies and hoped-for irresistible force – packed into a bone-jarring effort beside the stumps – nullified by an over-padded, lazy-arsed, immovable object, rocking forward on to his left leg to kill the missile stone-dead with a bat angled at 45 degrees. How much effort does that take?! On hot days it was especially maddening. And as the opening bowler in a team like Marlborough College Old Boys, you did this for as long as it took to tire and for the batsman to reverse the balance of aggressions.

Yes, I detested batsmen, and as a young adult I saw in the angry, rampaging Dennis Lillee a fellow traveller. There was no doubt, in his early years especially, that D. K. Lillee had a rabid dislike of willow wielders and an intense desire to dismiss them from his presence.

Such thoughts go through my mind as we wait for the man to bring the key to the rooms where justice will be dispensed. The umpire who made the booking with shaky anger four days ago was a hanging judge. But if I was Redmond Barry, who sentenced Ned Kelly, then, I am the beatified Mary MacKillop, defender of the oppressed, now.

As we (umpires and alleged miscreants) stand waiting in our two camps on the bitumen outside the clubrooms for the key-fetcher, my mind goes back to an earlier time, to another association at which Alf was umpires' adviser. It was to be a standard meeting of the men in white but, as no key was to be found to give us entry to our rooms, we strolled across to a power pole and gathered round it. Bathed in the light from above, we listened while the secretary read the correspondence and Alf gave his usual sound advice to round out a seven-minute meeting. If only they could all be like that. (Power poles have always been funny buggers, ever since a night of the 'wide games' our Scout troop used to play in Blenheim, New Zealand. On this night, we had embarked on a tracking exercise, and the trail-maker of our Pukeko [native swamphen] patrol made it easy for us by using an onion. What wasn't easy was that the sadist laid his 'trail' at the base of power poles through the heart of the town on a late-shopping night. As, on all fours, we sniffed the poles along High Street and out into the suburbs like savvy wolf cubs, our tender, virgin ears picked up crudities and oaths from passing cars that would have spun Baden Powell in his grave.)

Eventually, in Australia, our key, and the tribunal chairman, arrive and we file into the clubrooms where plastic bins are filled to the brim with Saturday's emptied cans and the floor is unwelcoming concrete. As Alf and his mate sit on either side of chairman Harold at a trestle table, we make our own seating arrangements, pulling up plastic chairs before the tribunal.

Clearly, we'd all rather be home watching *Cheers*, so Harold tries to make this a relaxed, informal occasion. It's not a court, rules of law don't apply here, we'll simply be expected to tell the truth, and he has no doubt that will happen. But it's not a kangaroo court either, and the normal procedures will be adhered to.

Now the chair turns its attention to me, telling me that 'we've all' had a chance to read my written statement of events, but, regardless of that, will I please read it for the convenience of the tribunal. This seems reasonable, except for a couple of things. Robert's daughter is playing on the floor in front of us. At once point she makes a grab for one of my shoes. It makes me uncomfortable. Is she grovelling on her father's behalf? Involuntarily, I draw my foot back. I feel like a Roundhead. Robert is a Cavalier.

Chairman Harold is concerned that my statement is larded with the 'f' word. He leans towards me, looking secretively left and right, as though someone might overhear him.

'It may be a good idea, as the "f" word appears throughout your statement, to use another word in its place,' he suggests. 'Why don't we say . . . "major" instead?'

So I begin, spelling out times and places, the state of the match, and Robert's mounting anger. 'When he was bowling to (player named), I heard him say major, but it was said quietly and he could have been talking to himself. However, the batsman drove the next ball for a single and (Robert) said slightly louder, "You major! Major it". I then asked (Robert) to tone down his language as he might be heard by people on the boundary. The next over he used the expressions "major shit", "major hell" and then just "major" on its own. In his next over again, at 2.40 p.m., when I rejected his lbw appeal, he looked at me and called me a major, and then added . . .'

My testimony now is interrupted. Alf leans forward and his expression suggests he has just trodden on a dog turd. But what he has to say suggests he's been off with the fairies.

'Excuse me,' he says, 'but what are you talking about? What . . . what's all this hogwash about major?'

I look to Harold for assistance, but he has turned to his left to stare, disbelievingly, at Alf.

However, this benign courtroom won't be hardened, especially against its own, and patiently the chairman explains our euphemism as a protection of Robert's cute moppet who is now dragging a plastic chair across the concrete, creating a sound like an untuned tuba.

Embarrassment is triggered in Alf's nervous system. Blood rushes to his face and, somewhere in the left hemisphere of his cranium, corpuscles jostle and fight for limited space, bumping into nerves as a consequence, knocking one towards another so that an electric charge is able to leap across the reduced space between nerve endings, so producing a spark that appears as a light in Alf's previously closed eyes.

The chairman's explanation has been the switch. Alf, now alert, a half smile on his lips, looks at me, then at Harold, and says: 'Well, I'll be majored.'

When the mirth subsides, Harold and his adjudicators listen to the evidence of Robert (he was only talking to himself when he used the magic words, and apologises for any offence he caused) and the pleas of his club official (Robert's out of work and the opportunity to play cricket with his mates is an important part of his support network and self-esteem). Then Harold thanks us all and asks us to step outside while he and his colleagues make their decision. 'Verdict' being eschewed; this isn't a court, remember.

In the warm night air, I gravitate to a group of umpires surrounding Don, who will lead the evidence in the next case to be heard. Don tells us a ripping yarn of wrongdoing, and as he rehearses its relatively complex details to the group, my own 'case', by contrast, appears stunted, increasingly tacky, brought by a thin-skin against a good, honest, working-class man (with a loving, dependant daughter).

Perhaps I'm an innocent instigator who's just been doing his job, but I am now wearing the black cap of Redmond Barry and I turn away from my peers to look for Robert. He is standing by his car, with just two supports: a cigarette between his index and middle fingers and his little girl clasped tightly to his left leg. I feel a strong urge to join his group, to be a third pillar of the support team. I walk over to him and the words come spontaneously: 'G'day, Rob.' (Note the solidarity implied by the diminutive.) 'Just want you to know, whatever happens, there's no hard feelings as far as I'm concerned.'

He clasps my proffered hand, shakes it, and says, 'Yeah mate, no sweat.'

This is a little disappointing, especially the bit about 'no sweat', which could have come from the speechwriter who gave us 'Aussie, Aussie, Aussie, oi, oi, oi'.

We talk about his daughter, curled into his leg, looking up plaintively at me, about our respective cars which are parked as companionably close as their owners, about our work, actual and hoped-for . . . about anything but cricket. The pauses are excruciating.

Then mercifully, the call to judgement comes and we file to the change rooms, all returning to our previous positions. That is except for Robert, who stands before the tribune in the middle (Harold) as though programmed to do so by generations of forebears who adopted the same supplicant position, awaiting sentence.

'Thank you, gentlemen,' says Harold. 'We've listened to both sides in this matter and we congratulate you both in giving your evidence succinctly and, we believe, honestly. But in considering all the evidence, we have felt inclined to believe that given by [our lot]. Robert, we hope you have learned from this experience and will return to the competition with a better understanding of what you can and cannot do in this game. However, in this case we believe your behaviour breached the standards that all players must adhere to. We have found you guilty of the charge brought against you, and we are suspending you for the next ten match days.'

There will be no standing around, no more awkward moments between accused and accuser. Robert pivots, heads straight for, and out, the door. Several of us walk after him.

I see him gather up his daughter and put her on the front seat beside him. No time for seat belts. The car is gunned to life, and as it heads down the car park towards the road it swerves, sending up showers of gravel, then lurches through the opening on to the bitumen and roars off into the night.

I feel stunned; empty; but manage the silly, random thought: I'd hate to be his wife, pet dog or cat when he gets home.

As I drive towards my own home, the Mary MacKillop rises in me, forming a notion that I will write to his club – no, make that the association and the tribunal – appealing the severity of the sentence, saying that I regret the outcome and am asking clemency on Robert's behalf. But this notion is like those ambitions and actions we dream in the ephemeral, twilight world of pre-sleep when best courses are clear and anything is possible – the dreams that melt away in the cold, hard light of day.

Somewhere on Sydney Road, dodging the tram tracks so the wheels won't slip and slide on them, I think of my 'adviser', the old pre-stroke Alf, and what a damned silly idea he would have deemed this appeal to . . . not clemency, but weakness. And silently I fall in beside him, hoping that mute inertia is the better part of valour.

Roses and Willows

Max's world was contained in a small, concreted backyard in the Melbourne suburb of Prahran. The hybrid border collie/husky pup yearned not just for canine company, but for the wide and wilder world beyond the high, brick fence. His owners were working people, and Max, in lonely puppydom, whined through days and weeks of boring, miserable separation anxiety.

Next door to Max were Daryl and Val Hood, and 'Hoodie', as he was known, was a workmate of mine at Pacific Publications where, between the two of us, we rewrote and battered into shape the unsolicited words of contributors to our weekly *Australasian Post* magazine. These non-staff writers were contributing to a journalism in which the thoughts and deeds of anyone in any place could be relayed, via a couple of rewriting sub-editors, to their great rural brethren around the nation. As human blotting-paper, Hoodie and I absorbed the ink-stained scribblings and typing of anyone with a story to tell. Submit it to *Post*, with a few good photos attached, and it might very well appear a week or two later alongside the jokes of (the late) Maurie Fields, the cartoons of Cedric the tramp and the Ettamogah Pub, and the giant Whopper crossword.

In the 1960s, I had worked briefly with Hoodie (me as a reporter, he as a sub-editor) at the Melbourne *Herald*. That was before it was bought by Rupert Murdoch and when it was Melbourne's only afternoon newspaper, a form and timing of media that, at least in English-speaking countries, has all but disappeared (unless, of course, they're giveaways, financed by their advertisers). Our paths hardly crossed at the *Herald*, and I didn't see Hoodie for more than two decades. Then, in the mid-1990s, still as a sub-editor, he joined the company I worked for and soon afterwards moved a mere ten metres across the carpet of our West Melbourne office – a paper dart toss belying the vast gulf in editorial attitudes and profitability of the respective mastheads: *TV Week*, from whence he came, and the battlers' *Aussie Post* to which he was closer in temperament and rather more drawn by its editorial philosophy. At least our stories, in the main, were real and earthy as opposed to the fawning sycophancy of the show business fan magazine-with-TV-programs he was leaving behind.

Like young Max, Hoodie yearned for a world beyond the confines of the *Aussie Post* office, which liked to give the impression its staff were homespun, regular country folk like the outback types we wrote about. We carried stories of an infinite variety, but most prized by the editors, who came and went in a dazzling succession, were accounts of killer crocodiles, sharks, snakes and buffalos, with tender mercies also extended to stories promoting formulae for hair regrowth and instant wealth. Down the back, beyond the staple fold, propping up classified ads for small-arms, knives, tattoos and advisers of the lovelorn, lurked columns by shonky astrologers and fortune-tellers.

We were telling of a disappearing Australia, of another place and another time, chronicling myths for . . . who? We weren't quite sure, even less sure of what 'they' wanted, despite 'reader surveys' and brainstorming sessions. One such session was in a Melbourne Cricket Ground superbox where an intense picking of brains by staff and management was leavened with twenty minutes of jokes told by Maurie Fields's son, Marty, and ended with a pep talk by the legendary (four premierships) VFL/AFL Aussie rules coach Tom Hafey. What Tom could contribute to our dilemma was far from clear. We, the workers, were already motivated by a combination of pride in work-performance and fear of unemployment, and the sudden and unexpected appearance of this bundle of testosterone produced an immediate reaction in at least one of the female journalists. Rolling her eyes ceilingward and uttering a word of single syllable, she brought upon herself, the following day, such wrath from management that the staff's MCG 'bonding' was rent asunder. The young eye-roller, popular with her workmates, was informed her career prospects were now strictly limited. As the bonding ligatures ripped and flew, it seemed more likely than ever that our colleague's prescribed future was shared.

Still, management and staff tried everything to revive the magazine's sagging fortunes. We hired Mike Whitney to do TV ads . . . we called in a TV current affairs crew and installed a tree as backdrop, hooking on to it the crows that adorn the Ettamogah Pub cartoons . . . we devised our own TV segments, and a new editor even managed to get his own Sunday morning radio show as putative opposition to the ABC's unassailable 'Australia All Over' with Ian McNamara. Our own 'Jacko' pushed the *Post* name between bush bands, ads and interviews, but our circulation lay as still and heavy as sump oil. We even changed our title, 'streamlining' the old *Australasian Post* to *Aussie Post*. A succession of columnists, including *Power Without Glory* author Frank Hardy, and rugby league guru Roy Masters, came and went. We simply couldn't afford them, not when the weekly prize for one of our readers' competitions was a floral laundry basket.

As *Post* began its prolonged death throes, the staff hit upon the idea of inviting our readers to write their own fictional short stories. Excellent. But when the idea came back from its excursion through management channels, a notable of Australian literature and literary talkfests had been attached, her well-paid brief being to select for publication the stories that duly began to pour in. 'Miss Brontë's' natural bent was along the lines of metaphysical cryptic-noire, and Hoodie and I duly scratched our heads trying to fathom what most of her favoured flock were on about. My own selection criterion of stories hanging proudly on a nail in a rural out-house waiting to give simple reading pleasure to a typical 'bushie' was being diametrically flouted. Editing required constant questioning and opinion-gathering across the newsroom, and cross words were said about the cryptics before us. After a year or so, when the throes had intensified to thrashing, the short stories mercifully became a deathly precursor of their host's impending fate. Reviewing the experiment, Hoodie and I agreed that a couple of old yarn-spinners had shown promise. So old, in fact, their simple, engaging, timeless prose was summoned up from crisp and yellowed leaves. But they were *Post* types to their bowyangs – Banjo Paterson and Henry Lawson.

None of it worked. As the magazine's circulation dropped below 50 000, then 40 000, and at last to 30 000, a crimson Kingswood sedan, its sides and roof emblazoned with *Post*'s icons, began touring outback roads with a reporter and photographer seeking out you-beaut Aussie bush yarns.

It sounded like fun, but Hoodie and I, desk-bound, weren't sharing it. Some days, Hoodie did it hard, his left leg jiggling a rapid tattoo, his head sinking on to the desk as he bemoaned the rationalisation that had us carrying a workload that once had been borne by four or five. But Hoodie had a dream. It was often expressed in the hang-dog tones of, say, Walter Matthau, as a desire for a 'country estate', and this cherished vision became a recurring dream/joke in which the whole office shared. (I made the Matthau comparison early on. Matthau's sad countenance was a clown's mask. Rather than be cast down by his glumness, the late comedian had the power to uplift; or so I found it, and so it was with Hoodie.)

What I didn't know about was the existence of Max the dog. Or that his owners, having departed for their day's work in inner Melbourne, would be replaced by Daryl and Val climbing that back fence where Max's world began and ended. Whereupon they'd hook a collar and leash on and walk him around the block or let him run free in a park. They did it regularly for months and when, at last, Max's owners revealed they were moving overseas and asked whether the Hoods knew anyone who might care for their dog, the couple were already well bonded to the long-haired pooch. Within seconds, they were its new owner.

Once or twice in our long parting, Hoodie had escaped journalism. For a while, he owned a pet shop. His affinity for animals, including Max, and their preferred milieu of the great outdoors had him couching his fantasies of escape from the grind of deadlines in terms of that evocative 'country estate'. He could have left us whenever he wanted, I thought, but Hoodie insisted he wanted to be around when *Post* met its fate, which could be a slow revival or, more likely, we thought, a hastier death. When, finally, *Post*'s circulation dropped to the life-threatening anaemia of 26 000, staff began to be off-loaded. I went to Bendigo. A few months later, Hoodie and the remaining Melbourne staff were scattered to the four winds as the magazine was dragged north to the company's Sydney headquarters, the Melburnians conspicuously uninvited. (The dear old rag, which came into being in 1864 as the *Australasian*, was sent to its rest in January 2002.)

When I caught up with him again, Hoodie had come to my neck of the woods, to the town of Bridgewater, just thirty-five kilometres north-west of Bendigo. The 'country estate' was a spacious, single-storey bungalow on the banks of the Loddon River. On the first day I visited, after soaking rain, his lush back lawn ran directly into the river's muddy water. I had arrived early on a warm, summer's day, and when Hoodie finally arrived and threw open the door of his van, Max sprang out and raced down that sloping lawn to plunge into the cooling river.

It was great to catch up with my popular colleague, who was loving the country life on his 'estate', which is beside a caravan park whose permanent residents, were they the magazine-buying type, would surely have plumped for *Post*. Hoodie had been picking grapes at Bridgewater's Waterwheel Vineyard and Winery and politely declined an offer to work a full week, instead of his two or three days. Appalled at the prospect of plenary labour, he later pulled stumps altogether, choosing to be a seven-days-a-week man of leisure.

It was at Waterwheel, with its 101 hectares (250 acres) under vines, that Hoodie met fellow grape-picker and cricketer Mike Rose. A singularly dedicated player, Mike seemed headed towards a new career of umpiring when I ventured to Inglewood, via Bridgewater, to meet him. Later, I wrote an article about him for my new employer, the *Bendigo Advertiser*, a regional daily:

Without the depth of non-playing support that keeps city cricket clubs buoyant, bush clubs often value their players in terms of 'putting in' and durability, ahead of runs and wickets.

At Kingower Cricket Club, in the Upper Loddon Cricket Association, they get double value from Mike Rose. The 46-year-old veteran is valued for everything – except in taking wickets, since his leg breaks are in mothballs, if not mummified.

The egg producer, who runs about 500 hens at his home off a dusty dirt track in Inglewood, forty-five kilometres north-west of Bendigo, has scored twelve centuries for Kingower seniors, guided it to one of its only two premierships in 1974–75, been secretary of the ULCA since giving up a five-year stint as its president in 1988, and – the feat that marks him as unique, at least in central Victoria – has not missed a single day as a player or umpire with his beloved Kingower in twenty-nine years.

'Our wedding was scheduled for New Year's Eve, 1976, to avoid a clash with the cricket,' says Mike's wife, Lynette, who has raised four equally cricket-mad children.

It was the same for the children's births. For the birth of elder son Ben, Lynette recalls being dropped off by Mike at the Bendigo Hospital on a match day in 1979, then being greeted by her sunburnt husband after the arrival of that same son who, in 2000–01, began captaining the Kingower seniors. Lynette bears no grudges for the absences. She's used to having Mike turn up to wedding receptions, having missed the nuptials, or racing off to cricket after an early wedding service to open a Kingower innings. It helps that Lynette's almost as cricket-mad as her husband. She was Kingower's team scorer before the family came along.

Now, on summer Saturdays, elder daughter Wendy, twenty-three, drives from Melbourne to keep the club's scorebooks. In 2000, Wendy completed a Bachelor of Applied Science degree in natural resource management at Deakin University and in mid-2001 was nursing an ankle broken in a match with her Inglewood netball team. An opening batsman, she joined Kingower juniors aged eight and was the first ULCA girl to captain a junior team. Wendy gave up cricket at seventeen when too old for the juniors. She's elder sister to opening batsman Ben; to David, sixteen, who captains Kingower juniors and joins the seniors in the afternoon; and Melanie, fourteen, who began playing with the local juniors in 1999 and is 'a pretty handy bowler', according to her proud dad.

The three elder children have been born with their father's ambidextrous quirk. All three are natural left-handers, but bat right-handed. Their right-handed dad was batting left-handed as far back as he can remember – that's when he played with Dingley in an under-16 competition in the outer Melbourne suburb of Springvale. And he's at a loss to explain his cricketing 'cack-handedness', other than to say 'I was told as a youngster that's the way it should be done.'

The Kingower club's records pull up short of an accurate analysis of games played and runs scored by Mike, who is one of just three life members in the club's sixty-two-year history.

'But it must be close to 300 games, at ten home and-away games per season, and we've made the finals pretty regularly,' he says. And at around 300 runs a season, he thinks he's scored some 9000 runs for Kingower seniors, for whom he began playing immediately on arriving in Inglewood with his parents and three siblings in 1971.

The most important runs he made for the club were 83 and 61 – the top scores in the 1974–75 grand final. The last of his three catches in that match disposed of opponents Bridgewater by a massive 275 runs and gave Kingower its most recent premiership.

But for Inglewood's single-season absence from the ULCA competition in 1971–72, Mike Rose would no doubt have played for his home town. But so desperate was the young man for a game of cricket on his arrival from Melbourne, he headed out to neighbouring Kingower, ten kilometres to the west, and has stuck fast. He was also an opening bowler on arriving at his new club, but switched to leg spin when he found it bursting at the seams with quicks.

Mike had opened the Kingower batting every year until five years ago when his son Ben and Mark Lamprell graduated from the club's juniors.

'I opened half a season with Ben, the other half with Mark, then told Ben I'd drop down the order to No. 7 the next season. We had plenty of players for the first game,' he says, 'so I volunteered to stand down. Ben dropped me to 12th man for the second match; I think he wanted to encourage someone who was thinking of playing elsewhere.'

'Playing elsewhere' never entered Mike's mind. For the past two summers, the selfless veteran has batted down the order, made himself 12th man or umpired, mostly the latter. But he was back in the action in 2000–01, batting in the tail 'when required', and changing into umpire's black dacks when not. He would have played in the 2000–01 semifinal except that the association couldn't find two neutral umpires so opted to draw one from each competing club. Naturally, Mike donned the white coat. The 'other' club, his home town of Inglewood, won by 150 runs and, in the grand final, Mike, umpiring again, stirred up some controversy by insisting that top-of-the-ladder Inglewood bat in a light drizzle, which duly turned into a downpour. No matter. Inglewood had the last laugh, beating its opponent Wedderburn on first innings.

The ULCA is based not only in Inglewood, but in Mike Rose's lounge room where a cabinet drawer is filled with the papers he shuffles and scribbles on each September to come up with the new season's draw. He expects to be ULCA secretary 'for the rest of my days', and cites the example of his club's previous president, Jack Gillespie, a retired farmer at Glenalbyn Grange, who remained in his post until his death in November 2000, at the age of eighty-five.

Hoodie and I edited many stories of characters such as Mike Rose. May each man share the enrichment of a long, well-earned retirement far from the city clamour.

Way to Go!

It was a hot, dusty day in the ironically named Green Gully, on the Keilor Plain west of Melbourne, and the game had sunk into a torpor. Or perhaps I had . . . I was sure the three decisions I'd given were right, but I was having to work hard on my concentration because the fielding team was all-but-silent, and that awareness of fieldsmen going through the motions can be contagious, making it hard to focus over twenty-two yards for five hours.

Then all of a sudden I'm frozen for the split second it takes to decide whether to zig or zag in response to a crashing straight drive that is coming at me at bail-height. More to the point, at groin height. This one's at lethal-missile speed, and a split second reveals it's not targeted at me but at the non-striker who, in any case, is close enough to provide a ricochet. The ball thunders into the splice of his bat. The willow, released from its grip, tumbles out to square leg.

Phew – close call! I observe the ball has gone to ground. But instantly I pose the question: what if, rebounding from the non-striker's bat, the ball had been caught by a fieldsman? Would the batsman be out? My cold sweat is as much about the fact that I would not have had a clue how to respond to the hypothetical appeal as it is about the just-averted realignment with the sopranos in my local choir.

I ask around, but no umpire at the pub that evening can recall a dismissal along the lines of my 'hypothetical'. I can hardly wait for Monday, just to phone my umpires' adviser. In fact, I have recently been talking to the Australian Cricket Board's (since retired) manager of umpiring, Tony Crafter, so I ask him.

Tony's answer is simple: 'Law 32.3 (e)', which says: '(A catch shall be considered to have been fairly made if) . . . a fielder catches the ball after it has touched an umpire, another fielder or the other batsman.' And for the purpose of this incident, 'the other batsman' includes the bat he's holding.

I've often thought that you could umpire this game for an entire lifetime and still encounter novel ways for a batsman to be given out or, at least, challenged by appeal.

Undoubtedly, cricket's most controversial dismissal is by lbw (leg before wicket). Almost since India (in 1932) and Pakistan (1954) were admitted to the Test arena, teams visiting the subcontinent have complained about its umpires' lbw bias against them. The slings have some justification: all too often appeals by subcontinent bowlers have been upheld by margins of four- or five-to-one in favour of the locals over the visitors. Brought up in New Zealand, I recall that before the Trevor Chappell under-arm incident on 1 February 1981, an early cause of NZ rankling over intermediary injustice was the mere two lbw shouts from the Kiwi bowlers upheld by Indian umpires on their home turf during a 1955–56 series, while the same gentlemen raised a finger fifteen times for their 'own' bowlers' appeals to balls hitting pads.

In the 1990s, with the advent of slow-motion replays, it became all-too-apparent that Australians and Kiwis living in glass houses shouldn't chuck cricket balls. Every season, Australian umpires have kept debates and arguments raging in pubs and workplaces over highly dubious lbws against visiting batsmen. And the guest, 'neutral' umpires have been no guarantee against lbw injustice.

In about every second match, Australian commentators tut-tut and second-guess in newspaper columns and the electronic media about applications of this highly subjective form of dismissal. Cricket authorities officially decry the media outbursts, which can so quickly become duelling headlines across oceans, with international sporting rivalries debased to mutual media slighting of umpires and officials.

Yet, paradoxically, in this electronic age of bringing sport to the world as it happens, when marketing is paramount to keep the game of cricket at the forefront of ever-increasing alternative recreations, the adage of 'any publicity is good publicity' holds true, and is probably advanced further by controversy over lbw dismissals than by any other aspect of umpiring.

In Hobart, in December 1999, an lbw decision against putatively the world's No. 1 batsman, Sachin Tendulkar, sparked up cricket writers half a world away. As Adelaide umpire Daryl Harper's finger went up in response to Glenn McGrath's insistent appeal, the cricketing world's press went into overdrive to place the crouching Indian captain on its front or back pages, circling the ball's contact point with Tendulkar's upper arm (some said it was his shoulder). Through the marvels of satellite television, slow-motion replays and freeze frames, the media conveyed Harper's decision as being more than questionable. India's own media – as happy as Pakistan's to ascribe to the decision an us-versus-them, even a racial, bias – went into a frenzy. Tendulkar himself refused to dwell on the controversial decision. The *Times* of India did it for him, insisting Tendulkar had been 'done in by umpire Harper'.

'The ball was still rising when it hit Tendulkar's shoulder,' complained the *Times*, 'and still Harper said it was out.'

Such umpiring decisions have consequences, not just for the batsman and his team. So it is entirely possible that Harper, being human and blessed with a survival instinct, was still over-compensating when on 8 November 2001, he kept his finger holstered and his hands at his sides to Chris Cairns's shout for lbw against Australia's Justin Langer in the opening over of the three-Test series at the Gabba. Commentators on both sides of the Tasman, having viewed the replays, concurred the missile that cannoned into Langer's back pad was zeroed in on middle stump. To their credit, Langer went on to score 104 and Harper joined the throng in admitting he'd got it wrong.

No batsman is happy with receiving the leg-before-wicket verdict, but as former Test umpire Lou Rowan points out, batsmen are in the worst position of all to judge the fairness of their dismissal by lbw. 'Having missed the ball altogether,' says Rowan, 'the batsman can hardly expect anyone to accept unquestioningly that he knew where the ball was going, unless it was obviously outside the line of leg stump.'

Rowan observes that it's unusual enough these days for a batsman to 'walk' on being caught behind the wicket, and it's almost unheard of for anyone to 'walk' before an lbw appeal is answered. However, Lou recalls that Queensland captain Mike Lucas did so in a 1971–72 Sheffield Shield match against WA. Hit on the pad by Graham McKenzie, he didn't look up, but simply turned and walked from the field!

The lbw Law, of course, allows for dismissal by body parts other than a leg blocking a ball's path to the stumps.

In the early 1990s, I took a two-year break from umpiring

to report on the progress of Melbourne's district senior competition for the now defunct *Sunday Herald*. On the afternoon of the final, 31 March 1990, with St Kilda veteran Warren Whiteside occupying the crease against a young Richmond up-and-comer named Paul Reiffel, I was lying by a sight-screen at the St Kilda Cricket Club's old Junction Oval ground on Fitzroy Street and looking at my notes when a loud 'clunking' sound from the centre caused me to jerk my head up. Consequently, some of the following in the next day's paper was from eye-witnesses rather than my own observation:

> Whiteside, fresh from winning a second Ryder Medal (Melbourne district cricket's award for the year's outstanding player, named for the Collingwood, Victorian and Australian great, Jack Ryder), opened with a single off David Saker to take his season's run tally to 600, then cover-drove Reiffel for two. Already genuinely quick, Reiffel responded with a succession of short deliveries to the chunky St Kilda No. 3. As a softening-up tactic it worked superbly; in Reiffel's twelfth over, after a snick to the boundary, Whiteside ducked to a searing delivery that kept low, struck the front of his helmet, deflected past diving 'keeper Gavin Holland and crossed the rope at fine leg. Whiteside, halfway up the wicket in search of a leg-bye, looked up to see umpire Len King's finger raised. King and fellow umpire Robin Bailhache, both Test and first-class veterans, acknowledged later the dismissal was unique in their experience.

More than a decade later, Whiteside recalls ducking to the half-tracker. To his astonishment, he says, the ball didn't lift as he was expecting:

> I kept my eyes on it for as long as possible and realised it was coming straight at me. My helmet was just two ear-pieces, it had no visor, and at the last instant I turned my head away. The ball hit the peak of the helmet and ricocheted away. I didn't know what had happened; at first, I thought it had bowled me. Then I glanced back and saw it running away past the 'keeper. I started running and was halfway down the wicket when the umpire raised his finger.

Whiteside wasn't hurt or dazed by the ball, but it was almost an hour later, while I was sitting with the scorers, that he poked his head into the room and asked of them: 'How was I out?' Whiteside's 'head-before-wicket' dismissal was vital to the outcome of the match as St Kilda, chasing 212, was dismissed for 210.

(Another clear memory of that day at the Junction Oval was the buzz going around the ground about a blond-haired kid who was turning them a country mile in the club's third-eleven: one Shane Warne. Later, there would be frissons to accompany the realisation Warne and I had played in the same lower-order team at St Kilda, me for two seasons in the late 1960s, he fleetingly on the way to ultimate glory, including selection by *Wisden* as one of its five cricketers of the twentieth century. The others are Sir Donald Bradman, Sir Garry Sobers, Sir Jack Hobbs, and Sir Vivian Richards, which raises the spectre . . . Sir Shane Warne?)

Whiteside, who played 213 district senior matches between 1978 and the end of 1999, found nothing particularly amusing about his 'head-before-wicket' dismissal. He did, however, chuckle at one earlier, equally bizarre, removal from the crease – even as it happened. He recalls:

> It was a match for St Kilda in 1986 against Hawthorn–East Melbourne at the old Glenferrie Oval. I played forward to a leg-spinner – I forget his name – and the ball hit me on the knee roll. It rebounded into the air, somewhere above my head. I had no idea where it was, but next thing it clanged on to the top of my helmet and bounced directly on to the bails, knocking them off. I was laughing after that one. I certainly wasn't laughing in the grand final a few years later – I was just confused.

These days, Whiteside, married to Kathy and with two children at primary school, enjoys a round of golf and works in Melbourne as a business development officer with an international freight transport company.

Cricket balls connecting with heads explains why cricket, over the past 200 years or so, has terminated more lives than any of Australia's four football codes.

My early cricket memories include my first visit to a first-class venue in New Zealand: Wellington's Basin Reserve where, in 1962–63, the local legend John Reid belted fifteen sixes in a first-class innings (against Northern Districts for whom the great All Black Don Clarke trundled medium-pacers as cannon fodder) – a record for sixes that stood for thirty-two years until Queensland and Australia's Andrew Symonds smashed sixteen of them on another oval of less-than-MCG dimensions, at Abergavenny, while playing for Gloucestershire against Glamorgan. Regrettably, I only heard the Reid innings by radio commentary. My visit to the hallowed Basin was a few years earlier, in the 1950s. My Dad and a younger brother, both uninterested in cricket, had just seen me into the ground and left to catch a tram along Kent Terrace (which Reid later peppered with his sixes) when a loud cry of 'Catch it!' went up.

Cricketers quickly gathered around a prone body measured out by a ball that had crashed into an unprotected skull. Soon a suited man ran on to the ground, followed five minutes later by an ambulance. The deathly hush that had fallen over the ground as they hoisted the stunned silly mid-on into the vehicle rather shook me up.

I experienced the same queasiness many years later when, umpiring a matting-on-concrete match in Melbourne's eastern suburbs, I stood in horror as a quickish bowler from the subcontinent swept by me, caught his front foot under the mat, flew through the air like the airborne Frank Tyson in his follow-through, performed a half pike, and crashed head-first on to the pitch. While he went into spasmic convulsions, I went into shock. It shames me still that while I was the closest to him as he began his thrashing and gurgling on the mat, I was not the first to render assistance, leaving that to a fieldsman who prised open the bowler's mouth to ensure he wasn't swallowing his tongue. The poor man's paroxysms had eased off by the time the ambulance arrived, and years later all I remember, further to the incident, was that the stricken bowler turned up, as batsman, the following week and kept his helmet on, even to the slow tweakers.

Probably the most famous dismissal by head-as-billiard-table-cushion within the game's higher echelons revolves around South Australian Eric ('Fritzy') Freeman, who was fielding at short leg to Seymour Nurse as the West Indies followed-on on the final day of the second Boxing Day Test of 1968, having scored 200 to Australia's 510.

Freeman's world revolved, too, that afternoon in Melbourne. The West Indies was 4/219 and going along nicely with Nurse and Gary Sobers having added 134 for the fifth wicket. Pressing for victory, captain Bill Lawry posted Freeman to short leg, a mere metre from Nurse and much too close for evasive action against the ferocious pull that despatched a short ball from spinner John Gleeson straight into the fieldsman.

'It collected me on the right side of my head,' recalls Fritzy:

> As I fell to the ground clutching a swelling lump, all I could hear was (wicketkeeper) Barry Jarman shouting, 'He's out!' I thought Barry was referring to me as I was on the deck and pretty stunned, but, in fact, the ball rebounded from my head down to Keith Stackpole some seventy metres away at backward square leg, and he accepted the catch – so he was talking about Nurse! That catch changed the match completely as Sobers also got out at the same score and the West Indies lost 6/61 to lose the Test by an innings and 30 runs [and eventually the series, 1–3]. I left the ground shortly after the incident but returned after ice-pack treatment.

Freeman, who nowadays comments on top-level cricket and AFL football played in Adelaide for ABC Radio, adds, 'In those days, there were no helmets. It was a freak dismissal and is often referred to by commentators whenever a player is dismissed in similar circumstances.'

Keith Stackpole, also an ABC Radio 'special comments' man, recalls he was at deep backward square leg, three-quarters of the way to the boundary at the southern stand end, instead of at his usual bat-pad or slips position, and was aware the ball had collected Freeman on its way to him. He remembers the shout of 'catch it' but didn't have much time to reflect on what was happening. 'It didn't go that high; I caught it at chest-height,' says Stackpole, and his recollection is that

Freeman gathered himself quickly. 'I'm pretty sure he was one of the first to congratulate me,' he says.

Officiating umpire Lou Rowan says of the incident, 'Freeman recovered quickly from a blow that might well have killed a lesser man.'

Like Freeman, Michael Slater's instinct was self-defence as Mark Butcher swept savagely at leg-spinner Stuart MacGill in the fourth Ashes Test at the MCG, in December 1998. Even in a trim, taut midriff such as Slater's, a doubling-up in defensive posture can create the anatomical equivalent of a baseballer's mitt. So it was that Slater, at short leg, even as he turned away from the ball, felt the blow, but managed to clasp a hand to the missile, holding it into his gut to complete the catch of the season. 'The full-blooded sweep nearly perforated Slater's navel, but stuck,' recorded the Australian edition of *Wisden Cricketers' Almanack*.

Slater and his team-mates' jubilation turned to disappointment the next day as England, despite conceding 70 runs on the first innings and witnessing Mike Atherton's first 'pair' in eighty-eight Tests, rode on the back of inspired bowling by Dean Headley (17–5–60–6), including a four-wicket haul in 12 balls, to win its only Test of the series, by 12 runs.

Occasionally, one man's physical pain can produce another's mental anguish. How's that? Lou Rowan, who had thirteen turbulent years as a first-class umpire, can explain. In the Adelaide Test against South Africa in 1963–64, Rowan, standing at square leg, failed to avoid a pull shot by Western Australian batsman Barry Shepherd. 'The result,' he says

> was a painful blow just inside the left hip, which left a bruise the size of a saucer. A sequel to this was ironic, as the shot would

> certainly have brought Shepherd 4 runs, but when the ball struck me he was able to run only a single. This was the last ball of the over, so that he then had to take strike for the first ball of the next over. With it, Trevor Goddard had poor Barry out, leg before.

Seven years later, in the 1970–71 Ashes series, Rowan was in the wars again. This time, in the fourth Test in Sydney, Graham McKenzie's square cut struck him painfully on the shin, shortly after which McKenzie had to retire when a short ball from John Snow struck him on the nose. The former umpire from Queensland observes: 'The moral seems to be that it doesn't pay batsmen to injure umpires with their shots. Yet retribution doesn't always follow. I made the mistake of turning my back on a Doug Walters shot in the England–Australia Test match in Perth in 1970–71 and for some time afterwards I found no pleasure in sitting down.'

Walters, too, was victim of an 'insult added to injury' dismissal. The boy from Dungog, NSW, who became one of Australia's most dashing post-war batsmen on either side of two years spent on National Service, copped the sort of physical pain he managed to avoid in army apparel in his State's third Sheffield Shield match of 1975–76.

On the batsman-friendly Adelaide Oval, Walters leaned back to play a pull shot against South Australian paceman Wayne Prior. The ball came through slower than Walters anticipated, causing him to try to stop his shot. Catching his sprigs in the pitch, he lost balance and, as the ball carried gently through to the 'keeper, crashed into his own stumps. Walters's first thought was that a stump had broken and gone through his leg. It wasn't until the fieldsmen had removed his pads that he realised what had happened – his left kneecap was halfway down his shin! Happily, when the masseur straightened his leg, everything went back into place.

Walters returned from Adelaide that night and went to see his doctor the next morning. The doctor was clearly in a happier frame of mind than his patient. He had been partying all night, and the party was still going at 11 a.m. when the troubled batsman called in. Walters recalls that the doctor assured him the knee would be okay in a fortnight, but wanted to see him in a couple of days. By then, Walters was black and blue from his hip to his big toe. Relaxed as ever, the doctor told Doug that's how it should have looked when he saw him the first time!

Walters recalls that he had physiotherapy twice a day for two weeks and then once a day (including electric shock treatment to the top and bottom of the knee), but it was three months after the accident before he played again. Unlike lightning, thunderbolts from pace bowlers tend to strike twice, or whenever it pleases the gods . . . in his first game back, playing for the NSW Association against a country side, Walters got whacked on the ligament of the same left knee. He got wise, he says, and thereafter protected his danger zone with two thigh pads joined together.

Any mug, fourth-change trundler might, under duress, admit that 'rubbish balls', clearly undeserving of a wicket, often claim them anyway. Former South Australian umpire Max O'Connell was officiating in a Shield match on his home turf when a ball from Queensland leg-spinner Malcolm Francke, who was hardly of the mug variety, slipped out of his hand. It bounced three times before reaching the startled middle-order batsman, John Nash, who, undecided whether to hit it for four or six, spooned it back for a caught and bowled.

Former Test captain and long-time Channel Nine commentator Richie Benaud very likely has seen more first-class matches than any living Australian. In the 1959–60 series in India, his third series at the helm, Richie helped engineer another 'defensive catch' which he rates as even more improbable than Michael Slater's.

Writing for this chapter, Benaud harks back to the second Test of that series, at Green Park, in Kanpur:

> N. J. Contractor was the batsman, and I had Alan Davidson bowling left-arm spin after he had finished his stint with the new ball. This was on a pitch without a blade of grass. Contractor, 74 at the time, swept Davidson and as Neil Harvey, at short backward square, ducked and turned away, the ball hit him and stuck between the back of his thighs. He fell to his knees and the ball stayed there. Neil carefully turned around, removed it and held it up.

Davidson finished with 7/93, but neither his heroic bowling nor Harvey's brilliance (or good fortune) could prevent Australia from losing the Test by 119 runs. As with the Slater reflex catch thirty-eight years later, Harvey's effort was contained within the Aussies' only loss of the series; their two wins over India were each by an innings, and two Tests were drawn.

Benaud rates the Harvey back-turned catch as one of the most remarkable he ever saw. Ironic, then, that he claims not to have seen his own amazing catch of Colin Cowdrey in the Lord's Test of 1956. A photo of the catch, showing Benaud, knees buckled, falling to his right and clutching the ball in his left hand at the end of an arm three-quarters extended above his head, is among the myriad framed photos and portraits in the Members' pavilion at the MCG. The photo caption is rather less conservative than the ambience of this cricketing sanctuary where lack of a tie denies entry. 'Catch of the century!' the caption shouts. 'Colin Cowdrey's cut, hit with tremendous power, is snapped up by Richie Benaud close in at point. Benaud later attributed the catch to reflexes – "I never even saw it," he said.'

Keith Stackpole, catcher of the Freeman deflection, nominates Mark Taylor's foot-to-hand catch at first slip off Michael Bevan to dismiss Carl Hooper in the second Test at the SCG in December 1996, as the most unusual catch he's seen.

The former Australian captain describes this remarkable dismissal in his book *Mark Taylor: A Captain's Year*:

> After lunch, Carl Hooper stands as our last stumbling block and, as chance has it, I bring about his dismissal in a moment I won't forget. I catch him at slip – eventually – off Michael Bevan via Healy's leg, my ribs, my hands, hat and finally foot . . . while lying on the ground. In all honesty, it was a bit of a stuff-up – and if it turned out to be a classic catch, well, it shouldn't have been. After fumbling around trying to get the darned thing under control, I did mean to kick it, although I had no clue where it might go. I was just hoping to keep the ball in the air so that Heals could catch it. As it turned out, it flopped back into my hands – and I finally took the catch. With Hooper gone, we go right on with it and close them down for 215 – a second successive comprehensive victory, by 124 runs.

Possibly the most highly acclaimed catch in the past two decades was the goalkeeper's tip-over-the-bar effort in the outfield by John Dyson to dismiss West Indian Sylvester Clarke in the Windies' second innings in Sydney in the summer of 1981–82. The Windies were on a run chase to give their pace battery time to skittle the Australians in the fourth innings. As the West Indies had lost the first match of a three-Test series by a mere 58 runs, there was a real 'edge' to the Sydney Test, as Dick French recalls in his chapter for this book.

Dyson himself recalls that, as the Windies' tail made clear their intention to slog, Greg Chappell posted him at deep mid-wicket, in front of the hill:

> I had already caught Michael Holding on the slog, and Greg said, 'It's a long boundary, I don't think they're good enough to reach it; go twenty metres in' [from the fence]. You're taught as a kid to do what the captain says . . . so, Clarke blocked a couple from [Bruce] Yardley then had an almighty slog and connected. I saw it clearly off the bat, and thought I was going to catch it in front of my face without having to move. But in the last twenty-odd metres, I realised the ball was higher than I'd first thought, and in the last second I knew I'd really have to jump for it . . . the leap was sideways and slightly backwards. The ball hit my hands perfectly, the left first and the right wrapped over it. I used to play soccer in the winter – I wasn't that year, so that I could concentrate on cricket – and I'd trained and played as a goalkeeper, so I just rolled like a 'keeper, pretty relieved to have caught it.

Even as Channel Nine's Bill Lawry went into high-register ecstasy and the director began preparing the first of countless replays, Dyson was on his feet and preparing to embrace an advancing stampede of team-mates.

'Bruce was pretty ecstatic about it. Greg was a little cooler; he just said, "Well, that's how to make an easy one look hard."'

Dyson had played first-grade soccer with Sutherland and St George (he's still playing, now with the Cronulla RSL), and most of the myriad of cricket fans who compared it with a soccer 'keeper's save didn't know how right they were. Asked how high he jumped to make the catch, Dyson doesn't hesitate: 'Seven or eight metres'. That might reflect the tedious frequency with which he's reminded of the catch, and the questions that invariably follow. 'In fact, I jumped as high as I could . . . there's hardly a week goes by when I don't get reminded of it. My only slight regret is that because of that grab, no one remembers I scored 127 not out in the same match to help save it.' (West Indies won the final Test in Adelaide by five wickets to square the series.)

Because it continues to be shown on TV, there are doubtless boys in backyards still pulling in the Dyson catch. After twenty-five years as a schoolteacher, John is still a friend of sporting youngsters – some 800 000 of them in NSW schools – as an officer with the State Department of Education and Training, working in its corporate relations and sponsorship unit to recruit and maintain sponsors for various school sporting programs.

One of the unluckiest dismissals is the run-out under Law 38, the notes attached to Section 2 of which say: 'If the ball is played on to the opposite wicket neither batsman is liable to be run out unless the ball has been touched by a fieldsman before the wicket is broken'. It's a rare summer that some bowler doesn't get a hand or finger on to a ball cannoning into the stumps beside him, thereby running out an innocent batsman, guilty only of backing up as he is supposed to do. It is surely the most infuriating form of dismissal for any batsman.

A malignant cousin of Law 38, Section 2, is the 'Mankad'

dismissal, upon which the non-striker will invariably curse the bowler who has whipped the bails off as 'punishment' for the over-eager single-sneaker advancing over the popping crease.

The eponymous Vinoo Mankad toured Australia with the 1947–48 Indian team and distinguished himself by twice running out Bill Brown while Brown was backing up too far at the bowler's end. In fact, Brown was run out in this manner several times. Mankad warned him before the first of these instances, but, notwithstanding this, Brown allowed his ingrained backing up habits to get the better of him.

Notorious for creating bad blood, the 'Mankad' mode of dismissal, in the mid-1970s, drove Harcourt, in central Victoria, out of the Castlemaine Association in which it had played for ninety years and into the neighbouring Bendigo District Cricket Association, where it stayed for almost two decades.

A long and bitter rivalry had existed between the apple and grape growers and sundry others of Harcourt, and the elevens produced by neighbouring Castlemaine, which is best known for its goldmining heritage and bacon factory. And when sixteen-year-old Martin Cairns strode to the wicket for his first A-grade match for the orchardist/vignerons and was immediately 'Mankaded' for backing up too far, tempers, naturally, erupted. A quarter of a century later, the Mankad perpetrator, now a prominent Castlemaine businessman, asks, understandably, that his name not be publicly linked with the incident – after taking some time to recall that, yes, he might have been involved in it.

But in 1976, at Camp Reserve in Castlemaine, officials and spectators of Harcourt strode to the wicket to remonstrate against the umpire's decision and his refusal to reinstate the young innocent at the crease. That night, the umpire found his car corralled. Harcourt, summoned to a tribunal, copped a hefty fine, but refused to pay and left the association. Next season the club took its bats and balls, drove over Big Hill and into Bendigo to renew its endeavours in that city's B1 turf competition. For Harcourt, which had been playing on concrete, that presented a challenge.

'The only turf wicket in Harcourt hadn't been used since the 1940s and it took some of the old-timers who had played on it to actually find it,' recalls Martin Cairns's younger brother, Andrew. In 1975, the old cricket ground in North Harcourt was found to be sprouting red gums. These were lopped and dug out and the reclaimed oval graded to produce what Andrew Cairns describes as 'one of the region's most picturesque grounds, surrounded by gum trees with a creek running beside it – an Australian version of an English village green'.

The next year, in the Bendigo competition, wicketkeeper and No. 3 batsman Andrew joined his brother, who also filled an important dual role as opening bat and medium-pacer. In counterpoint to his Mankad tale, Andrew spins a beguiling yarn from the early 1980s when Harcourt played Bendigo on that team's home pitch at the city's Queen Elizabeth Oval. 'We'd made about 180 and Bendigo was chasing,' he says. 'It was tight, and we needed three wickets and they needed 12 runs in a one-day match.' Andrew continues:

> One of our players was [noted playwright] John Romeril, an enigma, but a fantastic, articulate gentleman. He drove a Land Rover and wore creams, but over a blue singlet, with hobnail boots painted white in Dulux – he was the picture of an Aussie working-class cricketer. Our left-arm seamer Mark Santon was

> bowling; the batsman got an edge and I took the catch . . . two wickets left, Bendigo needing 12. The next pair scored 9, then we took another wicket. With the last pair together, needing 2 to win, Santon produced an in-swinging yorker which hit the No. 11 on the toe, right in front. The whole team went up as one, turning an appeal into a cheer. When the umpire failed to agree with us, Romeril strode to the wicket from deep fine leg, delivering a tirade – a Monty Python acid-spit – all the way to mid-pitch, where he stopped and bowed. Everyone, except the umpire, applauded. Romeril turned and walked theatrically back to the boundary. It was one of the funniest things I've ever seen.

Clearly inspired, Santon, two balls later, took the last Bendigo wicket and Harcourt, a one-run winner, entered the finals – but promptly went out again.

Australian opening bowler Alan Hurst, coincidentally now domiciled in Bendigo, was involved in the most recent 'Mankad' Test dismissal, in the final match that the Australian Cricket Board's XI played during the two seasons of Kerry Packer's World Series revolution.

It was the last of eight Tests (the first six against England) that 1978–79 summer, and Australia was one-down in the two-Test series against Pakistan after Sarfraz Nawaz had run amok on the low, slow Melbourne Cricket Ground wicket, capturing seven wickets for one run as Australia pulled up 71 runs short of its 382-run target.

Hurst, now teaching at a Bendigo primary school after a four-year stint as principal at another of that city's schools and a further four years running a computer business, recalls the dismissal of his fellow opening bowler Rodney Hogg in Australia's first innings of the first Test in Melbourne. The Hogg dismissal added to an existing lack of communication and unease, bordering on acrimony, between the two teams, and had a dramatic sequel in the following match. Hurst recalls:

> Sarfraz bowled a no-ball. Hoggie played forward and the ball dribbled off the bat to short leg. As he strolled out of his crease to pat the wicket down, [Javed] Miandad raced in from short backward square leg, ran behind Hoggie to whip the bails off, and appealed. Hogg had assumed it was a dead ball; it wasn't. Mushtaq Mohammed, the Pakistan captain, stood still and said nothing, so umpire Clarence Harvey, believing he had no option but to give him out, duly did so. Hoggie got more than halfway off the ground before Mushtaq ran after him, talked to him and invited him back.

Hogg's welcome back was short-lived. Harvey, under the Laws then operating, had no licence to reverse his decision and sent Hogg on his way again. The Law relating to umpires not being allowed to change their mind and reverse their decision was changed in 1980.

Former Test umpire Dick French says of the incident: 'Mick, in any event, could have asked the captain Mushtaq whether he wanted to call Hogg back, and Mushtaq did want that. Mick then should have gone along with the captain's request.' But no such niceties occurred in 1979, and Hurst recalls: 'Hoggie swung around, knocked two stumps out of the ground with his bat and marched off.' The bitter taste in everyone's mouth carried across the continent with the teams as they renewed hostilities, literally, in Perth a week later.

'The first two innings went as normal, Australia (327) taking a 50-run lead over Pakistan (277),' recalls Hurst. 'We made early inroads in their second innings and had them 9/263 when Asif Iqbal, who made 134 not out, was joined by Sikander Bakht.' He continues:

> I had bowled about four overs, and Sikander would sit on his bat for the first six or seven balls (eight-ball overs were still in place) then dash through to face a ball or two in case Asif hadn't farmed the strike completely. This had gone on for four or five overs when Trevor Laughlin, the 12th man who was on the field for Kim Hughes, drew my attention to the fact Sikander was cribbing – and not by a few inches. Hughes, who was acting captain because Graham Yallop was injured, was himself off the ground, leaving Andrew Hilditch to lead us. I asked Trevor how much Sikander was cribbing; his answer was, 'Two or three steps'. I hadn't even noticed. But the next over I did see that he was here to the wall [the wall in the lounge room of Hurst's Bendigo home is two metres away] out of his crease, and at the end of the over, Trevor asked, 'Did you see that?' I said, 'Yes, he's cheating. He's gone next over.' To my mind, it was blatant cheating, so the second-last ball of the next over, I just ran through, took the bails off, and he was two, two-and-a-half metres out of his crease. Sikander just stood there with his hands on his hips. [Umpire] Tony Crafter waited a few seconds, giving Hilditch a chance to say 'no', then raised his finger to Sikander to end the Pakistan innings.
>
> In the previous Test, Hoggie had wielded his bat behind him to knock down two of the stumps, and you could understand his frustration – you could imagine it, being called back then told to leave again. But Sikander, who had batted for forty minutes without making a run, stood there while Asif, the vice-captain, scattered all three stumps and gave us a tongue-lashing – one of the worst I ever heard on a cricket field.

Australia made 3/236 in its second innings to draw the series, but the tension and drama continued before the target was reached:

> We had made a good start, but then Rick Darling prodded a Sarfraz delivery to Sikander at mid-off. Although Rick's partner, Andrew Hilditch, hadn't left his crease, Sikander motioned as if to throw the stumps down, then lobbed the ball back to Sarfraz, who was a few metres down the wicket. The ball dribbled behind the stumps. Hilditch, being the gentleman, strolled after it, picked it up, and tossed it back to Sarfraz who jumped out of the way as if it were a bomb, and immediately appealed – again to poor old Tony Crafter. Tony waited a few seconds, looking deliberately at [captain] Mushtaq. No reaction, so Tony gave Hilditch out [for handling the ball], as he had to. It was the pay-back.

In the run chase, Darling made 79, Hilditch 29; Border 66, and Moss 38, were the not out batsmen. To add insult to Pakistan's injury, their bowlers (Sarfraz 0/85; Imran 0/81) took no scalps; as well as the 'handling the ball', there were two run-outs.

So an ugly series was drawn, 1-all. Hurst, the very antithesis of the fiery, cussing fast bowler of the Lillee/McGrath mould (his thoughtful commentary enhanced ABC Radio cricket broadcasts over a twelve-year career behind the microphone), feels no need to defend his 'Mankading' of Sikander. 'It happened – and I'll say this until I die – because he was cheating, taking an advantage of two or three metres on each of the last two balls of each over. This is fair dinkum stuff, it's not kids' backyard cricket, and it's gone on for four or five overs. If a batsman, playing forward, drags his foot a centimetre over the line, does the wicketkeeper give him a warning before taking the bails off?' Hurst asks rhetorically. 'In my mind, Sikander's action justified my reaction. Whereas if you look at what Sarfraz did, it was pure retaliation.'

The Pakistanis had included eight of their Packer WSC players in the two-Test series, which, Hurst says, 'made our performances, especially in Perth, very satisfying'. With the Perth Test over, captain Kim Hughes made a final bid to wash the bad taste out of everyone's mouth. Hughes ordered the Australians, armed generously with XXXXs and soft drinks, into the Pakistanis' rooms for an attempt at reconciliation. The gesture fell flat.

'I took in a couple of bottles of soft drink, sat down next to Imran Khan and offered him a drink,' recalls Hurst. 'I'd had little to do with him, but we were on speaking terms. Imran looked at me, shook his head and didn't say a word. As he took his boots and shirt off, I said something like, "it was an interesting game, wasn't it?" He gave a disinterested reply, excused himself and headed for the showers. Within five or ten minutes, most of the Australian players had been treated the same way, so we all headed back to our rooms. It was not what we were used to, after having just completed a series against the more sociable poms.'

Still, it was the fast bowler's best season. In that 1978–79 summer he played all eight Tests, including the losing six-Test series against England, and took 40 wickets (25 v. England; 15 v. Pakistan). His greatest triumph was in that final Pakistan Test in Perth, where he took nine wickets. Ten, if we include the 'Mankading' (we won't!). In 1979, Hurst headed off to England with another ACB, non-Packer side for the World Cup and a six-Test series in India. He managed two Tests of the

Indian leg before returning to Australia with a chronic back injury.

Watching him rise, painfully and with difficulty, from his lounge chair is to see that Hurst suffered in playing the game he loved. He admits he played his last five years only with the help of pain-killers as the result of a vertebrae link breaking about the time he played his first Test, against New Zealand, in 1974.

Hurst has an acute understanding of the exhaustion and agony Dean Jones went through in scoring his 210 at Madras in 1986–87. With his back almost 'gone', Hurst and Rodney Hogg shared three-over spells in the first, drawn Test in Madras in 1979 when temperatures averaged 42 degrees and humidity reached 93 per cent. Hogg twice left the ground with heat exhaustion, and Hurst remembers: 'You couldn't get air into your lungs because of the humidity and your head was pounding with the heat.'

After his second Indian Test, Hurst took the option of returning home rather than be placed in traction in an Indian hospital. As a result, Geoff Lawson flew out to begin his international career.

Alan Hurst is one of a legion of fast bowlers living with back pain after long careers. He even envies the great Dennis Lillee with whom he 'roomed' for four months on the Ashes and inaugural World Cup tour of England in 1975. Lillee had a season out of the game with eight stress fractures, which healed. That outcome is not in prospect for Hurst, and others. 'Two of my vertebrae just float; they don't link any more,' says the former fast bowler, who is matter-of-fact about his altered health, in no way engaged in self-pity. 'All that's holding [the two floating vertebrae] in place is ligament and muscle. There's no way you can bring the bones together without fusing them. An operation would require three vertebrae to be fused and two discs to be repaired or replaced, but even with today's technology, the surgeons can still offer only a 70 per cent chance of success. I've seen the results of that 30 per cent failure: one guy has had sixteen operations and, even with electronic stimulus to the muscles, he still can't walk properly. He originally had a very similar injury to mine.'

I met Alan Hurst while living in Bendigo. I'd got a job there in mid-1998 after *Australasian Post* off-loaded its Melbourne staff and relocated to Sydney. One of the best columns in the *Bendigo Advertiser*'s sports coverage was a weekly ramble through the international, State and bush scenery by the same Alan Hurst.

And when it comes to unusual dismissals, they don't come much rarer than this run-out, described in one of Hurst's columns about bush cricket. The central character was one Eric Horsted, who played cricket for Irrewillipe, a small town west of Colac in Victoria. Hurst wrote:

> In an accident as a kid, Eric lost his left leg when he fell off a horse-drawn plough. But he was fanatical about cricket and, with the aid of a wooden leg, became an outstanding batsman. Unknowing bowlers would often get a surprise when Eric came to the crease as he wore a pad only on his back leg. They got a further surprise when Eric pushed forward and the ball rebounded with a 'clunk' from his unpadded leg. Eric became adept at stealing leg byes from wayward bowlers. He made many centuries. In one game, when on 99, he was called through for a quick single. Unfortunately, as he started for the run, his wooden leg fell off and he was run out as he hobbled towards the other end. I'm told

his great sense of humour won the day as he walked off using his bat as support, with his leg tucked under his arm.

If Alan Hurst was a 'Mankad' instigator, Ian Redpath, who played sixty-seven Tests after making his debut against South Africa in 1963–64, remembers the hollow feeling of being on the receiving end. It was the drawn fourth Test against the West Indies in Adelaide in 1968–69, and Australia was chasing 360 to win. Redpath was batting with Ian Chappell 'and we were going fairly well,' he recalls. 'I was backing up when all of a sudden there was an appeal. I looked back and I was about a metre out [of my crease] and Charlie [Griffith] was standing with his hands on his hips and umpire Lou Rowan had his finger up. I said, "Well played, Charlie," and walked off.'

The dismissal was sweet revenge for Griffith, who, batting earlier in the day, had been run out after cannoning into the bowler Graham McKenzie. 'Charlie did not think of running a little wider and found McKenzie right in his way,' recalls umpire Lou Rowan of that dismissal. 'In the final countdown, Charlie was out by the proverbial mile. He was not amused and had plenty to say as he walked past me on his way to the dressing room.'

Rowan had equally little sympathy for Redpath ambling out of his crease prematurely. He remembers Griffith's appeal and Redpath 'looking at me with a rather feeble grin. As I raised my hand, I said to him, "You've had it, pal."

'Charlie came in for some intense barracking by the crowd,' continues Rowan. 'It was a most unusual dismissal and the first of the kind that I had experienced in first-class cricket. Comments and accusations about Redpath's run-out were plentiful. Some claimed that it was unfair. In my view, the batsman should be run-out because he had left his ground in an endeavour to gain an advantage for himself. Warnings are useless. Why warn a batsman for doing this, and not also warn him for batting out of his crease? The batsmen know the Laws and should obey them.'

Rowan swears that as the bowler delivered the ball, Redpath 'at times was four to eight feet out of his ground'. For his part, Redpath admits to keen embarrassment at his dismissal ('it doesn't happen very often in Test cricket') and to being a slow learner. In the next Test in Sydney, which Australia won by 382 runs to clinch the series, 3–1, the South Melbourne, Victorian and Test opener again lost concentration and strolled out of his crease. The laconic Redders admits: 'It was a bad habit of mine, of not watching the bowler's arm and walking as soon as he got into his delivery stride.' This time he was lucky; the bowler was the equally hostile quick, but more amiably disposed, Wes Hall, who halted in his delivery stride, waved the ball over the leg stump and said, so everyone could hear, 'Man, you'll never learn', and walked back to his mark, leaving Redpath's stumps intact.

Big Wes was right about Redpath, who still runs the antique shop he opened in Newtown, a western suburb of Geelong, in 1972. Redpath didn't learn. In a Shield match against Western Australia at the MCG in the mid-1970s, he was again the victim of a Mankad run-out, and again his opponent took pity. John Inverarity, the WA captain and one of the many friends Redpath made in the game, called him back, just before he crossed the boundary and the point of no-return.

While a frequent flirter with the rare Mankad form of despatchment, Redpath recalls the oddest dismissal he witnessed was in a district final in the early 1960s against

St Kilda, which was captained by Jack ('Darkie') Edwards, who later managed Australian Test teams. When Redpath's South Melbourne opening partner, Roger Miller, eased a single behind point, the St Kilda cover fieldsman conceded the run and lobbed the ball back to bowler Edwards, who raised a hand to try to catch it, missed and began strolling back to his mark, while behind him the ball dropped on to the stumps, running out the strolling Miller by an inch.

Wisden Cricketers' Almanack lists forty-six first-class cricketers who have been given out under Law 33 for 'handling the ball'. Only five have been Australians: E. Jones (for South Australia v. Victoria, in Melbourne in 1894–95); Peter Burge (Queensland v. NSW, in Sydney in 1958–59); Andrew Hilditch (Australia v. Pakistan, in Perth in 1978–79); R. B. Gartrell (Tasmania v. Victoria, in Melbourne in 1986–87); and Steve Waugh (Australia v. India, third Test, in Chennai in March 2001). The Australian *Wisden* recorded of the Waugh incident in Australia's first innings: 'Waugh, customarily the most vigilant and calculating of batsmen, had a rare lapse in concentration and became just the sixth player in 1539 Tests to be out handled the ball. He had survived a lbw appeal from Harbhajan, but as the ball bounced back towards him, he reflexively fended it away from the stumps with the palm of his right hand. His dramatic dismissal, for 47, prompted another batting collapse . . .' Tendulkar scored his twenty-fifth Test century a month before his twenty-eighth birthday, and the wily Harbhajan Singh took 8/84 (15 wickets for the match, 32 for the three-Test series) as Australia set India a seemingly modest 155 to win. After a mid-innings slump, the Indians struggled over the line with two wickets to spare to win the match and a memorable series.

Just occasionally, Australians have held up a scalp after invocation of Law 33. Most recent of them was fast bowler Merv Hughes, and the scalp was a prized one – no less than the since-transplanted tufts of Graham Gooch, in the Old Trafford Ashes Test of June 1993.

The legendary Dickie Bird was the umpire who condemned Gooch to become the first England player – and only the fifth worldwide – to be given out for handling the ball in a Test match. Bird recalls the incident in his 1998 updated autobiography:

> The England captain, batting from the front to try to prevent the Aussies from going one up in the six-match series, had made a magnificent 133 when, playing a ball from Merv Hughes down into his crease, he appeared to panic as it bounced back towards his stumps, and he knocked it away with his hand. Immediately, the Australian players appealed, and I had no option but to give Gooch out, although I felt very sorry for him, losing his wicket in that way at such a crucial stage of the game.
>
> Law 33 clearly states: 'Either batsman, on appeal, shall be out handled the ball, if he wilfully touches the ball while in play with the hand not holding the bat, unless he does so with the consent of the opposite side'.
>
> Gooch was obviously in breach of the Law, so I asked Australian captain Allan Border if he wanted to uphold the appeal. When he said he did, there was only one decision: 'That's out'. It was the first time I had given that particular decision in twenty-four years of umpiring first-class cricket. Gooch realised he would have to go as soon as he knocked the ball away. He could have used any other part of his body. He could have kicked the ball away, nudged it clear with his arm, or even headed it!

After his five hours and ten minutes of defiance, Gooch's dismissal proved to be the turning point. After he had gone, the remaining England batsmen were unable to hold out and the Australians eventually won that first Test by 179 runs.

There is nothing unusual about being given out lbw, but when seventeen batsmen are given out lbw in a single match, that is unusual. Unique, in fact. It happened to Dickie Bird and, as he explains in his book, although he was officiating, his role in the record was secondary. It happened when Bird umpired a Test between the West Indies and Pakistan at Port of Spain in April 1993. 'Mind you,' says the now-retired umpire, 'I only gave six [out]. My colleague, Steve Bucknor, was responsible for the rest.'

In 1992–93 at Kingsmead, Durban, South Africa played its first home Test match for twenty-two years. The other historic feature of the Test (against the Indian team captained by the since-disgraced and banned match-fixer Azharuddin) is that it was the first in which television replays, monitored by a third, off field umpire, were used. Now, that practice is universal for Tests and international one-dayers. Close calls had caused more than a century of controversy, even given the onus on umpires to give the benefit of any doubt to the batsman.

Although the electronic eye is ironing out the glitches at cricket's highest level, the run-out is still a trigger for controversy in sub-Test cricket, and will remain so.

The 'caught short' dismissal adds an often less-than-sanguine element to the game's history, and in a match at the Sydney Cricket Ground (then called the Association Ground) on 8 February 1879, a run-out caused a spectacular riot.

The England team was playing NSW and was led by Lord Harris, a baron who has often been portrayed as a doddering old toff. But in 1879 he was just twenty-eight and a pretty handy player; which was more than could be said for his team. The Englishmen, lacking the services of the mighty W. G. Grace, had lost the only Test of the tour by 10 wickets, five weeks earlier, and was on a return engagement with NSW, having lost the first match by 5 wickets. That summer presented something of a landmark in NSW cricket history, for it was the first time the State had dared meet an English team on level terms, each with an eleven-man side.

On the second day of the return match, a Saturday, England dismissed NSW for 177 in reply to its own first innings of 267. With the follow-on margin then only 80, the State's openers, Billy Murdoch and Alick Bannerman, were sent back in by his Lordship. The pair had put on 18 when Murdoch was run out. Murdoch, who later captained Australia in many Tests against England, had top-scored with an unbeaten 82 in the first innings, so much was expected of him in the second. The run-out was a close one. Disappointment for the crowd of 10 000 was immediate, and Murdoch's obvious displeasure fanned the emotion to anger. The *Sydney Morning Herald*'s reporter said the hooting began in the pavilion, where there were supposed to be several professional punters who stood to lose heavily if the Englishmen won the match. (Sound familiar?) Lord Harris sourced the trouble to the same place.

However, there were other contributing factors. One was that umpire George Coulthard, who gave Murdoch out, was a Victorian who had been brought to Sydney by Lord Harris. Another was that the English players had allegedly enraged the crowd by telling them they were nothing but 'sons of convicts'.

The *Sydney Morning Herald* blamed one of the English professionals for this, but both of them, Emmett and Ulyett, immediately wrote to the paper denying it and demanding a retraction since 'such a false report will cause a very bad impression among our many friends'.

The crowd's outrage over the run-out quickly turned into a full-scale riot. An estimated 2000 spectators swarmed on to the ground. The *SMH* said the invasion was begun by larrikins sitting at the bottom of 'the terrace', a forerunner of what was to become the Hill. The mob surged around the English players and the umpires. Lord Harris moved to protect the vulnerable Coulthard and was promptly hit on the body with a stick. The English player Hornby grabbed hold of the larrikin he thought was responsible and was marching him in custody to the pavilion when he, too, was assaulted. Hornby was hit in the face and had his shirt torn, but succeeded in getting his man to the pavilion and handing him over to police.

Australia's captain, Dave Gregory, was in the pavilion at the time of Murdoch's dismissal and could not possibly have judged the fairness of the run-out decision, yet he came to the conclusion, probably on the strength of Murdoch's account of the dismissal, that Coulthard was incompetent. Gregory told Lord Harris he wanted Coulthard replaced and, when the English captain refused, declared: 'Then the game is at an end'.

Vide Ray Illingworth in England's Sydney walk-off in 1970–71: throughout the melee, which lasted about thirty minutes, Lord Harris kept his men on the field for fear that Gregory might claim the match on forfeit if they left it.

With Gregory seeming determined to abandon the match himself and having called the two Australian batsmen back to the pavilion after the mob had been cleared from the ground, Harris turned to the other umpire, Edmund Barton, and asked whether Gregory could not be considered to have forfeited the match under the Laws of the game.

Barton, who was to become Australia's first prime minister, was then only three weeks past his thirtieth birthday and had not yet allowed politics to interfere to any serious extent with his cricket. However, he was already a man of some mettle, for he told Harris, 'I shall give it [the match] to you in two minutes' time if the batsmen do not return.'

Given the mood of the crowd, this would have been an incredibly courageous (or wreckless) thing to do. But, as with England's captain Ray Illingworth responding to umpire Lou Rowan's 'resume or forfeit' edict ninety-two years later, Australia's Dave Gregory opted to resume play. The crowd had other ideas. Twice, spectators stormed the oval just as play was about to restart and, at 5 p.m., with the mob still in control, play was called off for the day. It was resumed on the Monday and the Englishmen won by an innings and 41 runs.

The game's most famous run-out – of Ian Meckiff by the West Indies' Joe Solomon off the seventh ball of the final over to tie the first Test of 1960–61 – was as felicitous to the reputation of cricket as was the Billy Murdoch run-out damaging.

When the West Indies arrived in Australia in 1960, Test cricket was in a moribund state, weighed down through the 1950s by a surfeit of captains too afraid of defeat to venture risk, deserving of public indifference and empty seats – until, in Brisbane, the throwing arm of Joe Solomon sparked a nation's delight at Test cricket's first tie and gave clear evidence that the gods were smiling on Frank Worrell and Richie

Benaud in their publicly avowed intention to play purposeful, attacking cricket.

With the scores tied and two deliveries left as the sun cast its last, long shadows over the Gabba on 14 December 1960, Lindsay Kline, with the almost equally unaccomplished batsman Ian Meckiff at the other end, faced the fearsome Wesley Hall. The ball pitched in line with middle and leg, and Kline played it towards square leg. Solomon, renowned for his supreme skills as a fieldsman, moved swiftly to intercept and, with one stump to aim at, threw down the wicket. Umpire Colin Hoy raised his finger to signify Meckiff was short of his ground, and a lone cameraman froze the moment, creating one of cricket's best known images: a frantic, failing lunge, and five pairs of arms flung high in jubilation as Solomon's throw knocks a bail off. A riveting moment, not challenged even by the other Test tie in Madras in 1986 . . . though perhaps Warne's first Ashes ball of 1993, the unplayable leg-break that flummoxed Gatting and brought spin bowling back from the grave, came close.

Since the advent of helmets, buckled or with velcro to render them unlikely to fall on to stumps as batsmen duck and dive spasmically to avoid head-hunting quick men, the advent of errant headgear creating 'hit wicket' scorebook entries is rare. Caps are not likely to fall as batsmen dance down the wicket, or play any sort of shot, to the slows, and in the event of strong wind, caps are best handed to an umpire or otherwise discarded. So caps landing on wickets are as unlikely as a Glenn McGrath Test century.

Try telling that to the same Joe Solomon, then take a quick step backwards. In the second Test in Melbourne of that landmark series, Solomon, promoted to open the innings in place of Cammie Smith, was given out, correctly, after his cap fell from his head and dislodged the off bail as he played back to Richie Benaud.

For the second time in as many Tests, the unassuming Solomon's name was in the papers and another cameraman seized the moment, showing the famously honest wicket-keeper Wally Grout pointing to the fallen bail, leaving no doubt as to who he thinks is responsible. Umpire Hoy agreed with Grout, but the crowd, by now won over by the charm and brilliance of these West Indians, didn't. A big proportion of the 65 372 third-day crowd jeered Benaud, evidently believing he had acted unsportingly and ought to have recalled Solomon.

The fact that Benaud had stuck strictly to the Laws of the game cut no ice with them. Broadcaster and writer A. G. 'Johnnie' Moyes wagged his finger at the Melbourne crowd, writing: 'Whenever he [Benaud] started to bowl, yelling would continue and not for some time did the unruly mob cease its turbulence. It was a nasty scene and most discreditable.' Just what Moyes would have made of the Sydney crowd's displeasure at Murdoch's despatch in 1879 is a question of the boggling kind.

Solomon, for his part, admitted to writer and broadcaster Mike Coward, in Coward's *Calypso Summer* retrospective (published on the eve of the Frank Worrell Trophy series forty years later), that his 'hit wicket' in that second Test (won by Australia by 7 wickets) still baffles him. 'My cap fell on the wicket, and this is a slow bowler, not a fast bowler,' Solomon told Coward in a spluttered stream-of-consciousness. 'I'm not taking a bouncer . . . a slow bowler . . . play back . . . my cap fell off . . . hit the stumps!'

In recent years, cricket trivia buffs have been intrigued by a *Wisden* 'Unusual Dismissals' entry showing that H. Yadav, in a Tripura v. Orissa match at Cuttack, India, in 1997–98, was 'timed out'. This makes him the only man, in tens of thousands of first-class matches, to be dismissed this way! The relevant Law decrees that unless 'Time' has been called, the incoming batsman must be in a position to take guard, or for his partner to be ready to receive the next ball, within three minutes of the fall of the previous wicket. If this requirement is not met, the incoming batsman will be out – 'timed out'. In its 1999 edition, *Wisden* explained: 'Tripura No. 11 Hemulal Yadav became the first player to be given timed out, under Law 31, in first-class cricket. A drinks interval had been called at the fall of Tripura's ninth wicket [first innings], during which Yadav sat near the boundary, but the umpires said that he made no attempt to come to the crease after the break and they upheld Orissa's appeal against him.' Disappointing, really, for an ice-breaking offence. One might have hoped for something more exotic. A case of dysentery or Delhi belly (at the risk of cultural stereotyping) might have been more fitting. Perhaps a prolonged transaction with bookmaker 'John' behind the pavilion? In any event, it provided a footnote to a match otherwise unnoteworthy, with Orissa, Yadav's dispatcher, piling on 8/521 declared after winning the toss, then failing to nail its opponent (Tripura 235 and 3/187).

Up Before the Beak

Ooops, we've gone too far this time. 'Such is life' occurs to me. 'So, it has come to this' does too. And a few swear words.

In mid-1998, the ancient magazine on which I'd worked since 1990, *Australasian Post,* began shedding staff, just as its editorial group had been predicting it would. Any day for the past eight-or-so years we knew could be our last. And then it happened. Pacific Publications duly laid off all its *Post* staff, bar a couple, and moved the magazine to Sydney.

To stay employed and retain my salary, I had to go wherever needs took me. That was Bendigo, in central Victoria. I knew only one person there – a former girlfriend, and once I arrived, I desperately missed my ex-wife and family. A few years after our divorce, while I was still in Melbourne, my former wife had phoned me and asked whether I wanted us to be 'friends'. I had never stopped loving her, and I did! The causes of our split lay predominantly outside ourselves. In the interim, from her call to my retrenchment, I had sought her company at every opportunity and hoped for a formal reconciliation.

But my ex-wife had two hyperactive teenage daughters who, competing frenetically for their mother's attention, suddenly found common cause in me, their enemy, who absorbed far too much of that attention. At the end of a working day, then an eighty-minute return train/bus/walk to our home at North Dandenong in outer Melbourne, I was tired and sought only peace and quiet. And peace was anathema to the girls' constitution, just as it had been to me, a fellow hyperactive, at their age. TVs and stereos could not be turned down. Noise, and lots of it, was their balm. It ceased about midnight and, not being an astronaut with a hearing problem, I was constitutionally unable to withstand it. Differences between their mother and I became magnified. Shouting (mine) usurped calm consideration. We broke up, but in words that have the ring of a 1950s movie starring Gregory Peck, 'I loved my wife'. We were well matched, as she told me after her rapprochement phone call that arrived like a graduation gift, just as my separation counselling with a group of other wounded and divorced souls was wound up with ritualistic burnings of candles and papers bearing names of the late-betrothed.

But now I was taken off to the provinces where the local newspaper, thumping on to dewy lawns, required its sub-editors to work nightshifts. So much was missed: friends, loved ones, the restaurants and cinemas of Melbourne. Their replacement, as I arrived home about midnight, night after night, month after month, was a vicarious 'living' through the hazy images of my battered old TV set and the sharper images of books. And I was back at the place I had so wanted to escape from in my youth: provincialism. My initial working within it was to the south-east, across the Tasman, but it is a state of being and thinking beyond boundaries. And in Bendigo, where the editor asked me to be the feature writer between night shifts, my snuffling within the innards of this physically attractive city founded upon the discovery of gold in 1851, fast-tracked me, mentally, back to Blenheim, New Zealand, and to the flower-show results and Noxious Weeds Board prognostications I dutifully reported for the Marlborough Express in the 1960s.

I had given notice to my Emu Valley Cricket Association

(a notional entity encompassing the suburbs of Bendigo) of my intention to quit umpiring and, on my final Saturday behind the stumps I was, as it became all too apparent, free of the restraint that an ongoing commitment might have imposed. The umpires in this competition rotated through the three grades, and on this day I was in lowly division three. Not that that ever reduced my commitment to doing the best job possible in return for my $50 fee, which was paid by the players, some of whom, I knew, were dependent on Centrelink.

Emu Valley could rarely afford an umpiring partner. So this day I walked end to end, without the pressure valve a partner might unknowingly have provided, and unconscious at the outset of just how frustrated I was at events beyond the boundary line. I really had no awareness of carrying a molten core of anger until this final, post-resignation cricket match where a 'needling' captain got under my skin one hot Saturday.

A slope at one end of the paddock where we played constituted a part of the boundary, or so I thought. The point where the flat met the foot of the slope was sufficiently clear, I thought, to make the placing of small boundary flags along this 60-metre stretch unnecessary. (Local rules make mandatory the placing of markers at at least 20-metre intervals around the boundary.) In reality, I was guessing/hoping the demarcation between flat and slope would be clear, or that no lifted shot would land close, demanding judgement.

The knowledge this was to be my last match had made me careless. Of course, a demonic Murphy's Law lies in wait for such assumptions, and within ten minutes of the match starting, Ed, the toss-winning captain and opening batsman, hoicked a short one to this grey zone, landing it dangerously close to the notional line of demarcation. Four or six?

Ed turns to await my decision. I can't give one; have no idea what to signal. Then I remember, in blessed relief, the prescription for this situation: I ask the square leg umpire, a lower order batsman in Ed's team, who is closer to the landing point than me.

No idea, he signals with a shrug of his shoulders and disarming honesty. Again, as prescribed, I signal four rather than six, this being one of the rare occasions when benefit of the doubt goes to the bowler and the fielding team.

It's a warm day, much work lies ahead for both teams, and my decision doesn't go down well with Ed, who mutters, 'Let's at least keep the game honest.' This is red-rag material, salt to an open wound, but I mentally count the buttons on my coat, physically square my shoulders and swallow the verbal bile I want to hurl at him.

Eventually Ed is dismissed. I'm not involved in despatching him, and he departs, leaving me, in my mind, to click my heels above the dandelions and whoop my pleasure. But sitting with his team-mates on the timber decking of a tin-roofed, open shelter, the captain begins a verbal undermining, calling out in harsh judgement on my decisions through the afternoon. At one point, my signalling of a leg-bye is greeted by his jumping to his feet, arms raised in appreciation of an aberrationally correct decision. A colleague batsman given out caught behind from the softest of snicks is met with a clasping of the shoulders from a fellow-wronged.

The hours tick by, and what would be my satisfaction (at my own perception) of a good afternoon's decision making is displaced by a mounting resentment at Ed's visibly, audibly contrary view. But still I gulp back my instincts, which are to make a verbal reply.

At some point I give way, concessionally. It's aimed at the players' shelter, a modulated, measured, 'I'll speak to you after stumps, Ed,' which rather pleases me for its sensibleness. It gives me time to think, and for the remaining time before 6 p.m. I dwell upon the watershed we're both approaching.

My choices are clear: at stumps, I can do the necessary paperwork, scorebook-signing, pen my initials on the match ball, receive the 'all clear' from the captains and walk with dignity to my car. Or I can stay for a slug-fest with Ed.

What I don't appreciate is the latent cost of the afternoon's rigours. For five hours I have gulped back my instincts, which are to match fire with inferno. I have stored Ed's barbs in my memory, in a few cases jotted the trivia of time and quotations in my notebook, and at 6 p.m. I pull up stumps and pocket the bails.

My tormentor is already on the oval, striding towards me. I'm as unprepared as the Pompeians, and suddenly my preference for a dignified withdrawal from the gentle pastime of deliberating on cricketers' deeds and misdeeds is buried under the debris of my own spontaneous (verbal) eruption. It is triggered by Ed's gratuitous gambit: 'You haven't had a good day, but obviously you're new to umpiring so . . .'

Yeah, Ed, if fifteen seasons is new, I'm new.

Who knows how long I stood there haranguing him. Five minutes, as he said, later, or just the one or two I posited? The fact is, I had a truckload of verbs, nouns and expletives to unload and a couple of times Ed wanted to return to the (unflagged) boundary line he had just crossed. He walked towards me, then swerved to pass me. Arms akimbo, I blocked his way and all the time I was ranting.

Yet I retained a sharp awareness that I must not touch him, for to do so would, to him, constitute assault and take us to a higher tribunal than the one that was already beckoning with sirens and coloured lights.

In the pub, an hour later, some of my umpiring colleagues confirm, comfortingly, that, on their dealings with Ed, my adversary has proved a difficult customer.

'But you didn't call him "an arrogant little prick"?' I venture.

A silence. Then a helpful, 'Did you know he's vice-president of the association?'

Gulp. 'No, I didn't . . . thanks.'

Three weeks later, I stand before a three-man tribunal, flossing the consequences of my tete-a-tete with the captain and vice-president while avoiding, easily, the underlying causes of my contribution; perhaps at that point, they were not yet clear to me.

My counsel, three wise men of my umpires' association, including its president and secretary, are steadfast in their defence of me, presenting their case with such determination that the wronged gentleman – sweaty, feisty, provocative sportsman then; suited pacifist now – and his counsel jump to their feet to question 'just who is on trial here?'

I never liked these tribunals, where giant porkies and transformations from verbal aggressor to angelic innocence are standard. I'm determined not to undergo that change. I was a man behaving badly, and I'll take my medicine. (It's easy when you've already ministered your own dose of suspension/retirement, and rather like its flavour.) After the independent examiner who questioned Ed and me before the hearing has given his evidence to the tribunal, we, the adversaries, give ours, followed by equally offered, and taken, cross-examination.

The chairman despatches us to consider the evidence then, on our return, despatches me: suspended for the balance of the season.

I couldn't fault the verdict. It's the one I'd have given had I been the tribunal hearing evidence of this outburst, though its propensity to 'bring the game into disrepute' must have been limited by the fact that the two old stags who locked horns verbally did so beyond the hearing of anyone but themselves.

No, it's what followed that brought the game into disrepute. Being a newspaperman, it was a story too good to keep to myself. And the chap I told it to was also a newspaperman. So it had to leak. Like the Aswan Dam in flood.

On a slow news day, Ed and a fractious umpire made the page three lead, the local sports editor having written under the headline 'Bendigo cricket umpire strikes back':

> A Bendigo cricket umpire has been suspended for the rest of the season after a heated verbal exchange with a player.
>
> Emu Valley Cricket Association umpire John Gascoigne, a veteran of fifteen seasons, was rubbed out after he fronted the EVCA tribunal.
>
> A heated exchange between the long-time umpire and Emu Creek captain (Ed) in a division-three clash led to Gascoigne facing a report of 'bringing the game into disrepute'.
>
> It is understood to be the first time in the region's cricket history an umpire has been suspended.
>
> Gascoigne said yesterday the match was 'the most frustrating' he had endured in one-and-a-half seasons with the EVCA and more than thirty years' involvement with the game as a player, coach and umpire.
>
> 'There was a lot of sniping throughout the day's play. It started

early when there was an argument about whether a shot was a four or six.

'The Emu Creek captain [Ed] said, "Let's play it fairly." I told [Ed] I would speak to him after the match.'

When stumps were drawn, there was an argument between the umpire and the captain on field.

One of the umpire's comments was: '[If you were] any bigger, I might be tempted to take a swing at you.' A tribunal member asked if there was any physical contact, to which Gascoigne replied: 'There wasn't going to be unless he grew several inches after six o'clock.'

Gascoigne said he had decided before the match to resign from official duties, a decision based on working late hours and wanting a break from umpiring.

He said there were some comments he regretted.

Tribunal chairman Bob Colbourne said the panel had reprimanded Gascoigne and imposed suspension until the end of this season.

Mr Colbourne said it was the first time he had dealt with a charge against an umpire in almost ten years as tribunal chairman. He is also chairman of the Bendigo District Cricket Association's tribunal, and serves on football tribunals for the Heathcote and Loddon Valley competitions.

'On evidence presented, the umpire did admit to certain comments he shouldn't have made,' Mr Colbourne said. 'The incident was first investigated by the EVCA and then referred to the tribunal.'

End of story. Yes, I had been a very bad chap indeed and this burst of public exposure was undeniably embarrassing – as it should be.

In my letter thanking my fellow-umpire supporters at the tribunal, I felt the very least I could do was reassure them I would be making no return to their group, either for the following season or for any season thereafter. I didn't want my own embarrassment and shame tainting them, and the story of my indiscretion I felt would very likely precede me on to local cricket grounds.

But there was a curious coda. A few days after my suspension, while at work, I took a phone call from the president of the bigger of the two cricket associations covering the City of Greater Bendigo (a title conferred by a series of council mergers imposed by the Victorian Government in 1994). Naturally, the president and I referred to my fall from umpiring grace and, to my great surprise, he invited me to cross over and umpire in his association. To this day, I don't know whether he was joking. I assumed he was, and decided against calling his bluff.

Since then, merely watching, as a spectator, this graceful game whose name I write on forms inquiring as to my religion, has not been quite enough. I'd like to return to it as a player in a veterans' competition, but fear a chronic back injury would reimpose itself. So umpiring it will have to be.

I greatly look forward to my return. Older but wiser.

Part 2

On the Test Trail

Mel Johnson

They're Balls, Not Bombs!

My examiner, former Sheffield Shield umpire Graeme Jones sat at one end of a long table; I sat at the other end. I had studied hard to learn all the Laws of Cricket and here I finally was, sitting for my exam to become an umpire at the beginning of the 1972–73 season. Graeme asked, 'Are you ready to answer the oral questions?' I nodded. Then he hit me with it: 'What kind of beer do you drink, Mel?'

'XXXX,' I replied, surprised at his line of questioning.

'Congratulations,' Graeme said, 'you are now an umpire.'

And so began an umpiring career that spanned sixteen years.

That was late August 1972, and by mid-September, I was appointed to my first game, oddly enough with the third-grade team from Easts, the one I had to rather forcibly retire from. So there it was: Easts v. Souths, third grade, at the Bob Young Oval. I was by myself, there was no luxury of having a partner. And my first task was to give the opening batsman 'two legs'.

I'd always batted on centre, and I didn't have a clue what this batsman was talking about. Nobody trained us back in those days; we just sat for a silly little exam where I was asked what beer I drank, and my association was very short of umpires. So I had to ask him, 'What does two legs mean?' The batsman explained politely enough, but it was a less-than-auspicious start to my career.

I learned quickly and by Christmas 1972, I was umpiring

my first, first-grade game. From the outset, the first-grade players helped me enormously; fellows like Lew Cooper, Billy 'Wubby' Albury from Wynnum–Manly, Jack and Peter Evans from Easts and Donny Allen from Norths. As for Graeme's beer question: no, I didn't mind having a beer after the game – perhaps for longer than I should have, according to my wife, Jeanette – and we'd discuss the match, dissect it long and sensibly, so that, almost imperceptibly, the players during and after matches added infinitely more to my knowledge than the written Laws and my familiarity with them. They quickly taught me a hell of a lot about umpiring technique, what and how to do it, and so I made the first grade by December after four matches in the lower orders.

As with so many kids, cricket started for me with my Dad, Bill, who taught me and my brothers, Darryl and Lloyd, both the game's techniques and its largely unstated values. Dad, who was born in Barcaldine, in central-western Queensland, and played his cricket there as well as in Mackay and Rockhampton, was usually in the thick of our backyard matches where sibling rivalry would boil over from time to time. He had served with the RAAF in Milne Bay during WWII, later became a customs officer in Brisbane, and was proud of the fact that, playing as Mackay's wicketkeeper, he had the great Don Tallon as his opposite number when his team played Bundaberg. Dad was also a useful soccer player, and instilled in us as kids that the umpire's decision (his) was final. During all my years of umpiring I would often ask myself: what would Dad have done? It stood me in good stead all the way through my umpiring career.

As we got older the games moved out on to the road at Camp Hill, in Brisbane, and the neighbours would become our team-mates and opposition. Malcolm Morley was a fast bowler both on our street and for Easts in Brisbane. I seemed to handle myself pretty well against him, well enough for him to invite me as a thirteen-year-old down to Easts, to a playing career that lasted fifteen years with a club that produced such State or Test players as Peter Burge, Peter Allan, Ross Duncan, Tony Dell and Bob Paulsen. Current Test umpire Tony McQuillan played for Easts.

Just before joining the club, I was selected for the Queensland schoolboys' under-12 cricket XI and was made its captain. We played in Sydney for a shield that – like the Sheffield variety – Queensland had never won. Our team included Dick Marks, who later played centre for the Wallabies rugby union XV, Bill Buckle, who went on to play cricket for Queensland, and a wicketkeeper in George Negus, who made a name for himself in TV as a *60 Minutes* reporter, host of ABC's *Foreign Correspondent*, and later as chief executive of Soccer Australia. This constituted a fair bit of talent, and enough to win, convincingly, the shield in Sydney. Having joined Easts, I moved through the grades from the fourth-eleven, or C division, through to first grade in 1959–60 when I played alongside Peter Burge, Peter Allan and newcomer Bob Paulsen, and we were team-mates until 1963–64, by which time my teaching career had taken me into the bush regions. Eventually, I secured a job at Canberra Grammar School and, while in the ACT, became captain-coach of Queanbeyan Cricket Club – and the first paid coach of any cricket club in Australia. I represented the ACT until moving back to Brisbane in 1970 to take up another position.

I've lost count of the times I've been asked, 'How did you get into umpiring?' The answer is simple. After coming back from Canberra I rejoined Easts and played third grade. We'd just completed the first Saturday of a two-day match when I bent over to pick up something and suddenly realised I'd lost all feeling from the waist down. My back was damaged.

I was taken to hospital and told to lie still while they examined me and referred me to the first of a series of physiotherapists who told me things like, 'Get yourself another car, your one's going to damage your back', and 'Wrap yourself in cotton wool, you're buggered'. Eventually I saw a fellow named Peter Dornan, who ran the Toowong Physiotherapy Centre, and Richard Dunn, the Australian Rugby Union's physio, who were a shade more positive and asked me what *I* wanted to do. My answer – 'I want to be able to stand up and move around, initially' – earned me a series of exercises prescribed by Dornan. I followed these religiously until my first umpiring assignment came after a two-year break from cricket.

Two years recuperating meant Saturday afternoons were no longer filled with playing cricket. Naturally, I fell into some time-honoured Aussie bad habits, like having a drink and a bet. I also had a mortgage and two young kids and, consequently, after a couple of years during which I really was lost, my wife said, 'You love cricket – why don't you take up umpiring?'

That's how I found myself on an August night, with my examiner, Graeme Jones, answering questions on the game's Laws, such as 'What kind of beer do you drink?'

So, from taking on umpiring to keep me out of the TAB and the pub, I found myself in at the deep end, umpiring first-grade games, leading eventually to my 131 top-level games, including twenty-one Tests, thirty-eight Sheffield Shield matches (three of them finals), fifty-two one-day internationals,

State matches against visiting teams, McDonald's and Gillette Cup one-dayers, and a visit to Sharjah in 1984.

From 1970, regular meetings with Dornan and Dunn kept me on the cricket field through an umpiring career that was one of suspense, knowing the silliest little thing like placing the bails back on the stumps could induce a 'click' in my vertebra, ensuring I spent the rest of the day in agony. The back is still problematic, but manageable, so that I continue to play golf and do low-level exercise.

After a three-season apprenticeship in first grade, the selectors deemed me good enough to have a place in a Gillette Cup match between Queensland and Tasmania. I am eternally grateful to the three men who launched me on my career: W. E. P. ('Wep') Harris, Roy Littledyke and 'Horse' Pascoe. After a couple of seasons in first grade, I felt ready for the 'big time'.

To my dismay, my umpiring bosses made me go another season in first grade – yet, reflecting on my Gillette Cup experience, I realised how cricket-smart they were. That match was an eye-opener, to use an unfortunate term for one of my kind, and so much quicker and more intense than anything I'd experienced before. It didn't help that Jeff Thomson, who I'd never stood for previously, even in club matches, opened from my end. By the time I raised my eyes from adjudicating on his foot-fall, all I saw was the ball being passed from Greg Chappell at first slip to Phil Carlson in the gully. I had not seen the ball go down the wicket, the batsman, or John MacLean gloving it. It took me about three overs to catch up with Jeff. During that time, Mark Ray, Tasmania's opener, must have got an edge, which MacLean took, and the Queenslanders were all appealing as though it was a certainty. Well, I hadn't seen it and was in a dilemma until I heard Mark Ray's voice: 'For

Christ's sake, give me out. I hit the bloody thing!' So I did. I found out later that the Tasmanians were instructed not to walk and it was obvious from Mark's plaintive cry that he didn't want to be out there any longer than was absolutely necessary.

In 1975–76 I was appointed to my first Sheffield Shield match, Queensland against WA, at the Gabba. Two things stand out in my mind from that game: Mick Malone bowling from my end from the start of play until after the tea interval, and the great Dennis Lillee putting me in my place and teaching me a valuable lesson. Mick's effort showed very clearly that the Shield competition was not a place for the faint-hearted and gave me a benchmark for some of the 'pretenders' who came later. Dennis's lesson was a little more to the point. He was bowling to Trevor Hohns and letting the occasional short one rip. Trevor, who was not a good player of the rising ball, had played and missed repeatedly. Dennis became more and more agitated until eventually, he extended his follow-through and stood very close to the batsman, giving him the benefit of his knowledge and generally reading his horoscope. About halfway through his tirade, I called out to Dennis and suggested he return to his bowling mark. Dennis tersely replied, 'You wait your turn – I haven't finished with him yet,' and then continued the other half of his 'advice' to Trevor. After finishing with Hohns, he turned on his heel and demanded of me, 'Now, what's your problem?' My problem, I replied, was that I had jumped in too early, and wouldn't do it again, 'but you won't do that again, either, will you, Dennis?' I had no more trouble with Dennis that day, or any day thereafter. No real trouble, anyway.

Shield matches, one-dayers (domestic variety) and State

and touring sides came and went. Memories of those matches include a sickening injury to Kevin Badcock; Greg Chappell's lack of knowledge of the Laws; and Bob Willis's gearing up for the first Ashes Test of 1982–83.

Badcock's injury occurred during a McDonald's Cup match between Queensland and Tasmania at the Gabba. Tasmania was all out for 56. Viv Richards, who was playing for Queensland at the time, faced a delivery from Badcock. Richards flat-batted the ball with such power that poor Badcock was still low in his follow-through when the ball smashed into his cheekbone. Horrifyingly, it sounded as though a watermelon had been dropped three floors on to concrete. Fortunately, Badcock survived relatively unscathed after a couple of nights in hospital, but I can't ever remember seeing him play again.

My memorable encounter with Greg Chappell also occurred at the Gabba in 1982–83, when Queensland was playing England. Allan Lamb was batting and struck the ball powerfully about head high all the way to the mid-off boundary where Robbie Kerr took the ball at chest height. The force of the ball caused Robbie to stumble backwards over the little picket fence close to where it joined the big fence of the dog track. Under the Laws, my partner, Jim Taylor, correctly signalled 6 runs (and not out). Greg called out to me from first slip: 'What's going on here, Mel?'

I quoted the Law and said my partner was correct. Chappell then asked, 'How long has that been a Law?'

'Since 1980,' I replied.

'Well, I'll be buggered,' was Greg's response. It never ceases to amaze me that cricketers of all levels have a relatively small knowledge of the Laws of the game they play. If they sit down to play a game of Ludo, the first thing they acquaint themselves of are the rules. But, funnily enough, they either don't want to know, or rely heavily on the umpires to tell them, the Laws of Cricket.

The incident with Bob Willis, who was a very professional cricketer and a good bloke with it, occurred prior to the start of a Queensland v. England game. He told me that he could possibly be bowling a few no-balls, and would I call them all. A strange request, I thought, but there soon proved to be a succession of no-balls. Bob said he remembered that on a previous tour he'd had a no-ball problem bowling from the Vulture Street end of the Gabba, and what he was trying to do in this lead-up to the Test match was to adjust his run-up. The reason so many quick bowlers have become frustrated at overstepping at that end of the ground is simple: the run-up is ever-so-slightly downhill. Bob worked out that he had to add half a pace to his normal run-up if he bowled from the Vulture Street end of the ground. Problem solved, but not before extras provided a boost for the Queensland XI.

My first Test was Australia v. the West Indies, the third Test, at Adelaide Oval in 1979–80. My partner as I walked to the centre of that beautiful ground on Australia Day 1980 was Max O'Connell, who was standing in his last Test. Yet it seemed the butterflies in my stomach were less flighty than the ones in his. Max was like a flea in a bottle; he was everywhere before the match. He had me at the ground at 9 a.m., and he shunted me from one place to another, back and forth, up and down the grandstand steps. At 10 a.m. I said, 'Max – enough, I'll be worn out before the bloody match starts.' Max kept doing the rounds while I retreated to the umpires' room. He walked in at 10.55 a.m. announcing, 'Righto, we're going out.'

As we walked out to the centre, watched by 26 000 people, I was aware how unaffected I was by the big occasion and not the least bit nervous – until they played the National Anthem when my mouth went dry and then, could I have used one of those XXXXs!

Standing at square leg for the first over I was struck by how close the crowd was, and how quiet they were. It didn't last long. Max gave Gordon Greenidge out lbw and the crowd erupted. The noise was deafening, and right there, as my spine tingled, it sank in: this is Test cricket and I'm part of it. It was the turning point also to my enjoyment; I thoroughly enjoyed the match from that moment. I very seldom looked at scoreboards throughout my career, and I don't even remember the result of the game [Australia lost by 408 runs]. All I knew at the end of each day was how many wickets were down and, naturally, how many there were to go before the game finished.

It was not only my first Test; the Adelaide match also signalled my first run-in with a player. Colin Croft was a fair-sized lump of a fellow who made a name for himself by cannoning into Kiwi umpire Fred Goodall for not raising his finger on command. On this occasion he decided to bowl around the wicket and began running almost immediately into the danger area, so I mentioned this to him as he walked back to his mark. I braced myself for the barrage of abuse only the quick men can deliver; instead, he just said, 'Alright, I'll bowl over the wicket.' Almost involuntarily, I said, 'Oh, you big girl!' If looks could kill, my first Test would have been my last.

Now, twenty-two years after that debut Test, I remember vividly giving Croftie what he wanted as he bowled around the wicket in the same match: a raised finger for an lbw shout against Greg Chappell. The big man, who later got himself a commercial pilot's licence, must have been over the moon, but I was feeling far closer to earth; in fact, I was looking for a hole to crawl into. It was the worst decision I ever gave! And giving out the Australian captain left me in fear and trepidation, wondering whether I'd ever get another game in first-class cricket, let alone Tests. But Greg wasn't one to bear grudges, and I remain forever grateful.

Individually, Dennis Lillee bowled tirelessly through a heatwave on a dead, flat track – some ninety minutes of unrelieved toil with the sweat pouring from him, making that eyebrow flick to keep it out of his eyes. For all his efforts, he hadn't made much impression on the batsmen. But his team spirit and optimism were unquenchable and as he handed the ball to Geoff Dymock after his spell, I heard him say, 'Hang in there, I think you can get five if you put it there, and don't give 'em any room.' Sure enough, Dymock got five scalps in the innings.

At the other end, Lenny Pascoe, one of the great characters of the game, steamed in. His front foot was perilously close to the line at the best of times, and he was bowling to the great Viv Richards, who was flat-batting his bouncers back past him and to the cover boundaries. In those days, there was no limit to the number of bouncers that could be bowled. As Lenny walked back towards me, I told him he was starting to get too far over the line (I allowed a little leeway, but this was before TV zoomed in on such technicalities for all the world to see). Next thing, Viv was calling at me not to warn him. I figured he meant, 'Don't warn him, call him.' None of it. 'No,' said Viv, 'let him get closer, I just love it.' That, of course, only fired Lenny up even more.

Already I was finding the fire and brimstone of Test cricket was tempered by good humour. But what also struck me well before the end of my first Test was the comradeship of the Australian players, despite, it seemed to me, the fierce rivalry they show to each other in State games.

Sikander Bakht, the rake-thin Pakistan opening bowler, turned up in Sydney in a day/night game I umpired in 1981. Some of the Australian players reckoned he used his bat cover as a sleeping bag. The only thing inflated about him was his own opinion of his ability. At one point he bowled a bean ball (head-high full toss) to Rodney Marsh, who was never a good choice to commit that sin against. Marsh fended it off for a run and, as he sauntered down the pitch, he gave Sikander a gobful, mentioning his eating habits. I reckoned Rodney had handled it fairly well – even moderately by his standards – but as Sikander walked back past me, he had a grin that suggested the comments had made no impact whatsoever. I thought, bugger this, so I said to him, 'Come here.'

'You cannot warn me,' Sikander insisted. 'The ball slipped.'

'I'm not going to warn you, mate,' I answered, 'I'm going to give you a piece of friendly advice. You bowl another one of those to Rodney Marsh or any other Australian batsman and I guarantee you, they'll take you out behind the shed and they'll belt the shit out of you, and you can even wear your helmet if you wish.'

Sikander turned around quickly and said, 'Sorry, Mr Marsh.'

Another incident I was heavily involved in was the Dennis Lillee/Javed Miandad tussle in Perth in 1981–82. Miandad was a brilliant cricketer; a great improviser who had the game well and truly nutted out. Although he was not technically solid, he was a great fighter. During the match against Queensland early on that tour, Javed was captain.

As the rain tumbled down outside, Javed came and sat in our umpires' room. I assumed that because he knew I was rostered to umpire a couple of Tests, he was going to butter me up. At one point in the conversation, I asked him, 'What does it mean to you to be Pakistan's captain?'

His answer shook me up: 'I get to attend all the stonings at executions!'

'What do you mean?' I asked, shocked.

'They bury them up to their neck,' he replied. 'You start off with little stones, then gradually throw bigger stones and because I'm captain, I get my turn when the bigger stones are thrown.'

Gulp! 'That's terrific, Javed,' I said, thinking that was more prudent than the more honest: 'What sort of an arsehole are you?'

So we got to the Perth Test of 1981–82, which gave rise to the infamous picture of Javed with raised bat in response to Lillee's frustrated kick in the shins, with umpire Tony Crafter, the peacemaker, standing between them, preventing perhaps Test cricket's first two-man brawl.

The tensions started on day one when Australia was 7 down and Javed plunked himself at silly mid-off, casting a shadow in front of Lillee, who was batting. Javed jigged about as though he had fleas, spoke in what I assume was Urdu, the dialect spoken by Pakistani Muslims, and quite quickly got under Lillee's skin. I spoke to Dennis about it after stumps that day, and the great fast bowler admitted, 'This has been going on for some time. I got him out seven times in Pakistan (in 1979–80), but he wouldn't walk.' Apparently, the rules in Pakistan at that time, before so-called neutral umpires, were that if a star batsman nicked the ball he walked, possibly saving the umpire from having his house burnt down. According to Dennis, Miandad followed the rule to the letter – after he'd reached his hundred.

So when Miandad walked out to bat in Perth, Tony and I knew it was going to be 'on'. The plan, we already knew, was to hit Miandad – not necessarily with some short stuff but with the fielders' returns: to the back of the neck, his back, bum or the back of his legs. Miandad soon twigged to the plan. Filmed footage shows Graeme Wood and Lillee, with Miandad out of his crease between them, toying with the West Australians by shunting his bat over and out of the crease. And the only thing Lillee hit was me, in the shins, and it hurt like hell!

The tension between Miandad and Lillee continued to build during the match, but we reckoned they'd both been around long enough not to do anything stupid. Not long after, as I stood at square leg, I saw Dennis stand his ground as he got in the pathway of batsman Javed as he ran a single. The Pakistani had the bat by its handle, and ran it up the middle of Dennis's back. Dennis promptly whipped around and had a swipe at him with his left arm. Miandad wanted to carry it on, and raised his bat as if to hit Lillee, who swung a kick in the shins. All the while I was standing at square leg screaming out, 'Let 'em fight, let 'em fight – get rid of both of them.' Thankfully, perhaps, that didn't happen, but this was in the days when the Australians adjudicated on their own misbehaviour and all Tony and I had to do was tick a couple of boxes on a form at the end of the day's play. So when we got off the ground about five minutes after the players, we walked into our dressing room, grabbed our sheet of paper, ticked the boxes to indicate they were charged with assault and attempted assault, and walked back round to the players' dressing rooms.

In the Australian rooms, captain Greg Chappell's first words were: 'I thought I'd see you fellows sooner or later. Have you charged the other fellow?'

One of us answered, 'Yes, we've charged him equally.' So Greg took the form and said, 'This will be the minimum penalty, a $200 fine. We'll see what they do.'

We walked straight to the Pakistani dressing room, which was empty. Not a soul in sight. An attendant told us they'd ordered cabs and were 'just around the side'. We walked around the wall to find Miandad, still in his pads, batting gloves and helmet, holding his bat, and climbing into the back of a taxi. Just before he slammed the door, we managed to shove the charge sheet into his hand. Next morning the Pakistani management came to us and told us the incident had nothing to do with Javed Miandad; they wouldn't have any part of it. Consequently, we were obliged to appeal against the Australian decision to fine Lillee. That last day, Tony and I left the ground at about 10.30 p.m. after having written the whole incident down so that our attempt to have both of them convicted would stand up at a tribunal hearing.

The Australian Cricket Board determined the hearing would be the next night. We flew across to Melbourne and dashed by taxi to the ACB headquarters in Jolimont where Bob Merriman was to hear the case. VCR and tape were brought in. Graeme Wood was there to represent Lillee, but there was no sign of Miandad or any of the Pakistanis. During the tribunal meeting, no one could get the VCRs to work. One finally did, but the tape from the ABC was inconclusive. It showed Miandad's bat contact Lillee's back, but then the cameraman decided to point his lens at something else, missing out on a tawdry piece of cricket history. Proceedings in the tribunal quickly became farcical, with Wood saying he'd stood no more than two metres from the action and that Lillee had never, ever, kicked Miandad.

'What about the photo on the front page of the paper – how does that stand up?' someone wanted to know. The kick hadn't gone anywhere near Javed's pads, replied Wood.

I surmise that Merriman was going to suspend each player for a Test match, but when Miandad didn't turn up, he suspended Lillee for three one-day games and clearly hoped the Pakistanis would follow suit.

After the hearing, at about 6.30 p.m., Tony and I were smuggled down backstairs, booked into a taxi under the names of Smith and Jones, and driven to a motel – the same one where the Pakistanis were staying. As we entered the motel grounds, less than half an hour after leaving the ACB, some Pakistanis, including Miandad, greeted us with the news: 'He only got three matches, eh?'

'How did you know that?' I asked.

'Oh, we have our ways and means,' replied Miandad with a knowing smirk. Interestingly, Pakistan took no disciplinary action against Javed.

That set-up really was a farce, and the Lillee/Miandad incident quickly led to an end to the practice of players taking disciplinary action against their own. I still think each player should have lost a Test match in that case; the result sent out the wrong message.

The ACB selected me to umpire in the 1984 Asian tournament in the Persian Gulf immediately after the season's Sheffield Shield final. I drew stumps in the final at 6 p.m. and was on the plane to Dubai at 8 p.m. with my wife, Jeanette. We got off the aircraft at 3 a.m. and were bussed into a desolate-looking terminal. The board had given me a box of a dozen cricket balls as it had heard the sheikhdom was short of them. Good news for Sharjah. The ACB had also cautioned me that as this was a Muslim country, I had better not drink as alcohol was forbidden. Not great news, but I could put up with it for the twelve-day sojourn.

In the passenger terminal, which was filled with Indians and Pakistanis, an Indian gentleman walked up to me and said, 'Mr John,' (Indians always seem to call me that), 'will you come over here, please.' I went over and he asked me to sign a piece of paper. I read it, and it said: 'I hereby declare myself an alcoholic'.

I said, as you would, 'What does this mean?' It meant, replied the Indian, that if I signed, I could have as many drinks as I liked, so long as I didn't walk out on to the streets with them. I duly signed, and for the fortnight, I was able to have the odd drink behind closed doors trouble-free. But while I was signing the document and the luggage was being X-rayed, something much more sinister must have been going on because suddenly Jeanette and I were surrounded by security guards wearing gun belts, toting sub-machine guns and canes, and pointing at the box of cricket balls. They refused to open it, thinking they were bombs. When I went to open the box the guards scattered as though I was a suicide bomber. 'Don't touch, don't touch!' one of them screamed in English as I went through the actions of bowling a cricket ball. From my action, they got the message and put us on to a mini-bus to travel the twenty-five kilometres from Dubai to Sharjah. We were the only passengers of the fez-wearing driver, who was pulled up three times by soldiers who shoved their guns through the bus window as they asked for our passports. We could hardly fault the security arrangements.

The tournament's clay pitches, however, were definitely sub-standard. This was despite the organisers pumping desalinated water forty miles from the Red Sea to provide the only natural greenery in Sharjah. Dickie Bird and I, as the independent umpires demanded sensibly by India and Pakistan for the tournament, presided over the opening match between those occasionally warring neighbours. Dickie had umpired the tournament before, but this was my first time. Before the match started we were introduced to a posse of sheikhs and the people who shake, rattle and roll to put on the annual tournament, all of whom were protected by guards bristling with the automatic weapons I was getting used to seeing.

Those weapons were still in my mind when, to his first ball, Indian opener Ravi Shastri played back to a delivery that never rose from the clay. He was dead in front, and my finger went up, shakily. The crowd's noise sounded like machine-gun fire, and I almost cacked myself. I looked across to see if Dickie at square leg was ducking like me, but he was laughing, knowing that one of the local customs of barracking is to light a string of Tom Thumb crackers and drop them in a kerosene can! I wished he'd warned me.

Like everyone who's met him, I found Dickie Bird to be absolutely mad. The only time he appeared to bathe himself was when the two of us walked from our magnificent hotel down to a private beach. Dickie took off his right shoe and right sock, put his toe into the sea and said, 'That's good enough for me, I've had a dip in the Red Sea.' It wasn't so flash for those of us who travelled with him in cars in 38–42-degree heat; he wasn't the most popular passenger.

Perhaps the most interesting member of the Pakistani camp was a former Test player who we'll call 'X'. This was 1984, and bear in mind the bribery that has gone on ten and more years later. The tournament final was between India and Australia, and because of the Aussies' presence and the rule of independent umpires, I was ruled out and gave way to umpires from England (Bird) and Pakistan (Kazir Hyatt). I was paid US$1000 for each of my two matches. Two nights before the final, X, with a fine disregard for the written rules, asked me to umpire the game with Dickie. Having been instructed by the ACB to play down the 'independent umpire' rule, I told X: 'You want independent umpires – that's what you've got.'

X answered, 'We don't trust Kazir Hyatt because he will rob us.'

To put him off, I said, 'Well, I don't care about that.'

X tried another tack. 'Would $2000 make any difference?'

I said, 'No, that's it, you wanted independent umpires. You've got 'em, you stick with 'em.'

X continued, 'There's a lot of money riding on this and we don't want to lose it. I want you to do the game'.

I repeated my refusal. After that, my name was mud with the Pakistanis, and the ACB's advice to stand fast on the independent umpire issue seemed not only sound but psychic. Australia went on to win the final convincingly and I'm not sure whether X won or lost, but straight after I'd knocked back the two-grand, the reserve seats in the grandstand for Jeanette and me were no longer available. An interesting experience, though, and a forerunner of what we've learnt about the entanglement of cricket, bribery and bag-men.

Television replays, which became more and more popular as my career went on, could sometimes work in our favour. In

Melbourne during the 1980–81 season, with Australia playing India, N. S. Yadav, an off-spinner, was bowling around the wicket to Allan Border, who was batting at No. 5.

It was in the days when, if you got to lunch on day one without the MCG pitch cracking up and balls flying everywhere, you'd done pretty well. Late in the afternoon, Border swept at one from Yadav and in the midst of the dust and pebbles that flew up from the connection of bat, ball and ground, there lay a single bail. At square leg, I knew Border hadn't touched the stumps with his bat, foot, pad or anything else; knew, too, that the 'keeper hadn't taken it because the ball had hit him at ankle-height. I simply didn't know how the bail had got there. My co-umpire Rex Whitehead was unsighted by the dust and scree, but the Indian 'keeper was now making loud guttural noises which I assumed was an appeal, and kept pointing at the bail. After a spell of pondering separately, Rex and I ambled towards each other. Rex's opening gambit wasn't promising: 'What do you reckon we should do?' I don't know what made me do it, but I walked up to Border and said, 'You're out, mate.'

'How?' he wanted to know, quite reasonably.

'I don't know. Piss off.' And to his credit, he did.

Anyone who has been to the MCG will know that if you stand at square leg to a left-hander at the Members' end, the next player in has to pass you. It happened to be Rodney Marsh and, as he walked past me, I said, 'Did you see what happened on TV with that?' (The players can see the replays in the dressing room, just like everyone at home.) Rod said, 'Yeah, it just touched leg stump and bowled him.'

My reply of 'Thanks' was heartfelt, and at the next break as we were heading off, a large press contingent was waiting for my version of the dismissal. 'Border's dismissal was a bit controversial' was the tenor of their questioning. I was feeling pretty jaunty after Marshie's reassurance, so told them, 'No, quite clearly bowled, but the bastard wouldn't walk.'

So replays do work for us occasionally. They also came in handy for me as I stood in the last Test for Lillee, Chappell and Marsh at the fifth Test in Sydney against Pakistan in 1983–84. Lillee was bowling to Abdul Qadir late in the day, and for some reason he kept saying to me, 'I want the same number of victims as Marshie's got.'

I couldn't really understand that, because if he bowled it and Marsh caught it they were going to stay on the same tally anyway, but Dennis was starting to get paranoid about the whole thing. He thundered in and the ball flicked Qadir's pad going down the leg side. Dennis appealed and, as he was wont to do, ran all the way down the wicket before going into that pleading squat.

My first thought was, is he going to shit, or is he not? But without waiting for my response, he jumped into Marsh's arms, shouting, 'We've done it, we've done it!' But Rodney told him, 'He's not giving it out, Dennis.' Dennis turned to my colleague, Dick French, at square leg and said, 'Dick, the ball carried, didn't it?'

Dick, the diplomat, answered, 'It carried, but I don't know whether he hit it. You'd better go and talk to him.' (Me.) Dennis strode up the wicket and told me the two of us should retire together, or words to that effect, at the same time analysing my eyesight and a few other things about me. I was very confident I was correct, so said, 'Dennis, I'll back myself $100 on the replay. Do you want to be in it?' Snappily, he answered, 'No, he missed the bloody thing by a foot.'

Of course, the replays can work against you, as they did in Brisbane for a one-day match. Geoff Lawson and I didn't hit it off all that well, and the optometrist and fast bowler insisted that he bowl from the opposite end to where I was standing. But somehow the overs got mixed up and he had to bowl a few of them from my end. He bowled to Ian Botham and barrelled one down leg side; it clipped the pad on the way through. I wasn't going to call wide but, considering the animosity between us, thought there was nothing to lose and stuck my arms out to signal what Lawson feared was coming. The words he called me had the same number of letters as 'wide'. During the same over Botham backed away from one; so Lawson tracked him with the next one, as a good bowler should. It was just outside Botham's heel, so I called it a wide, too. The third one just brushed his pad on the way through, but wasn't wide enough to call, so Geoff turned around and said, 'Go on, call that a wide.' So I did. The replays showed I was a little harsh, but it was a case of my heart overruling my head. Another one I regret . . . sorry, Geoff.

Undoubtedly, the greatest technology introduced into cricket – many years ago – was the light meter. If the meters were set correctly, and ours were set by the TV crews, they gave tangible evidence to the players that the light was bad. And that meant, after hundreds of years of guessing, that we could be consistent. In Brisbane the magic number was 41. When the meter ticked over to that, we knew it was too dark to play. So before each match, we'd tell the captain that, at 41, we'd ask them whether they wanted to go off for light. If they chose to stay on, we'd tell them the meter reading would have to drop to 37 (the calibrations were in twos) before we'd grant another appeal.

On a Friday, just before lunch in a Sheffield Shield match between Queensland and the David Hookes-led South Australia, I saw Hookesy get a feather touch through to 'keeper Ray Phillips. Hookes, who was one of the most competitive players I ever met and questioned umpires' decisions constantly, didn't look at me, just scratched around as though unconcerned, but my finger was up. I had to tell him, 'You're out.' Hookes called down the wicket, 'The crowd's just come in to see me bat, Mel.'

'Well, they'll have to come back on Sunday then,' I answered. That set the tone for the match. For the first two days the meters hit 41 and the players went off early. Sure enough, on the Sunday South Australia was 3/270-odd, Hookes was in his 60s and the game's situation meant the Croweaters would want to stay at the crease to press for a win. Again, it got darker and reached 41. But Hookes wanted to stay. I said, 'Do you know the Laws?' and he said, 'Yes,' but I didn't think he did, so I said, 'You have to appeal back to us if you want to get off the field, and if the light meter gets down to 37 we'll grant it to you.'

He said, 'Okay, that's fair enough.' As luck would have it, SA lost three quick wickets and, of course, Hookesy was appealing all the time and asking, 'What's the meter showing?' I kept hitting the button and showing him: it was 41 and stayed there. Hookes insisted, 'But it's getting darker.'

'No, mate,' I said, 'it's just the Queensland light. It gets to an even level and just stays there a little while. When it goes, it will go very quickly.' But, secretly, I thought it was getting darker, too. In fact, I'd been continually hitting the meter's memory button and not giving him a true reading; I just didn't realise it at the time. When we came off and I realised what I'd done, I finally hit the right button and the meter was showing 33. We had played on through some serious gloom, but at least the outcome was not affected.

Another piece of technology that caused me some amusement was the electric jigger they introduced to the Sydney Cricket Ground to move the sight-screens. This had been preceded for yonks by a manual effort by a couple of pensioners who would have a few pots over lunch then, as the afternoon sun got to them, would lose peak performance, or have to be woken up before the screens could be moved. So the SCG Trust, or whatever they are, brought in this little jigger. On the day before the fifth Test to end the 1984–85 series between Australia and the rampaging West Indies, I went to the ground to trial this hi-tech breakthrough with Ray Isherwood, who was doing his first Test match with me. We pointed our gadgets – I had a blue one, Ray a yellow one – at the sight-screen and it would move whichever way we dictated. We were satisfied with the new product, but that afternoon a call came through to our hotel to say our pointing-things were too strong and were turning lights and television sets on and off, and setting the neighbourhood's roller doors in motion! However, the ground officials decided they'd stick with the technology, hoping the buffer of a crowd would blunt the instruments' circuit-breaking virility.

Next day, we arrived at the ground for the Test and went to our rooms high up in the clock tower. Half an hour before the start of play, Ray was not just nervous; he had his head stuck in the toilet bowl, wretching the butterflies from his stomach. I went to the window for some respite from the noise he was making and pointed my jigger at the sight-screen. I was fascinated as it moved ever so slightly. I thought this could be a bit of fun. People on either side of the sight-screen had out their thermoses with scones and cups of tea seated on their laps, and I started to move the big white screen.

I moved it left and watched fascinated as they waddled to the right, trying to balance their mornings teas. I'd wait a few minutes, then send the screen to the right, chuckling to myself as they teetered back again.

'Come and have a look at this, mate,' I called behind me to Ray, who had just come up for air. Ray came over and I said, 'Play with this for a while.' By the time 10.55 a.m. came around, Ray was laughing his head off, totally relaxed and ready for his big day.

The Sydney Cricket Ground was my favourite ground for umpiring. It had something about it, so that no matter how nervous or crook you were feeling, the SCG's electric atmosphere picked you up and focused the mind entirely on the cricket. Sydneysider Dick French and I umpired several Tests there. Neither of us minded a drink, and in our umpires' room a 2.7-litre refrigerator was always stocked with beer. The first thing we did on entering the room was check the fridge to ensure it was filled, ready for the end of the day's play. On a Friday night, after the first day of a West Indies Test, about a dozen people filtered into the room to share a drink with us and at about 8.30 p.m. Dick and I declared we'd take a shower and go and get a bite to eat. By this time our guests had gone, so Dick and I decided we'd knock off the last two bottles.

Next day we went to pick up our key from the downstairs bar. I heard Dick say to a bloke he knew, 'Kev, would you mind stocking the fridge for us?'

Kevin's answer – 'Oh, I stocked it for the Test match' – floored us.

Dick answered nonchalantly, 'We drank all that last night.'

Crestfallen as we walked out to restart the Test, we heard Kevin call out, 'Get those drunks off the field!' Hopefully, no one thought he was referring to us.

I also loved umpiring in Adelaide, at my home State's Gabba, and the WACA in Perth. I remember Bellerive in Hobart, where I umpired only a couple of one-day matches, as a freezing place and a batsman's paradise. Curiously, I didn't take to the Melbourne Cricket Ground – a huge mausoleum where umpires weren't made to feel especially welcome. On arrival, you'd negotiate a concrete labyrinth before coming to a sign marked 'Gents Lavatory'. You'd walk past the porcelain urinals to a tiny, windowless umpires' room. So at about 9 a.m. we'd change into our umpiring outfits and take all our gear and paraphernalia to the Members' room. Walking off the field and having the Members constantly in your ear wasn't very satisfactory, though, particularly after they'd had a few chardonnays.

I was 'lucky' enough to umpire three Sheffield Shield finals. The luck was qualified because my home State, Queensland, lost all three of them. In the first of them, in Perth in 1983–84, Queenslander Harry Frei came to grips with Dennis Lillee-as-batsman. Dennis was never that good against the short ball, a fact known to Harry and his team, and this was before the limit on bouncers. At one point, Lillee, who was making a habit of backing away, called out to Frei: 'How many Tests have you played, prick?' Harry's rejoinder was a beauty: 'How many VFL games have you played?' (Harry, a volatile character, once played for Footscray in the Victorian Football League, and Dennis would have done well to remember Harry missed a fair slab of his Australian Rules career through suspensions for punching.) The verbal sparring between Frei and Lillee went on for a few more overs, and as Harry walked past me to bowl again, he muttered to me, 'Mel, it'd be worthwhile doing three matches just to job this prick.'

I thought here's trouble, but let the over finish, then called the two together, leading them out to midwicket. 'Dennis,' I said, 'do you know how Harry feels about you?' Then, 'Harry,' I continued, 'do you know how Dennis feels about you?' They both nodded. 'Right, you both know how you feel about each other. How about we cool it?'

Dennis said, 'Fair enough, Mel, you won't hear any more from me.'

Harry replied, 'If you'd have been a VFL umpire, I'd have played more games.'

'Shut up, Harry,' I said, 'and get back to your place. That's the finish of it.'

Thankfully, strong characters like these two respond well to the sort of language they themselves deal out on the paddock. It was a great game, won by WA by four wickets, and my Sandgroper colleague Peter McConnell was as happy with the result as I was downcast. It didn't stop us having a drink after the match, and a pretty long one at that.

The other two Shield finals, crackerjack games, were in Sydney. In the first thrilling match in 1984–85 – won by NSW by one wicket, Peter Clifford held NSW together in the second innings when it looked for all the world as though Queensland would win its first Shield. At one point Jeff Thomson hit Clifford on the toe and launched into a huge appeal. Thommo's angled delivery pitched in the dust and rubble of the batting crease and I couldn't be sure of its course thereafter. Years later, Queensland officials reminded me of my role in robbing the State of its rightful reward that year. Pointing out that John Maguire had dropped two catches off Clifford never carried much weight with these fellows.

The same two teams played off in Sydney the following season with the match drawn and NSW retaining the Shield. All three Shield finals were probably the most memorable matches I ever umpired. Dad and my mother, Margaret, followed Queensland's Shield finals wherever they were played and attended the three I stood in. It was sad that Dad died before Queensland finally got over the Shield line in 1994–95, after sixty-eight years of trying. There were times in both Sydney matches when it appeared likely he would fulfil his dream – a hope he hid from no one and which probably put a little extra pressure on his son.

Dean Jones was always a very competitive character, and in one Shield match between the Vics and Queensland at the Gabba, the Bulls' Dirk Tazelaar curved a ball back into Dean. I clearly saw the ball take the inside edge before cannoning into Dean's pad and bouncing from his foot out to Robbie Kerr in the gully. The initial appeal from Dirk and the 'keeper was for lbw, but after I'd seen Kerr catch it, I raised my finger. Dean told me in no uncertain terms it couldn't possibly be out as he'd hit it. Naturally, I answered that was exactly why I'd given him out, and added for good measure, 'Look up at the scoreboard, you'll see C2 B8.'

'What do you mean?' Dean demanded. I explained that Robbie Kerr, No. 2 in the batting order, had caught a ball bowled by No. 8. 'No, he didn't,' said the Victorian, who was one of those blokes who was never out – in his own mind. If ever he was caught behind, he'd whip around and begin scratching his guard for the next delivery – it was always a pretty good clue he'd nicked it.

Jeanette and I have two daughters, Julie and Toni, both now married and with children of their own: Joel and Delyse to Julie, and Joshua and Mikayla to Toni. Jeanette and both the girls were tremendously supportive to me throughout my umpiring career and the frequent absences required, but I regret that through primary school and grade eight, Julie and Toni were teased, if not taunted, especially by their male classmates over the mistakes I may have made on the field of play. Eventually, they learned to cope with it and I was immensely proud and grateful to them for that.

I have mixed feelings about a more recent development – the third umpire. Simply, I don't believe he's necessary because it is a human game, of human elements – including frailties. And the third man subtracts from one of the fundamental Laws of the game: that the batsman gets the benefit of the doubt.

Cricket, to me, is a game in which you do what you're least best at, most of the time; so if you're a batsman, you spend most of your time sitting in the pavilion waiting to get out to bat, or waiting for everyone else to get out, so you can go out and field. If you're a bowler, the best you can hope for is 50 per cent of the action because you're not allowed to bowl both ends. Most cricketers spend 75 per cent of their time in the field or sitting in a pavilion. This is why the Laws of Cricket are framed so that the benefit of the doubt always goes to the batsman – give the blighter at least a quarter-share of the action.

My feelings are mixed because, obviously, in run-outs, stumpings and hit-wickets, the third umpire can ensure the right decision is made, so the bowler or fielder is rewarded for his effort. Again, my reservation is removal of the benefit of the doubt for the batsman. Let's say you have a Ricky Ponting who is run out by a couple of millimetres; he'd probably be given not out by the naked eye; a third umpire will deposit him in the dressing room for the rest of that day, and probably half the next one as well – not doing any of what he set out to do.

The third umpire, the all-telling 'eye', also tends to instil laziness in umpires 'on the way through'. With the video aide at square leg, Test and first-class cricket umpires don't have to move; the side-on decision will be made for them. Indian umpire Venkat is a good, or bad, example of that, rarely moving from behind the stumps at all. The trouble is, on the way to achieving the luxury of a third umpire, there is no such help – or excuse – for laziness. So the first-class and Test umpires make poor role models, which is the opposite to what we used to have.

Still, we have to accept crowd and home-viewer reaction to the 'third man' has been supportive of it; and one of the immutable laws of selling – or marketing, which is where the game's at – is that 'the customer knows best'.

No doubt the 'third eye' would have blinked into action at the moment of probably my most controversial Test match decision. It was the opening of 1982–83's fifth Ashes Test in Sydney. Kepler Wessels bunted the day's fourth ball to mid-on. I was at square leg and simply couldn't tell whether Wessels's partner, John Dyson, who took off for a run, had beaten the return that broke the stumps. So I gave Dyson not out. As the TV replay soon showed, Dyson was short of his crease by about eight inches. David Gower walked up to me and said, 'It's a bit early in the game to be making decisions like that,

Mel, isn't it?' None of the thirty-or-so English supporters who bombarded me with cards and letters bothered to sign their names, and one of the bulkier envelopes contained thirteen foolscap pages, with one capitalised word per page. It took me a little longer than usual to read: 'Obviously you can't see. That's why I am writing this in big print'. At the end of the Test, and series, I received another missive in the form of a large envelope containing a smaller envelope stuffed with cigarette ashes, and the message: 'You won the Ashes for Australia, so you might as well keep them'.

Accompanying the arrival of the third umpire in cricket was the Test match referee. My problem with these gentlemen is that they have a little too much power, or use too much power. The best referees always consult the umpires. They may say, 'I saw Glenn McGrath talking to a batsman. What was that all about?' The umpire may say, 'We quelled it on the field; it was nothing to warrant action.' But some referees sit with a check list and say, 'He said something to player X, therefore I'm going to fine him.'

The general public probably doesn't realise that many players are being fined off the field for relatively minor misdemeanours, and to me that's wrong. Players should be allowed to be players. I fear the characters of cricket, like Max Walker, Dennis Lillee and Lenny Pascoe, who really stirred people up and gave great entertainment, are being rubbed out of the game. Similar free spirits, I'm afraid, will simply be fined too heavily to be able to afford to be, or stay, 'characters'. Guidelines are needed to ensure the referees consult the umpires, and perhaps the captains, before taking any action. Still, only a tiny minority of referees have taken it upon themselves to be the be-all and end-all.

Of course, the spectators have their share of 'characters', and they become more numerous as the afternoon or night wears on. The more extreme version are known as streakers, and I saw my fair share of them, unfortunately, all of them blokes. The common thread, to use an inappropriate pun, is that none of them think their actions through, but that's inevitable with alcohol-related dares. In Adelaide, two characters tried to run from one side of the ground to the other where their mates were holding their clothes ready to jump into. Great in theory, but the 200 metres was more than they could handle. When they reached the middle of the ground they were exhausted, and I heard one streaker say to the other, 'Where's our clothes?'

'No idea,' puffed his mate. 'Hey – where are the security guys to get us out of here?' Dills! And they're least welcomed by the players, especially the batsmen, whose concentration is broken. There have to be more attractive ways of drawing attention and winning bets than charging naked on to a public arena.

MEL JOHNSON'S UMPIRING CV

72 first-class matches, between November 1975 and November 1987

Official Test matches – 21 (Australia v. England 7, West Indies 6, New Zealand 2, India 2, Pakistan 4)

Internationals – 13 (Queensland v. England 3, West Indies 3, India 2, Pakistan 2, New Zealand 2, Sri Lanka 1)

Sheffield Shield matches – 38

One-day internationals – 52, including 2 in Sharjah

Rex Whitehead

From Snake Gully to the 'G'

I'm not sure whether it was Yarra Baps v. Yarra Congs or Yarra Pressos. Then again, it could have been Paisley Street Baps v. the Streets. But it was to one of those fixtures that I first went to watch my father umpire a cricket match.

To the uninitiated, the teams were Yarraville Baptist Church Cricket Club, Yarraville Congregational Church Cricket Club, Yarraville Presbyterian Church Cricket Club, Paisley Street Baptist Church Cricket Club or Barkly Street Methodist Church Cricket Club. All clubs were keen competitors (along with others who had names I have long forgotten) in the Western Suburban Churches Cricket Association based, as the name implies, west of Melbourne, in the working-class suburb of Footscray in the mid-1950s.

As a youngster of six or seven, I would accompany my father, Ron Whitehead, and his partner, Syd Bates, and watch the day's proceedings. I would do this from the sublime comfort of our Ford Prefect parked next to the oval, which was one of four or five located on one spasmodically grassed parkland referred to by the locals as 'Snake Gully'. The name of the park was probably the encouragement in my choosing the front seat of the car rather than a closer vantage point.

I recall that Dad and Syd each carried the ubiquitous Gladstone bag out to the centre, some half-hour before play, to prepare the wicket. The pitch was matting over screenings which, under heat, generally turned rock-hard. The Gladstone bags carried all sorts of equipment needed to set up the wicket, but clearly the most valuable items were the wooden mallet, for banging the stumps into the granite-like surface, and lemonade bottles full of water. The water would be poured onto the surface where the stumps were to be placed, thereby turning the granite into sludge, similar to pre-mixed concrete.

The parkland's sporadic covering of grass was tufted, the sort that a dashing Jonty Rhodes type, when swooping on a loose ball from extra cover, could easily stumble on and break an ankle. Worse still was being in perfect position behind a thumping cover drive when a deviation from a tuft would cause the ball to rise alarmingly from a spot about three feet in front of the fielder and head straight for his forehead or, more frighteningly for the lads of the west, an area about two feet lower. Not only did the cricketers of the WSCCA possess fine cricketing skills; they were courageous to a man.

The parklands were surrounded by paddocks. Beyond the vast playing area, occupied by the flannelled fools, there was nothing. This openness, coupled with the barren nature of the playing surface, created a fair amount of dust. Anyone familiar with a northerly wind in Melbourne during the heat of summer will recognise here the fatal ingredients for a dust storm. The wind would blow dust and pollens through the air at an horrific rate and I can only guess at the difficulty confronting Dad and Syd when the question was posed as to a caught behind from a thin edge, particularly if one was positioned at the southern end. How they managed to keep their eyes open, or to see anything at all, is a matter of some conjecture. It was probably why Dad spent most of the summer with an almost permanent squint.

Once play started, I would try to keep score. By this time,

I had already decided that bowling was for mugs and the glamour position was that of a batsman. It followed, therefore, that my only interest was in keeping score of the batsmen. The bowlers' statistics were of no interest. Dad would call play and I would score runs to the respective batsmen, generally named after some distinguishing feature which was usually the colour of the cap, so that my scoresheet would look something like this:

Red Cap 12221134422111 44

Blue Cap 22111224432443

Invariably, my scoring efforts would be stymied by a most unfortunate set of circumstances. The Blue Cap would get out, and guess what? The new batsman would appear, also wearing a Red Cap. In the dust and pollen haze, there would be no other way of distinguishing the batsmen, so I would give it away.

I must have been pretty keen on the game because I can recall accompanying my father to the cricket as my regular Saturday activity until I was old enough to play in the WSCCA under-16 competition.

My father had been a leading umpire in the association since before the war and for many years was honoured with the appointment to stand in the association final. Years later, one of his colleagues, Arthur Thurston, related the story of Dad umpiring a match during the war, when he was home from the army on leave. (Remembering my mother, I don't know how he got away with that.) Anyway, it came time for my father to catch a train back to wherever he was posted (probably northern Queensland), and he was forced to retire. Arthur told me that all of the players from both sides clapped and cheered him as he left the ground. In later years, I was to go on to umpire Test cricket, but never in my career (nor in the vast majority of umpires' careers, I venture) was I cheered from the oval. Jeered – yes, cheered – never.

My family's involvement with umpiring the great game had in fact started with my paternal grandfather Norman, who umpired in the Victorian Sub-District Cricket Association. My Uncle Bill (Dad's younger brother) umpired in the Glenroy Cricket Association and, following his retirement, in the Rosebud Cricket Association. So there was indeed a family connection to 'wearing the white coat'.

From the outset, I have loved the game, its traditions and its culture, but umpiring was never something I aspired to during my playing days, or at least, not until the very end. Given my father's connection, I always had respect for umpires and never possessed any negative views of their part in the game. I can also say, with absolute honesty, that I never copped a rough one from the umpire, probably because there is little area for doubt when the stumps are spread-eagled behind you.

As soon as I could, I started playing in the WSCCA. I must have been about ten, and played in the under-16 competition for Barkly Street Methodists Cricket Club, affectionately known as 'the Streets'. I can already see former players and umpiring colleagues raising an eyebrow given my known partiality towards a glass or three of the amber fluid. But it is true; I played for a Methodist church (not that many of the players actually attended proceedings on Sundays).

I fielded in one of two positions: fine leg or third man, which required running the length of the oval after each over. The kids we played against were huge in a way only a small kid can understand. I remember this big ugly quick called Ron, who was a tearaway fast bowler for Paisley Street Baps. He was bloody terrifying, and I was amazed at how even the bigger kids didn't get killed by him. Only recently, I met Ron again as a result of our mutual passion for the Western Bulldogs Football Club in the AFL. It was the first time I had cast eyes on him for forty years. He is still ugly, but amazingly, he has shrunk. I stand at about 6 feet 2 inches under the old scale, which must be well short of his height forty years ago, but these days he is only about 5 feet 7 inches!

A couple of years later the Streets folded and I went to play for Paisley Street Baps. By now I was thirteen, taller and a bit more developed. The year was a highlight for two reasons. About halfway through the season, we were playing on Myers Flat, one of those huge parklands holding six cricket ovals. One of those ovals is now named the Merv Hughes Oval and is the home ground of Footscray Cricket Club, for whom Merv still plays as captain of the second-eleven.

On this particular day, there was a big northerly blowing and all bowlers had trouble running up into it. By this time, I fancied myself as a bit of a quick. The only trouble was that nobody else at the club and, in particular, the captain, shared my view. In desperation, the captain asked, 'Who wants to bowl into it?'

'Pick me! Pick me!' I shouted, and with a look of resigned despair, the skipper threw me the cherry. Taking my well-rehearsed fifteen-step run-up, I charged into the breeze and gave it the lot. Into the gale, it only just got there, but throughout the morning the opposition batsmen seemed mesmerised by the contradiction of the long run-up and the gentle trajectory of the delivery. But to everybody's amazement, including my own, I finished with a match-winning 5/17.

After the game we headed off to the local milk bar for a

bottle of Coke. The guys were abuzz with my performance and I was lapping it up until the skipper said, 'I didn't know you bowled "offies".'

'Me neither,' was the chorus from the rest. So that's what I had been doing, I thought. At that precise moment, my career as an offie was born.

By a strange coincidence, later that day a Victorian match was being televised and one of the bowlers was Ian Quick who, despite the name, was an off-spin bowler, who toured England in an Ashes tour. Quick had an exaggerated action that had his arms swinging in and out in the delivery approach. I was most impressed with this and immediately adopted the same action.

When next I turned out for Paisley Street, I was offered the ball as first-change bowler to ply my offies. 'Do you think the shine has been removed sufficiently for my spin to have its maximum effect?' I enquired of the skipper. 'Not yet,' he responded, 'but you won't have to wait long.'

'Right arm over,' I advised the ump and immediately launched into my Ian Quicks. Quick must have had it right because I took a bundle of wickets in what was left of the season and finished with an average of 3.3 runs per wicket. How do I remember it so precisely? The bloke, who won the association bowling average that year, finished with an average of 5-plus. I was ineligible for the award, as I had bowled one over short of the minimum number required to qualify. I went along to the presentation night and noted that the trophy for the winner of the bowling average was a shaving kit – a useless article as far as I was concerned because I was destined not to shave for at least another three years.

My season that year was special for two reasons. In

addition, and of far greater significance to my bowling feats, was our achievement in reaching the final against Kingi Baps (the Kingsville Baptist Church Cricket Club). I opened the batting on the first morning and thrashed the attack for a brilliant 29, made in only two hours. I remember I was 25 not out when we lost our fourth wicket and in strode Alec Oldfield to the crease. Now, Alec had just turned sixteen, but looked about thirty-four. As he had for the whole season, Alec pummelled the attack smashing sixes at will. When he got out, he had compiled 55 while I pushed steadily on to 27.

On the second day, we bowled out the opposition for a score well short of ours. This was no mean feat as they had both Graeme Joslin and Tony Hargreaves in their side, both of whom went on to become very good district cricketers with initially Footscray and then St Kilda for Joslin, and Richmond for Hargreaves. I officiated at many district first-eleven games involving both and that final was regularly discussed, with our achievements embellished over time.

To any aspiring batsmen reading this chapter I would like to pass on a tip that I picked up in our second innings of the final. We had already won the game and were playing out time. I opened the batting and had reached a comfortable 7, all singles, when my batting partner called me through for a quick single. At this point I digress for a moment. I don't know how many times I had asked my mother to get me a pair of tight-fitting jocks for cricket. On reflection, I think the fact she was a woman was the reason she failed to comprehend the important purpose of my request. Anyway there I was, taking off down the track, responding to my partner's call in a situation where cricket commentators excitedly shout, 'He'll have to be quick!' I started to fear the worst about a third of the way down the pitch when I felt my box inexorably and irrevocably leaving its designated position. Now the challenge was to reach my ground not only before the fieldsman returned the ball but also before the box ventured further down my leg. I was doomed from the moment I donned those loose jocks. At about two-thirds of the way down the pitch, my box wedged itself at the back of my knee, meaning I was suddenly unable to bend it, like someone who has pulled a hamstring in a 100-metre sprint. I was run out by ten feet.

When I later told my father of my fate, he instructed my mother to acquire the appropriate under-clothing forthwith. I remember buying my first jockstrap as though it were yesterday. There is no doubt about it; you're not a man until you own a jockstrap. The second innings failure, however, did nothing to dampen the spirits of the premiership win, which, despite a lifetime's involvement in sport, remains my only premiership success. The only downside was we all had to go to church the next day as part of our celebrations.

The following year, my best mate, Lindsay James, convinced me that my cricket career would be better served by moving into the Footscray Cricket Association and playing with him at Footscray United.

I played under-16 and then open age for a total of eight years with the club. After that time, I still hadn't established myself in the first-eleven, despite having moved the club to change their rules to allow me to play at the highest level when still a junior. My last year in particular was disappointing and I finished the season a disillusioned cricketer.

The City of Footscray has two favourite sons: Ted Whitten, the greatest Australian Rules footballer ever, and Charlie Sutton, captain and coach of Footscray's only premiership team. For some years I had enjoyed the odd ale at Charlie Sutton's pub, located a couple of Whitten's with-the-wind torpedoes from the Western Oval, now called the Whitten Oval. Like all suburban pubs in those days (pre-pokies), Charlie's had its regulars. They were, in fact, the pub's lifeline.

Included among the locals was Jack Collins, who at the time was a Sheffield Shield umpire, later reaching Test standard and officiating in Packer's breakaway cricket; Keith Butler, also a Shield umpire; Bruce Neate, a VCA first-eleven umpire and former player; Peter Collins (Jack's brother), a former VCA umpire; and an Irishman, Terry McKenna, a long-standing captain of Footscray's third-eleven and the most argumentative bastard after a few beers I ever met.

I would stand and listen to these blokes regale each other with stories of their umpiring experiences for hours. Jack and Keith would talk about players such as Bill Lawry, Bob Simpson, Brian Booth et al from a first-hand basis. Such was my love of the game, they would leave me spellbound.

After a poor season with Footscray United, and at twenty-two years of age, I started to think about the possibility of umpiring. All the experiences of the umpires at Charlie Sutton's, and my fond memories of accompanying my late father to the cricket (he had passed away a couple of years earlier), started me thinking more positively towards wearing the white coat. Finally, I reasoned that if I could umpire a level of cricket better than that which I was capable of playing, then I would be in front. I was of the view that I might be capable of playing third-eleven cricket, but there was no way I would ever be at second-eleven standard. Given that the twos played on enclosed grounds, which were mainly VFL football ovals, that would be another superb experience.

Encouraged by the umpires at Charlie's, I went to the winter umpiring classes held over a period of about eight weeks at VCA House and attended by budding umpires and anybody looking to improve their knowledge of the Laws of the game. The classes were run by the VCAUA's umpire's adviser, Bill Smyth, who, in my view, possesses a knowledge of the Laws of the game unparalleled in this or any other country of the world.

I quickly learned that, like most cricketers, my knowledge of the Laws was limited in the extreme. Apart from the very basics, I knew nothing. The atmosphere of the whole thing captivated me: the richness of the clubby décor of the VCA boardroom, the names on the honour rolls, the casting of pearls by Bill and the beers afterwards at Lou Richards's pub while the leading umpires of the day debated all matters cricket.

At the conclusion of the classes, the VCAUA set an exam for those aspiring to be added to its panel. I was warned to study hard because the exam would be difficult. Examination night was in two parts. In part one we were given a piece of paper with four questions and asked to answer the questions verbally before a panel of three assessors, including Bill Smyth. The questions were incredibly complex and one remains in my mind to this day. Here it is:

> Q. The bowler delivers the ball, which is a no-ball, and is driven by the batsman who in so doing, breaks the wicket at the striker's end before the ball is deflected by the bowler's hand and breaks the wicket at the bowler's end with the non-striker out of his

ground. The ball continues on and crosses the boundary. A fieldsman returns the ball to the bowler. When the bowler is part way through his run-up for the next delivery, a fieldsman calls, 'How's that?' If you are the umpire at the bowler's end what do you do before the appeal, on the appeal and after the appeal?

Wouldn't you just love to see Tony Greig and Bill Lawry ponder that one? The answer went something like this:

Before the Appeal

1. The umpire would call and signal: 'no-ball'.
2. On the ball becoming dead, the umpire would signal to the scorers: 'no-ball'.
3. The umpire would call and signal to the scorers: 'four runs'.

On the Appeal

1. The umpire would prevent the bowler from delivering the next ball.
2. The laws at the time allowed an appeal up to the point that the bowler entered his delivery stride. On this basis, the appeal stands.
3. Given an appeal covers all ways of being out, and working on the basis of precedence in terms of chronological order, there are grounds to examine whether an appeal for hit wicket is valid. Given that the original delivery was a no-ball, then the striker cannot be given out hit-wicket.
4. Given that an appeal for hit-wicket is invalid, the umpire would rule the non-striker out – run out.

After the Appeal

1. The umpire would cancel the signal and the score of four runs.

2. The umpire would check with the scorers at the next break in play to ensure the score of four runs was deleted.

Part two was a written exam, which took me the full three hours allowed. This was also tough, particularly for those in trades or occupations that did not require a lot of written communication. I was fortunate in that my profession at the time required a lot of writing on a daily basis.

A week or so later, I received a letter from Jack Ledward, secretary of the VCA, advising me that I had not been accepted onto the umpires' panel and recommending I go to the Subdistrict Association to begin my career. This held no appeal for me whatsoever and I decided, bugger it, I will continue to play.

A short time later, David Richards (later to become executive director of the International Cricket Council, but then in his newly appointed position as assistant secretary of the VCA) phoned me to say that a candidate who had been appointed to the panel had declined the offer and, in David's words, I was 'next cab off the rank'. So there I was, accepted onto the panel because some unknown person had pulled out. To this day, I don't know who he was, but I'm thankful he couldn't make it. And the letter from Jack Ledward? It hangs framed and overlooking my bar, alongside another letter from Alan Barnes (then secretary of the Australian Cricket Board of Control), advising of my first appointment to an international match, being Australia against the West Indies at the MCG, some seven years later.

Appointments to VCA matches occur on a very structured basis. Selection to the panel is not an easy process as successful umpires from suburban associations, of which there are many, are encouraged to join. Once appointed, promotion is only achieved on the basis of sound performance. There is never a shortage of umpires on the VCA panel.

Coming into the first game, I realised how little I knew about the practical aspects of umpiring. In those days, the tuition was restricted almost entirely to an understanding and knowledge of the Laws. Practical issues, such as how far back do I stand at either the bowler's end or at square leg?, had not been considered. Virtually all of the other additions to the panel had come from suburban associations and brought with them some degree of experience. That could be either a plus or a negative, depending on whether the habits acquired were good or bad. In my case, I had to rely entirely on my playing experience and perhaps some memories of Snake Gully.

I guess like all firsts, I remember my first game vividly. It was a special day for another reason, for at about 1 o'clock in the morning our first child, Roxanne, had been born. As any first-time father knows, this is a draining experience in itself. By the time I got to the ground, having managed to get lost on the way, I was somewhat stressed. Fortunately, I had an experienced partner in Adrian Crawford, who introduced himself on my arrival and explained that he had already fixed the stumps in my absence, and who generally had a calming effect on the whole situation.

Shortly after, we strode on to the field to officiate in the VCA third-eleven match between Northcote and Hawthorn–East Melbourne at Northcote, another of those parkland areas with a number of ovals overlapping. I stood at the end elected by the Northcote quick to begin play. It was a typical, early October day in Melbourne with the sun shining but the wind cutting a hole right through you.

The opening bowler, after marking out his delivery,

removed his short-sleeved jumper and handed it to me. This was followed by the removal of his long-sleeved jumper and finally his cap. I gathered them together under my arms and readied myself for the first delivery of my career. With everybody ready to go, I called, 'Play.' Immediately, my lack of practical knowledge about the profession in which I was embarking became apparent. The bowler moved into his delivery stride and I took immediate note that, in fact, it was a legitimate delivery as the feet had not reached over either the return crease or the popping crease. So far, so good. The ball, however, pitched some ten inches off the cut portion of the pitch and straight away I recognised this as a wide and accordingly called and signalled such in a triumphant manner. The only trouble was both jumpers and a cap fell to the ground as a result of my outstretched arms, causing me to regather the clothing in a hurried and ungainly manner so as few people as possible would notice. I think with the exception of the twenty-two players, two scorers and my colleague, few others noticed. First lesson learned – hold all discarded clothing in one hand. I was a fast learner. I can honestly say I never fell for that one again.

The rest of the day, in an umpiring sense, was rather uneventful but tiring. After pulling stumps, I quickly changed and rushed into the hospital to see my wife Carol and our beautiful new daughter. This had been some day. When visiting hours were over, I went out and got pissed.

There was only one other day during that season that has stayed in my mind. I umpired Fitzroy v. St Kilda third-elevens on the same parkland as my first game at Northcote. This was on another oval and Fitzroy's home ground. On the second day, the temperature was touching 40 degrees with a northerly blowing hard. It was one of the toughest days that I ever stood. The two captains were Bob Bitmead, who had previously played for Victoria and toured New Zealand in an Australian second-eleven, and Eric Seccombe, a highly credentialled first-eleven player with St Kilda over many years. After the game, Bob and Eric gave us the umpires' report and asked us to fill in our own names. They had marked both my partner Alan Scaife and myself with the highest marks possible and added their own comment of 'outstanding performance'.

I am sure they gave us the form to complete because they wanted us to see their assessment. They had obviously recognised the difficulty of the task under such oppressive conditions. It was the only time I ever saw my own report in any game I umpired. I remember going home and, through exhaustion, being physically ill throughout the night.

After the completion of each day's play during the year, I couldn't wait for Monday night to come along so I could get to Charlie's and talk about my experiences with the other umpires. So many times I would be explaining something I had done when suddenly they would all look aghast at one another and then exclaim, 'You did what?' This was generally the forerunner of being told I had stuffed something up and warned not to do it again. But mostly, I just listened to the senior blokes talking about their days in the middle, whether it was at district first-eleven level or State cricket. In one season, I accumulated knowledge that might have taken years to acquire without these mentors. Even the mad Irishman Terry McKenna was helpful by giving a player's perspective, often referring to us as 'you cheating bastards'.

At the end of the year, I was rewarded with the semifinal and the final for the third-eleven competition, a rare occurrence for a first-year umpire and due almost entirely to what I learned at Charlie's. At a meeting of those umpires allocated to finals, Bill Smyth made special mention of my achievement in my first year. Rare praise indeed from the Master.

The following season, I was promoted to the district second elevens. In only one year I had achieved my ultimate goals of reaching that standard and officiating at all the major grounds where, for years, I had been a spectator supporting the Bulldogs. In those days in summer, the surface of the grounds was magnificent: flat, fully grassed and a far cry from the grounds of my playing days at parklands such as Snake Gully.

All of the ovals had operational scoreboards and, where necessary, sight-screens. But best of all, the pitches were perfectly marked out with painted white lines and, top this – the stumps were already in place with only the bails to be positioned. No need for the Gladstone bag here! Just to be in the rooms where the greats of cricket and football had been was a buzz for a boy from Footscray. But the best of them all was the Albert Ground, the de facto home ground of the famous Melbourne Cricket Club. *This* is a cricket ground. Its quaint clubhouse, scoreboard and general surrounds make it my favourite. While I have visited Lord's and the Oval, I have not seen cricket played in England 'on the village green'. I have relied on word pictures painted by Neville Cardus and others to fill my mind with such romantic impressions of the game and I imagine the Albert Ground to be the perfect venue for cricket, as Cardus saw it.

I looked forward to every game that year. Being appointed to the main grounds was part of it, but there was also the opportunity to see some big name players up close as they were entering the twilight of their careers in the twos. The standard of cricket was markedly better than in the thirds and, in tandem with that, the difficulty of umpiring increased proportionately as the game quickened up. I must have had a good year as I found myself appointed to the second-eleven semifinal. The most gratifying aspect of being appointed to finals was that it represented the only recognition of your standing. Praise from players was a rarity and we never saw captains' reports.

I headed into my third year looking forward to what might unfold. But what I didn't expect was my appointment in the first round of the season to the first-elevens, and guess where?! Footscray v. Essendon, at the Western Oval – my first time at the ground which, to a local lad, was the shrine to both cricket and football. I can't describe the joy I felt.

There was only one concern. By then, Lindsay James was captain of Footscray. We had grown up together, going to the same school. We had played cricket and football together and all the other things that young blokes do, we did together. We used to go on holidays together. We had acted as a groomsman at each other's wedding. We worked together at Rothmans and, when we built our homes, we built in the same suburb and in the same street. When we were having lunch together on the Friday before the game, Lindsay said to me in a matter-of-fact sort of way, 'I'll give you a lift tomorrow if you like.' To this I replied, 'Pig's arse!' He was clearly offended until I followed up with, 'Look, buddy – tomorrow I don't know you and you don't know me.' He was obviously nonplussed, but agreed to my wishes.

As is the custom in district cricket, my colleague Vern Smithwick and I strode on to the Western Oval about twenty minutes before play to meet the captains and to supervise the toss. We gestured for the skippers to come over and, when they arrived, I offered my hand to the Essendon captain and said, 'Rex Whitehead', to which he responded, 'Keith Kirby.' I replied, 'Pleased to meet you,' and, turning to Lindsay and offering my hand, said, 'Rex Whitehead,' to which he replied, 'Lindsay James – pleased to meet you.' The charade was complete.

This was some match, with the teams including John Grant and Keith Kirby (Essendon and Victoria) and Ray Bright and Alan Hurst (Footscray, Victoria and Australia). It was a one-day fixture, played on a sticky wicket as this was in the pre-covered wicket era. Bright was close to unplayable, taking 6/10. I felt pretty comfortable all day. Then it came time for Lindsay to bat. He took strike and shortly after was comprehensively bowled. Easiest decision I ever made.

I was to umpire Footscray with Lindsay as captain on a number of occasions after that initial appointment. We were both professional enough to realise that we both had our jobs to do and went about it without fear or favour. What happened on the field stayed there and life continued on. However, there was one occasion I recall which didn't exactly delight him. Footscray were in the field and a Prahran batsman shouldered arms and allowed the ball to hit the pad, before taking off and completing one run. Lindsay and the fieldsmen in slips were vocal in their criticism of me that I should not have allowed the run as no shot had been offered. I told them all that I knew what I was doing. After the game as we were having a beer, Lindsay waited till I was on my own and came over and said, 'Remember the leg-bye you allowed today? I realise that there was probably something in the Laws that led you to rule as you did, but could you explain it to me so

I know in the future?' I replied, 'Yep – temporary insanity!' He said, 'Good – I'm about to complete your umpire's report. Could you tell me how many 't's there are in shithouse?'

District cricket was a full-on competition played with a ferocity that probably goes unnoticed unless you are out in the middle. In some instances, it was a tougher competition than Shield cricket. Certainly, a district semifinal was no place for false hearts as it was a cut-throat entry into the final. District cricket in Melbourne had its noted characters and competitors who seemed to inspire the best and worst in the opposition.

Without question the Daddy of them all was St Kilda's Nigel Murch. This bloke was a big, blond Adonis, who possessed a powerful physique and a similar personality. Depending on his mood, he could be the most threatening figure in the game or the most entertaining and amusing character ever met. Two incidents stick in my mind – the first was related by Jack Collins when umpiring a district match. A new batsman playing his first senior game came out to bat with Murch in full flight. Nigel had beaten him all ends up with three successive deliveries without hitting the stumps or enticing a nick. After the fourth such occurrence, it all got too much for Nigel who extended his follow through to within three feet of the batsman and, peering into his face, yelled, 'Not only can't he bat, but isn't he f—ing ugly?!' The batsman was out soon after.

On his retirement from district cricket, Murch played for Malvern in the sub-district competition. By this time his pace, which had been hostile in his prime, had given way to fast–medium at best. A young fellow with an air of cockiness came to the crease and immediately smashed one past Nigel and, in running to the non-striker's end, uttered something like, 'Too easy, old man.' This was a huge blow to Nigel's self-esteem. With the next ball, he summoned up every bit of strength he had and pitched a short, rising delivery dead on line, which the lad could not evade before being struck flush on the jaw. Murch charged down the wicket and, standing over the batsman now prostrate on the pitch, remarked, 'Old man, eh? About $1200 worth of dental work, I'd say!'

In district cricket, the hardest thing I had to do was no-ball a couple of bowlers for an illegal delivery. In both instances, the players involved were moderately successful first-eleven bowlers and being spoken about as possible State players. In considering the issue of fair and unfair deliveries, it is necessary to look at the history of the Laws.

For those who can remember (and I confess here, that I am relying on anecdotal evidence, because of my relative youth), back in the late 1950s and early 1960s there existed a number of bowlers in Australia with doubtful deliveries. The era, if you like, could be called the Meckiff era, without being unfair to him as he was one of a number who were 'suspect'. The difficulty for umpires, and indeed players, was that the Law at the time required the umpire to be absolutely satisfied that the ball had been 'thrown' (delivered illegally) before he could call him. In other words, the Law favoured the bowler with the suspect action. In the mid-1960s the Law was reviewed and took on a 180-degree change whereupon it required the umpire to be absolutely satisfied that the ball had been properly bowled. Therefore, under this wording, if there is any doubt in the umpire's mind as to the purity of the delivery, then it is incumbent on him/her to no-ball the bowler. The clear intent of the law-makers was to rid the game of those who were considered suspect, and rightly so, in my view, as the nature of the delivery action – that is, with a straight arm – is one of the defining issues which separates cricket from other sports.

Considering the history of the Law and its current wording, I am strongly of the view that there exists in Test cricket today a couple of bowlers from the subcontinent, Muralitharan and Dharmasena, who clearly breach this Law. One is so blatant that his delivery would fail under the previous Law.

The whole question of illegal deliveries in international cricket is not assisted by the policy of removing the responsibilities from the umpires in dealing with the issue by demanding they mention suspect actions in their report rather than deal with it according to the Laws of the game.

As to the two bowlers I called in district cricket, it is worth noting both disappeared from the district scene almost immediately. The interesting issue with these bowlers, whom I called in two different games each (and who were strangely not called by other umpires at the time), was that on each occasion it came as no surprise to the bowlers' team-mates. Clearly, they were aware of the fact before I intervened. Despite this, it was a very tough call that gave me no joy. On a grander scale, it disturbs me that bowlers with suspect actions can rise through domestic levels to the Test arena without umpires along the way doing their duty.

My first appointment to officiate at the MCG was for a State colts fixture followed by an Australian colts v. Australian schoolboys match, from which an Australian under-19 team to tour England was to be picked. The teams included Geoff Marsh, Dirk Wellham, Wayne Phillips and a diminutive David

Boon. I can clearly recall Boon coming out to bat at about number six as a tiny sixteen-year-old, and thinking to myself that this kid will be able to talk for the rest of his life about the day he played on the MCG.

At the time, Mark O'Neill, son of Norman, was bowling. He put a short one down to Boon who tried to hook it off his nose, only to get a nick and send it straight into the snoz, causing it to bleed for some time. When it finally stopped, O'Neill and his team-mates learned that it had not been a good idea to pin Boon, who proceeded to smash them all over the paddock for a brilliant century. Despite many visits to the MCG for Shield and Test cricket, I never saw the ball hit cleaner than Boon did that day. He was selected to tour England and never looked back.

After some three or four years at district first-eleven level, including a couple of semifinals, I found myself appointed to my first Sheffield Shield match, Victoria v. Western Australia, at the MCG. I stood that match with Robin Bailhache, who simply never made a mistake. Geez, he must have thought I was ordinary.

Standing in the middle of the MCG is an awesome experience, even without a crowd, and I needed to keep pinching myself to make sure it was really me who was standing there. It hadn't been all that long ago that, armed with an esky and accompanied by a few mates, I had been standing in Bay 13 soaking up the atmosphere of a Shield match. It didn't seem much further back than that when, with my family, I had been there watching Sam Loxton batting for the Vics. Now, here I was, standing in the middle of it.

At State level, my most memorable match was the 1979–80 Gillette (forerunner of the Mercantile Mutual) Cup final between Victoria and New South Wales, played before a crowd of 45 000 and televised nationally. I remember it being a fierce contest with plenty happening for the umpires. I recall that Jim Higgs was 12th man for Victoria that day, but his only involvement in the game was to carry the drinks. For this (which I might add he performed with some aplomb) he was paid $1200.

After the match and presentations, I was sitting in the dressing room with my colleague Dick French and feeling absolutely stuffed, such was the pressure and intensity of the job. Ken Jacobs, then assistant secretary of the VCA (now executive director), entered the room and handed us our remuneration for the day's efforts – the grand sum of $22.75 each. I thanked Ken for the board's abundant generosity and suggested that I would have offered to buy him a drink at the Hilton later, but I didn't have enough money.

My first international was a one-dayer between Australia and the West Indies at the MCG. The Windies won the toss and batted, with Gordon Greenidge and Desmond Haynes opening. Dennis Lillee opened the bowling from my end and was quick – real quick. Greenidge got out shortly after the start and Viv Richards came to the crease. There had been much speculation in the press surrounding his fitness and there was some doubt as to his availability until he entered the arena to loud jeering and hoots from the crowd. I could not believe it. Here was the world's premier batsman being treated in this fashion, for no apparent reason. It must have inspired Richards because he peeled off the highest score (at the time) for a one-day international of 156 not out. I have neither before, nor since, seen batting like it. He absolutely hammered everything that came his way and the faster Lillee bowled, the harder he hit it.

I vividly remember one shot off Lillee where he planted his front foot down the track and smashed the ball over mid-off one bounce into the fence. Such was the power of the shot that Haynes, who was the non-striker, exclaimed (as he watched the ball go over his head), 'Faaaaaaark!' Couldn't have said it better myself. Actually, a similar remark was made by Lillee but with a vastly different intonation.

At one stage, Greg Chappell brought on Allan Border. It must have been for comic relief. Richards crashed the first ball so hard and high that I lost it, but assumed it went over the Southern Stand roof. I stood there, momentarily bewildered. Finally, I reasoned that I had better arrange for a replacement ball. As I was moving towards the players' gate and passing Greg Chappell at slip, he asked me, 'Where are you going?'

'To get another pill,' I replied, to which he responded, pointing to the ball in Border's hand, 'What's wrong with that one?' Talk about feeling like a goose, I thought, as I trudged back to square leg. When the innings was closed, Richards left the ground to a standing ovation, rightly deserved and a fitting tribute to an innings that will be long-remembered by all who saw it.

International one-day matches are certainly different. I was officiating the day that Greg Chappell came out to bat with seven innings behind him without score. At the time he was reported as declaring that it was not that he was batting poorly, it was just that he was getting out. I dreamt of using that one. I thought it would be perfect next time the media was giving me a thrashing to respond with, 'It is not that I am umpiring poorly, it is just that I keep giving shockers.' I wonder how the media would have responded.

Anyway, on this particular day, Greg strode to the wicket

with the crowd abuzz. Just as he was about to take strike, some wag let a duck out on to the arena. This did not make Greg a happy man. After the duck was recaptured and taken away, he settled over his bat to take strike. The ball was delivered and Greg confidently allowed it to go through to the 'keeper. The crowd roared its approval. He had actually lasted one ball. The next delivery was angled down the leg side and he attempted a glance and headed off for an easy single to a thunderous reception from the crowd. When I signalled to the scorers that it was, in fact, a leg-bye, I thought I was going to be lynched. Greg would have approved. It was, in fact, the end of the over and he asked me if I could loosen one of the straps on his pad. As I was doing this, he said, 'Actually, it's killing me. I'm not used to batting this long!'

On another occasion, I was umpiring Australia v. India in a day/night match in Sydney. Border got a hundred, and thousands of fans swarmed on to the oval. I stood at the bowler's end, ensuring that nobody could souvenir the stumps or bails. Alongside me was the Indian bowler, Dilip Doshi. Just then, a nine or ten-year-old, freckle-faced kid ran up to Doshi and from a distance of around ten feet, yelled, 'All Indians are poofters!' Doshi, despite his best endeavours, was never going to catch the tyke as he haired off before jumping over the fence in front of the Hill. I mused that he was probably an Australian opening bowler in the making. All the prerequisites were there.

My entry into international cricket coincided with two issues, both of which have often been described as the undoing of umpires, namely the introduction of the 'big screen' to the MCG, which was the first venue to get one, and the introduction by Channel Nine of multi-camera placement and the slow-motion replay.

When the big screen was introduced to the MCG, Robin Bailhache and I had a number of informal discussions with the then secretary of the Melbourne Cricket Club and former Australian captain Ian Johnson on the issue of what should and should not be shown on the screen. We were at pains to point out that it was one thing for a cricket follower to see an umpire make an error on the television screen at home. It was another matter to show that live in front of 70 000 spectators, particularly late in the day, when some of the lads in Bay 13 had become tired and emotional. While I am not sure whether our advice was of any consequence, I am convinced that withholding such evidence is a prudent judgement.

In the matter of television replays and different camera angles, I guess the big discovery to the cricket-following public was that now they could see that umpires make mistakes. Let me tell the reader, there was nothing new in that – it simply meant now the entire world knew. In the early days, one or two commentators were clearly gleeful when they happened to pin an error on the umpire.

I assume I speak for my colleagues when I say that the run-out errors definitely surprised me. This was never a decision that I personally had a problem with, yet the slow-motion replay caught my colleagues and me out on a number of occasions. Some commentators took pleasure in each incident, saying things like, 'He was out by a foot and, look, the umpire has given him not out.' I once discussed this issue with a television technician, who pointed out to me that the batsman was out of his ground, not by a measure in distance but by a measure in time. He went on to say that in the scenario offered, the batsman was out by 1/64th of a second, being the time it took for the bat to travel over that distance. It therefore becomes immediately apparent that no human being can be accurate inside that degree of error.

A final comment on that issue: prior to the introduction of the third umpire, viewers saw a number of errors in run-outs. Not once, however, was there an occasion where an umpire gave a batsman out when he had made his ground. The principle of giving the batsman the benefit of the doubt was applied in every instance. From time to time it might have been nice if the media had allowed themselves to acknowledge this fact and, indeed, to applaud it.

As to the third umpire and replays, I sincerely hope that no further intrusion into the game is taken using this facility. I strongly believe that sport is all about human success and failure, including that of the umpire. The whole culture of the game is at risk if we, say, look to the third umpire who might use some technical device to adjudge an lbw. The principle is that the fielding side enquires of the umpire whether in his opinion, certain requirements of the Law have been met. Note the words 'in his opinion'. Part of the charm of cricket is the subjectivity of the decision-making process, which adds to spectator/viewer interest in forming their own opinions as to the correctness of the decision. It gives all of us the opportunity to own a view. There is an anxiety aroused while the umpire considers his decision, which may take two or three seconds, yet feels like an age, so that when that decision is finally delivered there is often great excitement and emotion. This creates a certain theatre about the occasion and I would hate to see that lost or diluted as it is while waiting the faceless, third umpire's decision. Sports like American Football can use replays at will. It is a plastic, stop-start game anyway. Cricket is better than that.

After a couple of seasons doing one-day internationals, I was appointed to umpire my first Test match, Australia v. India, at the SCG in January 1981. In fact, I was appointed to do the series of three Tests. At age thirty-two, I was one of the youngest ever to be appointed to Test level in Australia. The first Test match was in Sydney. Never in my life have I been as nervous as I was before that game. My father-in-law came into the rooms before the game (he went on to umpire cricket in the Bellarine association) and I was so nervous I couldn't talk. As we went out on to the ground to begin play, I looked up to the heavens and said, 'This one's for you, Dad.' I am sure he was watching and probably wondering why I was walking out there without a Gladstone bag. Greg Chappell ran past and said, 'G'day,' while I responded with something incomprehensible. My hands were shaking so much that I had trouble putting the bails on. Fortunately, my partner was the laconic Queenslander Mel Johnson. Mel is the most laid-back fellow and I couldn't have been matched with a better bloke.

Lillee opened proceedings from my end and it wasn't long before there was a big appeal for a caught Marsh bowled Lillee. The batsman had just feathered it off the glove. I put the finger up and at the same time all the nerves disappeared, probably because I knew by then I was into it.

A little later, Lillee was replaced by Lenny Pascoe. Now there's somebody different. He was bowling to one Sandeep Patil, who played three cover drives over second slip and down to the boundary. This did not impress Lenny, who screamed down the pitch, 'You're nothing but a mongrel #$+&% and [pointing to his forehead] the next one's going to get you right here.' Welcome to Test cricket, Rex. The queer thing was it did. Hit him on the head, that is. Now get this. Lenny starts wandering around in great despair, wringing his hands and generally being full of remorse. He was moaning to his mates, 'You don't think I've killed the poor bastard, do you?' Two minutes earlier he had threatened to. Actually, despite a bit of blood, it was more of a glancing blow and after a short retirement Sandeep re-entered the fray and throughout the series proved himself to be a good bloke and a batsman of rare quality.

This was also the first occasion Lillee had opened the bowling with Rodney Hogg. Hoggy was also different, a fair dinkum larrikin, but you had to like him. Lillee always worked feverishly on the ball to keep the shine. Hoggy, on the other hand, wasn't much into this. After Hoggy's first over it came back to Lillee in a bit of a mess and Dennis let him know it. Another over and no change. Again a rebuke from Dennis. Neither Dennis nor I could believe it when it came back after Hoggy's third, once more unshone. This time Dennis really let him have it. Hoggy responded, 'But I can't do it.'

'Why not?'

'Because I'm not wearing the right pants.'

With blood rushing to his head, Dennis turned to me. 'Did you hear that? He can't polish the ball because he's got the wrong f—ing pants on!' I couldn't help it. It broke me up.

Greg Chappell made a brilliant double century, but Doug Walters played the shot of the match. He unleashed a pull shot off Ghavri that went crashing into the fence and which I completely lost sight of before I heard the loud bang on the advertising hoarding. Non-striker Greg Chappell, clearly impressed with the shot, turned to me and asked incredulously, 'Did you see that?'

Greg gave me a funny look when I replied, 'No.'

Australia won the Test, so it was off to Adelaide for the second match. I had never known heat like it. For the first three days, the temperature reached 43 degrees. Soon after lunch, on the first day, my mate Tony Crafter, a native South Australian, told me that a gully breeze would come through midafternoon and cool things down, presumably like Perth's Fremantle Doctor. Twenty years on, I'm still waiting for that gully breeze. The match was noteworthy for Sandeep Patil's 174 and Kim Hughes's 213, and for the Indians giving me a bagging through the press after the game.

The third Test was played at the MCG. The highlight came in India's second innings when that 'patron' of cricket umpires, Sunil Gavaskar, was batting with his intriguingly named partner Chetan Chauhan. It was the first time in the series that Gavaskar had looked like getting some runs and he had reached 70. Lillee was bowling from my end, the Members', and needed one wicket to equal Richie Benaud's Australian Test record. He pitched one on off stump and the ball cannoned into Gavaskar's pads at about shin level. There was a huge appeal and I determined that the ball was going to miss leg and off, but middle was in real trouble. I raised the finger skywards.

Gavaskar stunned everyone by holding his bat aloft and claiming he had hit the ball. Lillee would have none of this and after charging down the pitch pointed to the precise spot on Gavaskar's pads where the ball had hit. Gavaskar, sensing Lillee's angst, decided to take his leave. In so doing he had to walk past me. As he approached me, he said, 'I heet thet bull weeth ma bet.' To which, with commendable conciseness, I replied, 'Pig's arse!' At this point he grabbed Chetan and said,

'We go.' And they were off, ready to catch the next Air India flight to Madras.

Now, you have to picture this. Here am I, umpiring my first Test match in my home town, at the MCG. My wife Carol, my mum, my children Roxanne and Clayton, my mother-in-law and father-in-law, are all sitting in the stand watching and one team doesn't want to play because of me. As I walked after the reluctant batsmen, I was in the process of quoting the Law on 'refusal to play' when my mate, Mel Johnson, called out. He was standing alongside Greg Chappell, no doubt discussing the affairs of the day. I wandered over to join them and Greg said, 'This is easy. As soon as they are off the oval, I will appeal and you can award the Test to us.' Under the Laws, in a technical sense, that was correct. But I replied to Greg that this was a Test match and no Test match was going down like that as long as I was umpiring. It must have impressed him because he later wrote in his book covering the series that my comments had brought home to him the seriousness of the occasion and the sanctity of Test cricket.

Finally, to everyone's relief the incoming batsman, Vengsarkar, and Chauhan re-entered the oval and the game continued. The whole episode took on gigantic proportions within the media with newspaper front pages and television and radio news all headlining the walk-off. Later that night, Richie Benaud introduced a segment on television claiming that Channel Nine had the technology to examine the correctness or otherwise of the decision.

In the first instance, they showed the ball travelling frame by frame in reaching the pad. As that was inconclusive, they then raised the sound volume from the microphone at the base of the stumps. Richie said, 'If the ball did hit the bat, you will hear two distinct sounds.' The volume was so raised that in its final travel the viewer could hear it actually move through the air until, with one dull thud, it met the pad. 'There's one umpire who can sleep well tonight,' said Richie. Bill Lawry, who was presenting the show alongside him, leapt into his hysterical, falsetto timbre to announce, 'I don't care what that says, I still believe Gavaskar.' Good on ya, Bill! History now tells us that India went on to win the Test match and square the series, 1-all, something it could not have done had Gavaskar's wishes been met.

Some two years later, I umpired my fourth and final Test, the Boxing Day match in Melbourne, Australia v. England. Later that season, I was to announce my retirement from all cricket at the age of thirty-four, an age when most umpires are still learning the game and when another twenty years might have been possible at the highest level.

Why retire? From the players' perspective, the major consequence of Kerry Packer's World Series Cricket arose with players, quite rightly, finally being paid a reasonable sum for 'putting on the show'. Moreover, rather than being treated as sometimes almost irrelevant and dispensable by the authorities, they were accorded greater respect in all manner of their relationships with the game's administrators. Sadly, though, this was not the case with umpires who, unless they had very supportive employers, found the intrusion on their business lives, alongside the meagre return in fees, difficult to reconcile. More importantly, there existed at that time an almost cultural cringe by administrators against showing support for umpires and developing their skills for the greater betterment of the game. At any time we were quite aware that we were only as good as our last game; a situation which, for my part, hardly justified risking the full dedication to my permanent career.

Despite these concerns, I can say that umpiring cricket gave me far more than I could ever give back and, as I said on acceptance of my life membership of the Victorian Cricket Association Umpires' Association (an honour I cherish like no other award), there is no finer body of men than the members of the VCAUA, or for that matter, any other devotee of the game who wears the famous white coat.

When people ask me to relate my fondest memory, it is without question hearing the voice of cricket, Alan McGilvray describe the following: 'And now it's Lillee from the Paddington end to Gavaskar and past Mr Whitehead standing in his first Test.' Here was the man whose voice *was* Test cricket, whether I heard it on the radio while lying on the beach, or at a house party in the middle of winter when McGilvray would paint word pictures of the Oval, describing the heroics of Miller, Archer, Benaud, Washbrook and Hutton. Fancy the great man calling my name and referring to me as Mister! What a thrill for a boy from Footscray who first knew cricket at Snake Gully.

REX WHITEHEAD'S UMPIRING CV

16 first-class matches between December 1978 and January 1983

Official Test matches – 4 (Australia v. England 1, India 3)

Internationals – 3 (Victoria v. New Zealand, Pakistan, England)

Sheffield Shield matches – 9

One-day internationals – 15

Dick French
I Should Be in France

It was February 1979, the 'rest' day of the fourth Test between England and Australia, and my wife Margaret and I were driving to a friend's place for an early evening meal and a chat before preparing for the fourth day's dramatic events.

As we drove past a newsagency, we couldn't help but notice the placard outside. The now defunct Sydney *Sun*'s banner read 'LBW Uproar – Photo'. I immediately thought this must be some reference to my co-umpire adjudging Geoffrey Boycott out lbw in the first over of England's second innings, and I said to my wife, 'We better get a paper and see what they're saying about my mate [Robin Bailhache].'

Margaret hopped out of the car, bought the *Sun*, climbed back in and announced: 'It's not Robin they're getting stuck into – it's you!' And there it was, on the front page, with a photo of Derek Randall being hit on the pads and me shaking my head. Keith Miller was reporting the incident as Randall being 'plumb', adding: 'Umpire French in years to come will no doubt be asked by his grandchildren about this Randall decision he gave, or rather didn't give, and which gave England the series in 1978–79'.

All very well, Keith, I thought, but it's not your decision or anyone else's. It's simply the opinion of the umpire, who happens to be me. The only problem on this occasion was that Randall was nought at the time, and went on to score 150. But I kept the article; it's now flatly desiccated like a long-dead butterfly in one of eight scrapbooks that chronicle my career and the hundreds of matches it encompassed. That very few of the articles are complimentary doesn't subtract from the enjoyment I get from occasionally browsing through them.

I can't remember when I first took an interest in cricket, but clearly recollect my father taking me to the first Test match played in Sydney after WWII. It was the day in December 1946, after Don Bradman and Sid Barnes had each scored 234. I can recall Len Hutton smashing the ball all over the place in a brilliant short innings, before hitting his wicket.

Like Australia's fortunes on that day, the weather must have taken a turn for the worse, because I recall Dad saying, apropos of nothing happening out on the ground: 'Remember, son, always take a jumper with you to the cricket.' Advice I adhered to strictly for the next fifty years.

My enthusiasm for the game thus kindled, I can say with the greatest pleasure and pride that I've since seen every Test match subsequently played at the Sydney Cricket Ground, a ground I fell in love with in 1946 and which remains very special to me. Sitting on the Hill with my dad that year, I could never have dreamt that one day I would be out in the middle umpiring a Test match or of the pride and sense of achievement that would bring.

Attending Sydney Boys' High School later in the 1950s was also a bonus, as the school was directly opposite the SCG. It was a simple matter to skip a few periods and watch Lindwall, Miller and company in action, courtesy of the free passes we were given as members of the school's first-eleven, although my academic record no doubt suffered from these self-imposed absences from the occasional class.

My interest in the Laws of Cricket and, by definition,

umpiring, began when in a school match I was adjudged out stumped off a no-ball. My protest to the umpire got me nowhere; just a good dressing down from my parents when they heard about my dissent. Armed with a copy of the Laws of Cricket (1947 code), I finally got Dad to admit the umpire had been wrong on this point of Law, as distinct from the fact of dismissal.

From that day on I studied the Laws intently and still do today as something new always seems to crop up. Amendments to the Laws continually reflect the changing nature of the game, and major rewrites occurred in 1980 and 2000. I was honoured to have some direct input through the Australian Cricket Board on the year 2000 Law rewrite in the late 1990s, and no doubt there will be many other changes as the years roll on.

My undistinguished playing career was notable only for a match with City & Suburban against a NSW Cricket Association team on the SCG in 1969 when I ran out my batting partner while he was 99. An uncomfortable moment in any context, but Graham Reed was a great personal friend who went on to umpire Shield cricket.

So I turned my attentions to qualifying as an umpire. This meant I had to attend four weeks of intense study of the Laws, in lectures given by Tom Brooks and Ted Wykes, who used an old Ducane manual stop-frame projector. A week later a group of us sat for an oral exam. Former Test umpire George Borwick was one of the examiners, and in spite of much head-shaking from George at some of my answers, I managed to pass and was awarded my certificate in 1969, although several years went by before I took up umpiring in Sydney grade cricket. These days NSW Cricket's umpire-training committee consists of ten expert lecturers using sophisticated, state-of-the-art training manuals and videos, and multiple-choice written papers are used to examine prospective members who must achieve an 85 per cent pass mark. As the current NSW state director of umpiring, I now oversee all this activity and marvel at how far we have come in the past thirty years.

My initiation to umpiring in Sydney fourth grade in 1971–72 brought with it a complete culture shock. I quickly learnt that a good knowledge of the Laws of Cricket was just a small part of the art of umpiring. I was dealing with real people in real, pressurised situations, requiring skilled man-management and imposing new, unparalleled demands on my concentration, with wayward players, captains and weather, unfamiliar grounds and a host of other distractions not covered by the complex Laws. But after a season of observation and presumably favourable reports from captains and officials, I found myself promoted through the grades and, eventually, to first grade, which was a pretty intense standard of cricket.

We were then – and promising rookies still are now – put through colts, second XI and other representative matches, performing over longer and longer hours, to see how we'd go before being considered for promotion to Shield matches. Naturally, the promotion pole from first grade to higher honours becomes slippery fairly rapidly.

In the umpires' room at the SCG there is an honours board with the names of all umpires who have officiated at Sheffield Shield level since the NSW Cricket Umpires' Association was formed in 1913. There are only seventy names on it, which gives some idea of how difficult it is to attain that level – not how difficult it is to get a decent sign-writer, as one wag suggested! With a membership of more than 800 umpires in the State, it can be seen that less than 1 per cent of members are going to reach first-class level.

To reach the next levels – one-day internationals, then Test cricket – is even more daunting, and currently NSW has only five living umpires who have officiated in Test cricket in the past forty years. So it's an ambitious rookie who considers he can become a Test umpire without a lot of effort, pain and good old hard work; but it can be done.

After three seasons (1973–75) in first grade, minor representative matches and second XI games, I was finally appointed to my first Shield match in February 1976 – NSW v. WA – with Test umpire Tom Brooks as my partner. My allowance, or fee, for the match was $65. But the experience was beyond price and I was fortunate to have a sympathetic employer, the AMP Society, to release me from my accounting duties for four scheduled days and the first of my forty-four Sheffield Shield matches. 'Scheduled', because it rained non-stop for the first two-and-a-half days so that by the time I finally got onto the ground I was a nervous wreck. It was not made easier by my introduction to the WA captain, Rodney Marsh, who in making a point to his team-mates that this was my first game, attempted to put me at ease by commenting, 'Dick, I want you to know that I always walk when I'm out.' Tom Brooks, a veteran of some twenty Tests by this stage, responded: 'Rodney, it's pretty hard not to walk when your three stumps are scattered all over the ground.'

The match finally got under way after lunch on day three, a day made memorable for my first decision in first-class cricket: giving Bruce Yardley, the Test off-spinner, out caught behind following a raucous appeal from Len Pascoe and ten others. I thought, great – this is my first decision, and on my beloved SCG. To my horror, Yardley advanced down the pitch after being out, holding his cap and complaining the ball had clipped it. Len solved the situation brilliantly: 'Piss off, you bloody sandgroper,' he said, 'or I'll wrap the cap around your neck.' Yardley took a left-hand turn and walked off the ground.

I must have gone reasonably well in that initial match, because I was selected to officiate in the next Shield game, NSW v. South Australia. The authorities were experimenting with a new type of ball – Steeden – a good cherry, I thought, with pronounced seams and one side printed with 156 G, the metric equivalent of five-and-a-half ounces. As we walked through the gate on to the hallowed turf, and before dropping the ball for the fielding captain to pick up, my co-umpire looked at the gold 156 G on the ball and exclaimed: 'Look at that, Dick – made in 1969.' I'm glad the players didn't overhear that comment, which would tend to confirm that most of us are lacking in the eyesight department.

Late in the day I met Ian Chappell for the first time. I hadn't been introduced to him before play started and he finally arrived at the crease after the fall of a South Australian wicket. The sun was getting in my eyes at square leg on the eastern side of the SCG, so I decided to cross over to point. The Laws say that is perfectly in order provided you inform the batsman of your intention. As I crossed over and passed Ian, I said, 'Just going over to point, Ian.' His response, 'I don't give a f— where you stand,' shook me up momentarily, but as I walked quickly to take up my new position, Chappell followed and added, 'While you're at it, you can tell your equally incompetent mate that's he's not watching the no-balls.'

My 'incompetent mate' temporarily ended Ian's problems with the alleged no-balling on the very next delivery, giving him out lbw. But it was an early demonstration of how the former Australian captain managed to disturb a few feathers on his way through.

By 1977 the umpiring match allowance had been increased to $100 for Shield matches, and Australian cricket was in disarray with the defection of players to World Series Cricket. A number of former Test umpires had been approached to officiate in the rebel games. The hefty contracts offered made my $100 match fee look very paltry by comparison, but to my knowledge none of the then current group of first-class umpires was offered a contract to defect. There was certainly no point in my being offered the Packer/PBL money to switch, as no amount would have enticed me from the chance to umpire a Test match in Australia.

And then it happened: Robin Bailhache (Vic.) and Reg Ledwidge (NSW) had been selected to umpire the second Test between Australia and India in Perth in December 1977, but eight days before the Test was due to start, Reg suffered a cerebral haemorrhage and sadly died a few days later. Shortly afterwards, Austin Chapman and I were officiating in a Shield match in Sydney, wearing black arm bands as a mark of respect, when I received a call from ACB secretary Alan Barnes inviting me to umpire in the Test in place of Reg. I accepted, but had very mixed emotions and trouble concentrating for the remainder of the Shield match. I was to be the sixty-ninth Australian Test umpire since 1877.

The Test match in Perth, played just before Christmas 1977, was one of the hottest matches I had ever controlled. I knew none of the Indian side and only half the Australian team.

I had never met Rob Bailhache, but he proved to be a tower of strength and support on my nervous start to Test cricket. 'Don't be nervous, old son,' he said, ten minutes before play was due to start. 'Just think, seventy-five million Indians will be watching you [on TV].'

The match went fairly well for both of us, and Australia, under Bob Simpson, won a close encounter by two wickets. Back in Sydney, Margaret presented me with a letter from Bhopal in India, in lovely handwriting under a gold embossed letterhead. From a female, and no doubt a princess, I decided. The letter, which has pride of place in one of my scrapbooks, begins: 'Dear Mr Richard French, undoubtedly you are a great umpire . . .' Yeah, nice start, I thought. It continues: 'But either your eyes are a bit weak or you are a great big cheat'. And on she went, two pages of vitriol on my performance in Perth. But her heart was in the right place – she finished the letter with 'God be with you'.

A week later I was fortunate to be selected with Max O'Connell to officiate in the third Test in Melbourne, and I felt much more satisfied at having achieved this selection at last in my own right. The satisfaction was short lived, because India had three top-line spinners: Bedi, Chandrasekhar and Prasanna, and umpiring them on the then-dodgy Melbourne pitch was not easy. It wasn't easy for the Australians, either, India winning by 222 runs to keep the series alive.

By the time the fifth Test came around in Adelaide, the series was level at 2-all. Max and I were appointed to the match, which proved to be the most difficult I'd had to date. There were several close and controversial decisions, and feelings were running high, particularly among the Indians, who were letting the match slip away by the end of day three. Bishan Bedi regarded both umpires as 'not very competent'. Australian captain Simpson countered by saying he was 'completely satisfied with the standard of umpiring'; Bishen, he reckoned, was 'clutching at straws'. In any event, I had plenty of clippings for my now swelling scrapbooks, and was rather pleased when the match ended on the sixth day with Australia prevailing in another close finish [by 47 runs].

This Test was also notable for me as, at last – in the umpires' room after day four – I met the great man, Sir Donald Bradman. His first words to me were: 'Mr French, by what Law did you not allow Bishan Bedi to bowl today before lunch?' I had decided not to let Bedi bowl on this particular morning, because he failed to take the field at the start of play, remaining in the dressing room nursing what was no doubt a giant legacy from the previous rest day in the Barossa Valley. I considered it would be unfair to allow Bedi to bowl immediately he came on to the field an hour after play had started in considerable heat, so ruled that he could not bowl for another hour. Bedi was not impressed, but I was convinced his proposal amounted to unfair play. This I explained to Sir Donald. 'You were quite right,' he agreed, and walked out of the room. It was interesting to note that in the 1980 rewrite of the Laws, this particular Law was changed to accommodate this very situation. It wouldn't surprise me to learn The Don had had some input.

After this 1977–78 series, the usual call went out for neutral umpires to stand in Test matches. The fact of that neutrality is now taken for granted, but I've never been in favour of the system. It is very, very difficult to get appointed to a Test match in Australia now, and currently we lack depth in Test umpiring experience because of the chances thus limited. The few top umpires of each country tour the world, officiating in Test matches, but their inevitable retirement leaves a big hole in local ranks. I remain sceptical of the worth of so-called neutral umpires. It proved an abject failure when temporarily introduced to the Sheffield Shield competition several seasons ago and was quickly abandoned.

During the second year (1978–79) of the great schism of World Series Cricket, the England side toured Australia under the captaincy of Mike Brearley. I'd have to say Brearley was the finest captain I ever saw in the middle, although Mark Taylor was not far behind. Brearley was a most astute tactician, erudite and intelligent, a pleasant personality and great leader. The contrast with his counterpart, Graham Yallop, was striking, and England won the six-Test series by a 5–1 margin.

Around this time I was transferred by my employer to Adelaide, so I had the added problems of buying and selling homes, taking time off from work for cricket, organising new schools for my three sons, and generally settling in to a new environment. But the Adelaide people were great and the SA umpires made me feel most welcome: my concerns about a possible adverse reaction to taking the spot of a local umpire in first-class cricket proved unfounded.

I thoroughly enjoyed my time, albeit a brief eleven months, in Adelaide. Max O'Connell and I, now fellow Croweaters, were back in tandem for the first Test against the Poms; this in spite of Geoffrey Boycott complaining, predictably, about me giving him out twice lbw in the South Australians' match against the tourists ('Ball pitched on middle and leg cannot hit leg stoomp, oompah'). The Test in Brisbane brought more controversy when I warned Bob Willis for bowling bouncers at Australia's opening bowler and No. 9 bat, Rodney Hogg. Willis got a bit upset at this, and Brearley came down the pitch to talk to me, explaining that he and Yallop had reached an agreement about the use of bouncers to unrecognised batsmen. I politely pointed out that no one had bothered to tell the umpires of this arrangement, which in any event was contrary to the Laws of Cricket. It all got sorted out in the end, but the press, as usual, made an issue out of it.

In any sport there are events and memories that stand out and bring a shiver to the spine when they are recalled. One such incident was during the third Test in Melbourne when Hogg bowled Boycott for one, thus causing the loudest sustained roar I have ever heard from a sporting public. I was at square leg at the time and noticed the wicket smashed a fraction of a second before the huge noise reached us out in the middle. Australian patriotic fervour was at its peak with the rival rebel series being played elsewhere in the country, and the jubilation of the Australian players and spectators was wonderful to see. It was just as well the Aussies derived maximum enjoyment from the Melbourne Test because it was the only match the home side won in the series (by 103 runs). On reflection, the only full-throated roar from an Australian crowd to match the Boycott dismissal in my experience was that which greeted Sydney Swans full-forward Tony Lockett's after-the-siren point on the Sydney Cricket Ground that put the Swans into the 1996 AFL grand final. This time I could cheer as a supporter, and what a feeling!

The fourth Test of the 1978–79 series brought with it my refusal to raise a finger to send Derek Randall on his way – the incident that so fired up Keith Miller – and by now my bulging scrapbook was telling me (no, reminding me) that controversy and Test matches in these days of probing TV lenses and slow-motion replays are inseparable. Bailhache and O'Connell, both of them more experienced than me, confirmed they, too, kept scrapbooks of their 'other' jobs and made the point that while they were great to browse through in winter, the books were best left in the cupboard during summer or, at least, were not to be taken to heart. Still, when I look back at all these documented incidents after such a long time, I feel more grateful than ever to have played a small part in Australian cricket.

Towards the end of the summer, my AMP employer chose to transfer me interstate yet again, this time to Melbourne, causing further dislocation to my family. Surprisingly, amid the confusion I found myself in Melbourne on a Saturday in late March with absolutely nothing to do. I found the Victorian Cricket Association's phone number, phoned an official, Bill Price, and asked him if by chance they could use an umpire. Indeed they could, said Bill, who directed me to Gosche's Paddock to preside over a fourth-grade district match. Fine, except I'd never heard of Gosche's half-dozen acres, and when I eventually found it, play was delayed because my co-umpire had left the new ball in the public toilet/change room and it had been stolen. Some introduction! But my three seasons impressed me greatly with the standard of the Vics' district cricket, administration, the grounds and the VCA Umpires' Association. When I joined the VCAUA in 1979 there were six first-class umpires on its panel: Bailhache, Jack Collins, Kevin Carmody, Bill Copeland, Ray Isherwood and Rex Whitehead. So it became difficult to get a Shield match, let alone a Test. (How quickly the situation can change: in seasons 1999–2000 and 2000–01 there were no Victorian umpires on the national panel, with a new one appointed in season 2001–02.)

It was around this time, with the 'peace treaty' and merging of World Series and traditional cricket in time for 1979–80, that the ACB decided on a national panel to officiate in Tests and one-day internationals. Victorians made up most of the panel and it was great to meet fellow umpires from other States at specially convened ACB umpires' meetings over the following years. Sections of the press wanted to take the changes further, with three umpires to stand in Tests. Thankfully, the suggestion was rejected by both the umps and the authorities. Oddly, though, about twelve years later, the three-umpires system was trialed for two seasons of Shield matches before being assigned to the scrap heap. In all my travels I met no umpire in favour of such a system. With umpires rotating each session, comments from players out in the middle, such as 'Your mate would have given that out lbw this morning' did the game no good. One umpire would always miss out on the sometimes dramatic final session of the match, and the broken continuity produced additional demands of concentration and pressure. I think the ACB has got it just about right at present with its five-man panel and space for adding emerging umpires via a supplementary panel.

The 1979–80 season in Melbourne was notable in that I was selected to stand in the district final as well as several Shield and one-day international matches. Sydney, in fact, hosted the first one-dayers to be played under lights. A young Merv Hughes ensured the Melbourne district final was a memorable affair, the Footscray fast bowler starting his run from near the sight screen. The St Kilda batsmen almost needed their own screen to mask their sensibilities from the incoming paceman: moustached Merv was indeed a fearsome sight! Hughes cannoned one ball into the pads of the Saints'

England Test match spinner-in-residence, John Emburey, and demanded a favourable lbw decision. I said 'not out', whereupon Merv demanded to know what the ball was missing. I responded, 'Merv, it would have just missed the leg bail.' Hughes: 'Yes, and I bet you failed at geometry at school too.' He got better with his repartee as the years went on.

Like his mate Jeff Thomson, Len Pascoe was pretty slippery both with his *bons mots* and the pace of his bowling. In a one-day international at the MCG in 1980, Len opened the attack to Geoffrey Boycott. The England opener tried to glance a full-length delivery slanting across his pads and I heard a distinct click before it was gloved by Rod Marsh. All the Australians appealed, delighted at having got rid of this dour, supremely focused character before he could do any damage – or so they thought. They were in full celebration, but, frankly, I hadn't a clue what had happened, which is why an important, often-invoked Law gives benefit of any doubt to the batsman. So, not for the first time, I invoked it and hoped the TV cameras agreed with me. The ultimate party pooper, I called out in the loudest, clearest voice I could muster: 'Not out.' The hugging stopped. Pascoe glared at me, glared back at Boycott, then called beyond him to Marsh: 'Hey, Bacchus, before you give the ball back to me, take the splinter out of it.'

Season 1980–81 will always be remembered for the underarm incident on the Melbourne Cricket Ground at the end of the third World Series Cup final on 1 February 1981. I remember it well because I had umpired the second final the day before; Australia beat the Kiwis quite easily in an undramatic match that gave no clue of the seismic events about to unfold. The deciding final was packed with drama right up to the final delivery of the day when Trevor Chappell played carpet bowls with an unwilling Brian McKechnie and launched the international incident that still rumbles quietly on, especially across the Tasman when the two teams resume conflict in either the short or long form of the game. I felt so sorry for the umpires, Peter Cronin (SA) and Don Weser (WA), on that day. They were clearly distressed when I met them at the gate to help them off with the stumps, bails and balls. And, believe it or not, I still have that ball, an innocuous-looking projectile that is scuffed and tatty as though it had been bowled all afternoon on rough concrete. Mind you, plenty of others reckon they have the same ball. I've seen one in Wellington, which its owner insists is *the* ball, and others in Perth and Melbourne. But my New Zealand friends who visit me in Sydney love to take photos of my ball, and it's a great discussion point.

The season was also interesting for a letter I received from an anonymous writer after a Shield match in Melbourne. Even though I wasn't the umpire involved, I offer it as an example of the sort of mail we sometimes get:

> Dear Mr French, that's where you should be, IN FRANCE. You are either a bloody cheat or incompetent. Your giving out Martin Kent was sheer robbery; ask all your commentators down there. The ball would have missed the leg stump by inches. Similarly the lbw of Broad. I am not sure whether it was you or your equally incompetent mate [no, the letter was not from Ian Chappell], but it came off Broad's bat. No wonder Victoria wins matches. It reminds me of that Victorian umpire Barlow, I think that was his name, who was the only umpire in Australia to no-ball Eddie Gilbert. Fair go, mate.

And then there was the telegram Mel Johnson and I received just prior to a one-day international in January 1981: 'New Zealand complaints about Australian umpires appear to have pressured and intimidated umpires,' it read. 'This is explanation for decisions favourable to Australia. In the match in January ignore pressure and give fair decisions – Cricket Fan.'

The VCA cricket final in 1981 between Carlton and Richmond was notable in that I no-balled former Test and Shield fast bowler Ian Callan thirteen times in his first two overs.

Callan: 'What am I doing wrong?'

French: 'Perhaps you might try and move your bowling marker.'

Callan: 'I'll move it, alright.' And with that he picked it up and proceeded to throw it out of the ground. No wonder his nickname was Mad Dog.

The summer of 1981–82 opened with the announcement of the umpires on the national panel: Bailhache, Whitehead and French (Victoria); Crafter, Cronin and Martin (SA); and Johnson (Queensland). Predictably, the other States without representation, particularly NSW, went into print at the failure of their own systems to gain nominees. Twenty years later, NSW was doing very nicely on the national umpiring scene, with two – Darrell Hair and Simon Taufel – on the five-member national panel. Thank heavens selections are not made on a State basis.

That summer Pakistan and the West Indies visited for three Tests each against Australia, and clearly Pakistan was not happy with the standard of umpiring in its matches. Robin Bailhache and I officiated in the third Test in Melbourne on a very poor pitch. Pakistan won this game and, curiously, no complaints were forthcoming from its hierarchy. One positive came out of the match: the Melbourne pitch and centre square were dug up at the end of the season.

Just before this Test, Robin and I stood in a one-day international between Australia and Pakistan in Adelaide. Greg Chappell was dismissed for 38 by a bowler named Ijaz Faqih, and an excitable Javed Miandad yelled out from his position in the covers: 'Faqih, you beauty, we get him.' At least that's what he claimed he said. Greg thought Javed had sworn at him with the 'F' word and told me so on his way off. We gave the Pakistan skipper the benefit of some very grave doubt. It was interesting that the controversial Pakistan manager, Ijaz Butt, apologised to Chappell after the match.

The first West Indies Test that summer was relatively peaceful and Australia won it by 58 runs. But the second match was both dynamic and nothing short of traumatic for co-umpire Mel Johnson and me. We had many tight decisions to judge amid the brilliant batting, bowling and fielding of both teams. John Dyson's catch off Sylvester Clarke deep in the outfield remains the greatest catch I have witnessed from the middle. The crowd on the SCG Hill gave John well-deserved acclamation for a long time afterwards. But West Indies vice-captain Viv Richards turned on a nice little tantrum when earlier I had given Bruce Laird not out from an attempted hook that seemed to balloon off his neck and was caught by Richards at third slip. Richards exuberantly flung the ball high in the air, with his ecstasy quickly turning to anger when I said 'not out'. Richards said, 'You don't see that, man, you don't see nothin.' At this stage Laird was in some distress with a red weal having formed on his throat, so maybe I got that one right, in spite of a headline the next morning in the Murdoch press: 'French

Cuts Up Aussies', which was a reference to two decisions against Graeme Wood and Dyson in their first innings. At least Ian Chappell went into bat for me, saying he didn't see too much wrong with the decisions. Mel and I were pleased when the match finished early in a draw because of bad light.

In the middle of 1982 my employer transferred me back to Sydney. This was a period of both joy and regret, as I had fitted in well with the Victorian environment and made many business and sporting friends in the three-and-a-half years I had been there. But life moves on, and the next challenge was to get re-established in the Sydney cricket scene, as England was due to tour Australia again in an Ashes series later that year.

During early December I was in the middle of the third Test in Adelaide and feeling rather guilty as I left Margaret to handle all the organisational details of settling into a new home at Carlingford, a north-western suburb in Sydney. One newspaper did an article on umpires and pointed out that I held the unique record of umpiring Shield cricket in three States. By the end of the season I had increased this to four; Peter McConnell and I officiated in the very first Shield final, in Perth in March 1983.

The Adelaide Test went fairly uneventfully, but I recall Rodney Hogg asking for a bottle opener on the field to open a bottle of soft drink that he had planted in one of the holes used to store helmets. I always carried a lot of odds and ends on to the field, and Rodney knew this and was going to take the mickey out of me when I couldn't produce an opener. But I had him beaten: I had one tucked away in my pocket. During that Test Derek Randall performed rather poorly – a duck in one innings and very few in the other – and as Australia was cruising towards victory on the last morning, Derek swooped on a ball hit by John Dyson and tried to run him out, shying at the stumps, missing, and watching it go for four overthrows. 'Bloody hell, Dick,' he said, 'I've just given away more runs than I've scored in the Test.'

Just prior to the Adelaide Test I stood in a Shield match in Sydney, where the *Daily Telegraph*'s Jim Woodward's story appeared under the headline: 'Hookes Accused – Unfair Play Rap By Umpire'. I had decided that David was indulging in unfair play by moving a fieldsman quickly backwards at deep square leg as the bowler (Hogg) was in the process of his run-up. I called, 'Dead ball', spoke quietly to David, and all was resolved amicably. But at the end of the day co-umpire Alan Marshall and I received a delegation of press reporters wanting to know what had gone on out in the middle. We had to be very circumspect talking to the press and I was surprised at the article that appeared the following morning. The match was also notable for one of the biggest hits ever seen at the SCG. Big Joel Garner, batting for South Australia, took a step down the pitch and lifted left-arm spinner Murray Bennett into the third row of the top deck of the M. A. Noble Stand – an awesome hit.

The fifth and final Test was to determine the outcome of the Ashes series, and it followed on from the announced retirement of two officiating umpires of that series, Robin Bailhache and Rex Whitehead. It didn't take long for renewed controversy to emerge when play started late on the first day due to rain. John Dyson was ruled not out in a close run-out appeal, and Greg Chappell was adjudged lbw. Mel Johnson and I were somewhat grateful for the shortened first day, and as we retreated up the stairs to the sanctuary of the umpires' room, one SCG member greeted us with: 'You blokes should be ashamed of yourselves.' I suggested he come along to our umpires' summer coaching classes, but he didn't accept that invitation.

Further controversial decisions emerged as the match went on. The press was fairly supportive of Mel and me each day, although one paper, previewing the balance of the match, insisted the English tourists faced another 'confrontation with umpires Mel Johnson and Dick French' the next day. Nothing could have been further from the truth. I found Bob Willis and Greg Chappell to be very fine captains and sportsmen who always played the game in the right spirit.

The season ended on a dramatic note with the inaugural Sheffield Shield final played in Perth between NSW and Western Australia. NSW won a fiercely fought match by 54 runs, but not before Peter McConnell and I reported Mike Whitney on a charge of crude and abusive language contrary to the spirit of cricket. Words had been exchanged between Whitney and Rod Marsh, who had just been dismissed, and the incident no doubt didn't look good on national television, the medium in which Mike later forged a successful career. Mike was found guilty and fined $50, but he bore no grudges against the umpires. He even had a drink with Rod after the match! I always liked Mike Whitney, with his competitive nature and good-natured banter in the middle. He is the proud father of triplets and once told me, 'Dick, I'm the only bowler to get a hat-trick with two balls.'

It was around this time that I could see no value in wearing old-fashioned butchers' white coats on cool days out in the middle in club and State matches. After my first season of umpiring back in 1972, a fellow low-grade umpire and I had put forward a motion at the NSWCUA's annual general meeting that white coats, which were compulsorily worn every day, could be dispensed with. Despite much head shaking and muttering from old-time umpires sitting down the front, the motion got through, so I managed to get my name in the annual report for the first time. In the 1980s, it was time to do away with coats altogether in club and NSW Shield matches. We replaced the coats (mine was taken by one of my sons for a fancy dress party) with white pullovers and white sleeveless jumpers, and these were very popular. My good friend and former top umpire Ross Emerson is to be congratulated in running with this, ordering supplies and dispensing them very efficiently. I could never work out why the other States were so slow to adopt a similar change, but eventually all States scrapped the coats, leaving only Test matches where they are worn, no doubt so that sponsor National Grid could feature prominently on the coat jacket.

Mel Johnson and I launched our 1983–84 season by making a thirty-minute umpires' training film in Brisbane, believed to be the first such video made in Australia. The hardest part was rehearsing our lines prior to filming, and Greg Chappell's introductory speech took longer to film than perhaps he intended. The film was sold all over the country, with sale proceeds ploughed back into the States' umpiring associations.

The second Test of that summer between Australia and Pakistan was notable for the amount of rain that fell on the Gabba and eventually washed out the match. I have photos at home of Mel Johnson and me wading bare-footed out in the middle for a final inspection before calling off the match. We abandoned play at 1 p.m., but by 6 p.m. the ground looked bone dry. Another hour and we might have played.

At the end of the third Test in Adelaide, which followed the Brisbane wash-out, and which was very trying on the last day with Abdul Qadir spinning the ball as much as Shane Warne at his best, I was surprised to read a comment from Zaheer Abbas who was quoted as being 'extremely pleased with the standard of umpiring in the Tests. Full marks to the umpires'. It's not often Australian umpires get this sort of comment from touring captains.

The fifth Test in Sydney had another rain-delayed start and Mel and I were soundly booed as we walked on to the field and again when we walked off at 6 p.m. We were lucky to start at all; the SCG had just acquired a new super-sopper and the Channel Nine helicopter gave a thirty-five-minute display of low flying to complete the job.

Around this time plans were under way for the NSWCUA to celebrate its seventy-fifth anniversary, and after much preparation from a lot of our umpires we formed an anniversary committee to handle a slap-up dinner and other events. One innovation was to produce a menu for the official table in braille, and in a room full of umpires this was well accepted, especially by one of our members who sold hearing aids for a living! At the dinner I was invited to propose the toast to cricket, and I managed to get my hands on some club captains' match reports on umpires' performances. Here is a short selection of what I quoted in that speech:

1. This umpire is unfit to umpire any class of cricket.
2. Had a good match – only gave eight doubtful decisions this week, a vast improvement on last week.
3. Spoilt a good game with his absurd interpretations of various rules.

4. Obviously doesn't understand the lbw Law because he gave me out twice this way in the match.
5. No doubt had a bad bout of fibrositis in his right arm, as the highest he raised it all day was to put his hat on, which he had left in the pavilion after lunch.

It was a grand evening of humour and repartee. The braille menu reminds me of a letter I received from a ten-year-old boy six months before I retired. He wanted some information on the Laws of Cricket and wrote: 'Dear Mr Richard French, I'm writing larger than I normally do because I understand you don't see very well.' No doubt, blind jokes and references are a fact of umpiring life.

Twice in my umpiring career I had the pleasure of seeing a bowler take 9 wickets from the end in which I was standing. One was Sir Richard Hadlee, the other Robert 'Dutchy' Holland, who in December 1984, took 9/83 for NSW against SA. Holland took the first 9 wickets to fall, but opening bowler Geoff Lawson had Tim May lbw, ruining Dutchy's chances of gaining cricket's equivalent of a hole-in-one at golf. In Brisbane in November 1985, Richard Hadlee took 9 in Australia's first innings, catching the other wicket himself. It was one of the finest pieces of bowling I can remember, with unerring accuracy, swing and cut off the pitch from a relatively short run-up. One's concentration had to be at its sharpest when umpiring Hadlee.

During the one-day series in 1984–85, there was the usual drama over umpires' interpretations of 'wide' balls. During an Australia v. Sri Lanka match at the SCG, Rodney Hogg bowled two steepling deliveries in his first over that passed over the batsman and wicketkeeper Wayne Phillips and ran to the boundary. Rod was not impressed with being called for eight 'wides' in the first over of the match, snatched his hat and headed for the boundary in – as a paper reported the next day – 'high dudgeon'. When he returned to bowl over number three he said that I was threatening his career. Hang on, I thought, I'm an umpire, not a selector. But Hoggie was never one to hide his feelings.

Several months later there was a tournament to celebrate the centenary of Victorian cricket and Peter McConnell and I officiated in a day/night match between India and Pakistan. We were on the field for seven hours without hearing one word of English. Only once did it come close: a rejection of a caught-behind appeal resulted in a comment from somewhere in the covers, which sounded a lot like the magic 'F' word. In this match, my partner and I broke a long-standing code of ethics by holding conference whenever a wicket fell, thereby preserving our sanity.

Cricket has a great way of sorting people out. In a Sydney club match in October 1985, I gave the Northern Districts' likeable captain, Ross Turner, out 'handled the ball', on a solitary appeal from the North Sydney captain, Trevor Chappell. In spite of my best endeavours to get Chappell to withdraw the appeal, he stood firm, so I had no option but to give Ross out. Feelings were running pretty high, but Ross had the last laugh later in the day when Chappell was dismissed for a duck. Ross told me later over a drink, 'Dick, I want you to know I always walk when I handle the ball.' Ross Turner has gone on to be a very capable cricket administrator, working for the MCC at Lord's and, more recently, with the ACB in Melbourne.

Further drama erupted in a McDonald's Cup match in Sydney in December, 1985. In fact, the match ended in chaos and controversy. Western Australia, chasing a NSW score of 235, needed only 3 runs from the final delivery of the game to snare victory. Tim Zoehrer deflected the last ball off paceman Dave Gilbert past 'keeper Greg Dyer, and immediately scampered off for the required runs. Zoehrer and partner Wayne Andrews completed the run and then Dyer broke the wicket, jubilantly throwing the ball high in a victory gesture. Andrews started walking towards the pavilion, then saw his partner sprinting towards him for a second run, which would have tied the game. So Andrews turned and scampered towards the other wicket before the pair joyously sprinted to the dressing room believing they had forced a tie. In the meantime, I had signalled one leg-bye, ruled the second run a 'dead ball' and called 'time'.

All hell broke loose. A deputation of WA team officials came into the umpires' room demanding to know why the match was not a tie. I repeated a number of times that the ball was finally settled after a distinct break in play after the first run. WA captain Graeme Wood was not impressed, storming out of the room, slamming the door and muttering, 'Bloody eastern seaboard umpires.' The finish to the game caused a bit of press comment, and next morning ACB umpires delegate from Perth, Bert Rigg, phoned me and said curtly, 'You were right,' and then hung up.

When the Indians played Australia in the drawn second Test in Melbourne in December that year, Kapil Dev, the Indian captain, put on a turn about the standard of umpiring in Australia. Rain prevented India winning the Test on the final afternoon, which would have given Kapil his first win in nineteen Tests at the helm. At one stage during the match Kapil was bowling from my end when he cannoned a ball into David

Hookes's pads and appealed loudly. I said 'not out' and signalled a leg bye as the batsmen ran a single. 'Mr Umpire, that was definitely out,' said Kapil. David Hookes walked past Kapil and replied: 'Turn it up, Kapil, that's only out in Calcutta, mate', a none-too-subtle allusion to the standard of umpiring over there. Team manager Venkat, now a leading international umpire in his own right, later issued an apology to Ray Isherwood and me on behalf of the team. 'The public may have misunderstood Kapil's words,' offered Venkat. 'He was just upset.'

Jeff Thomson played one of his best games on the SCG during an action-packed Shield final between NSW and Queensland in March 1986. When he completed his final over, he took his cap from me and walked out towards square leg and the Bill O'Reilly stand to generous applause. One wag from a private box in the stand yelled out: 'Go on Thommo you idiot, now you can go fishing.' Jeff looked up, took his cap off, and replied, 'I can't. All the prawns are sitting up there next to you.'

Thomson was certainly the fastest bowler I ever saw, and as well as being quick-witted, he was pretty slick with numbers, too. In a one-day international in Sydney in 1979–80, Thommo was at his tear-away fastest. Towards the end of an over, most bowlers ask how many balls are left as they walk back to their mark, and the umpire will glance down at his counter and it might be one, two, or whatever. Well, in this final season of eight-ball overs before Australia joined the rest of the world in plumping for six, Jeff asked me: 'How many?' I looked at my counter and answered, 'Four.' Thommo's reply floored me: 'What's that – four gone or four to come?'

By early 1986 I was having recurring knee problems. Many operations over the previous fifteen years had not really fixed the problem. Leading surgeon Dr Merv Cross decided to operate on my left knee yet again, this time inserting a splint and screws, and I was out of action for many months from the winter of 1986. Later on, in the late 1990s, I had to have two total knee replacements, but I knew even in 1986 that my days of umpiring were limited.

In the Australian winter of 1986, following my knee operation, Margaret and I went on a trip to England and Scotland for the Commonwealth Games in Edinburgh. On our way through I stopped at Lord's to view a match and met H. R. 'Dickie' Bird for the first time. Subsequently I've met Dickie on many occasions and found him to be a delightful, if somewhat different, person. At Lord's on this occasion Dickie told me the story of the great Sir Alec Bedser and Jack Crapp travelling together to Leeds for the fourth Test in 1948 against Bradman's all-conquering Australian side. As Dickie tells the story, Bedser parked the car in the hotel car park where they were staying, while Crapp went into the foyer to register.

Receptionist: 'Oh, bed, sir?'

Crapp: 'Er, no, Crapp.'

Receptionist: 'Certainly, sir, first corridor down there and to your right.'

Well, Dickie tells me it's a true story.

England toured Australia in 1986–87 and made a clean sweep of everything on the tour: the Ashes, World Series, and the Challenge Cup series held in Perth to celebrate the forthcoming America's Cup series of races. The Boxing Day Test was notable for England winning the match and the series within three days, and my scrapbook mercifully records no controversies. I can recall, however, Greg Matthews asking me late one day during the Test how many overs were left to bowl. I said: 'Greg, this will be the penultimate over of the day.' Greg gaped at me and replied: 'The bloody what?'

When I returned from Perth from the lengthy Challenge Cup one-day series early in 1987, I was allocated to day two of a Sydney fourth-grade match at Woollahra Oval, which is next to Royal Sydney Golf Course. During the afternoon it was a problem concentrating and umpiring the predominantly young cricketers, and I can clearly recall one boy's father approaching me to enquire how his son was to be recorded out. And standing at square leg late in the day I was startled when a golf ball lobbed next to me from a wayward shot from next door. The golfer was not deterred; play was held up while he lofted the ball back on to the fairway, no doubt illegally, but still a great shot and an interesting interlude to the cricket match.

Season 1987–88 opened with a Shield match in Newcastle and my co-umpire Rocky Harris and I were forced to report fast bowler Geoff Lawson for dissent in an incident involving Allan Border. Geoff was officially reprimanded and apologised to both umpires, but over the years many umpires had difficulty relating to the competitive fast bowler. Indeed, I can recall in one Shield match rejecting an appeal by Lawson for a caught behind off opening batsman Geoff Marsh, and as Geoff walked back past me to bowl the next ball, I suspected he was swearing. I called him back and said, 'Geoff, are you swearing at me?'

'No,' said Lawson, 'I'm swearing at myself.'

'In that case,' I replied, 'would you mind not using my name so much as you walk past?!'

The Boxing Day Test in December 1987, between Australia and New Zealand had everything – controversy, great cricket, and the game going down to the wire at 6.49 p.m. on day five, with Australia 9 wickets down and Richard Hadlee bowling the last over to Mike Whitney. The game ended in a heart-stopping draw. This was the Greg Dyer 'no catch' match where NZ batsman Andrew Jones was adjudged out caught behind. As I recall the incident from square leg, Jones tried to leg-glance fast bowler Craig McDermott, and Dyer, diving to his left, came up with what appeared to be a magnificent catch. My co-umpire Tony Crafter looked across to me to check whether the ball had carried, as indeed it had, and I indicated so to Tony. What we both didn't know was that one behind-the-wicket TV camera had picked up the ball momentarily bouncing out of Dyer's gloves and then getting scooped up again. It was all too quick for the human eye, and these days Andrew Jones would probably have been given the green light by the TV umpire, and thus given not out. This incident was seized on by the media as poor sportsmanship by the Australians, but I felt sorry for Dyer who genuinely appeared not to know for certain whether he had caught it. I don't think I helped the cause at the end of the Test when Tony and I were interviewed by a *Melbourne Times on Sunday* reporter, with me wearing a T-shirt with the logo pronouncing the product 'The great Aussie Life Saver'. Perhaps I could have been more circumspect in my choice of T-shirts that evening.

Later in season 1987–88 the McDonald's Cup matches were played with orange balls to determine whether they were better to use and see than the standard white balls. In my view, this was an experiment that failed, the orange colour merging into other colours at the ground. The balls also lost their colour very quickly and, generally, barely lasted the distance. We were asked to put in a report at the end of March and, to my knowledge, orange balls were never used again. I am still of the opinion that normal red balls should be used for all one-day matches, day and night. The current crop of white balls are always being replaced, as the leather does not last and scuffs up too easily.

After three first-class games early in the 1988–89 season, it was obvious my knees were not up to standing for four and five days on the trot, and I decided after much soul searching and discussions with family to announce my retirement from all cricket. I duly notified the ACB, the NSWCA and all my close umpiring friends, and was amazed at the letters that arrived from all over the country. Even some current and former cricketers congratulated me 'on my retirement', which I guess could be interpreted either way. So although in my capacity now as the NSW state director of umpiring and an umpiring selector I continue to travel to many grade matches, first-class matches and minor representative games, I have never officiated a single match on the field since the day I stopped. Initially, it was a real culture shock.

I guess no input would be complete without some reference to the future of the game and my thoughts on electronic aids, 'third umpires', and the role of one-day cricket vis-a-vis Test cricket. So, for what they're worth, here are my opinions on developments in umpiring and the game in general.

Electronic umpiring aids

I have never agreed with electronic umpiring aids for umpires, using a third umpire to give the red or green light on close run-outs, stumpings, hit-wicket decisions or close-to-ground catches. These aids are justified by their supporters as being in the interests of getting decisions right, but this seems a poor argument to me. In my entire career perhaps only twice would this aid have been most helpful, which is hardly enough to justify the expense of installing and operating the equipment. Umpiring decisions are based on the facts in front of the umpires, similar to a court of law, and any benefit of doubt must go to the batsman. I get the impression these days that the delicate balance between bat and ball is tilting towards the fielding side, and we must be careful not to destroy this balance.

Nevertheless, I accept that the system is here for the foreseeable future and indeed may even be extended to include all catches, including faint snicks, and – worst of all – lbws as technology advances. Even no-balls might be on the agenda; so the mind boggles at what might be in place in, say, five to ten years down the track. But umpiring could perhaps be improved if the third umpire, usually selected from the top bracket of umpires, was actually officiating in another match, thus gaining more on-field experience. Maybe thought should be given to recently retired umpires taking over this role in future.

International panel of umpires

The concept of the international umpiring panel was introduced some years ago to pacify those administrators who wanted to project the image of 'neutral' umpires around the world. In fact, this very expensive exercise did just the opposite. Until the end of the 2001–02 season, each of the ten Test-playing countries nominated two umpires (England four) and they were allocated to Test matches around the world. The fact that there may be ten better umpires from England and

Australia than the twenty or twenty-two nominated made no difference, so in many cases the best umpires were not being selected. I believe Sydney first-grade cricket would have some umpires better skilled than some I have observed at Test matches in recent times. It is a very expensive exercise and presents less opportunity for local umpires to officiate in Tests in their own country. As I mentioned earlier, a similar system was tried several years ago in Shield cricket, and it simply did not work. The umpires at the elite level needed sympathetic employers if they were to get the required time off to umpire. It disturbs me in my current role as state director of umpiring to observe the number of umpires unemployed or working part-time.

In April 2002, the ICC identified an elite panel of ten umpires worldwide to officiate in Test matches around the world on a full-time basis, supported by a supplementary panel of twenty umpires who would stand in one-day internationals in the various countries alongside local umpires. Thus the umpiring of international matches has finally moved to a true system of 'independent' umpires, and time will tell whether the cost of this huge logistical exercise is worthwhile; as indeed we will have to wait on the extent of the emerging problem of inhibiting the development of local umpires.

Full-time umpires

The Australian Cricket Board has recently introduced two-year contracts for umpires on the national panel. This is an improvement on the previous system, where much uncertainty prevailed regarding selections, and where some umpires had to forego promotions in their employment because of umpiring commitments. Now, umpires with time on their hands can be employed as part-time umpiring development officers, and this is good for cricket generally. The major flaw here is that some States don't have umpires on the national panel, so there is no opportunity for development work in that State, further compounding the problem. A better solution would be for the ACB to provide development grants to each State and let local associations employ people with the right attributes to improve umpiring standards.

Umpiring accreditation

All umpires throughout the country are now being invited to become accredited before advancing on to higher levels. The National Officiating Program (all sports), led by former Australian Rules umpire Bill Deller, has been working this initiative through with the ACB to give our umpires a much more professional background and competency level.

One-day cricket and Tests

There is no doubt the advent and development of one-day cricket has brought great changes and improvements to the standard of cricket worldwide, with attendant financial benefits. But Test cricket remains the ultimate pinnacle of selection for both cricketers and umpires and the fact that Australia has had only eighty-five Test umpires in more than 120 years suggests how difficult it can be to reach this elite level.

Cricket administration

The level of expertise of cricket administrators in Australia is extremely high. I never cease to be amazed at the input of these talented people, most of whom act in voluntary positions and in their own time. Some are out night after night attending meetings, presentations, AGMs, selections and other functions from junior cricket to the highest ACB level. The running of first-class cricket in Australia is very professional, with business plans being managed by dynamic people. At the umpiring level we have a national umpiring manager, who is a full-time employee of the ACB, and local State directors of umpiring charged with overseeing recruiting, training, developing and selecting umpires. It follows that the relationship between cricketers, cricket administrators and umpires has never been better. The advent of scorer members in State umpiring associations has added a new dimension to cricket in recent seasons.

When I ceased umpiring during the 1988–89 season, I expected that after the necessary knee operations (which, in fact, did not cease until August 1998, at which point I had a new pair of titanium knees), I would have more time to play golf and more uninterrupted time in both my senior financial position with the AMP Insurance Group and a lot of other non-cricket-related activities.

In fact, the opposite happened. I was elected president of the NSWCUA, the second-largest umpiring association in the world (after the English ACU&S Association), and held the post for ten years, until 2000. The NSW Cricket Board some years ago appointed me as the NSW State Director of umpiring, which has proved to be very interesting and rewarding and involves close association with the ACB and the other States.

Then followed appointment to the State and representative panel of selectors, and I now oversee local appointments to each game in Sydney where 150 umpires are allocated to matches in the various grades. This is a huge logistical exercise.

In 1996, two events occurred about which I remain very humble and proud. Firstly, in the Queen's Birthday honours list of that year, I was awarded the Medal of the Order of Australia for services to cricket. It was a very proud moment when the NSW Governor, his Excellency Gordon Samuels, presented me with my 'gong'. Later that same year I was made a life member of the NSWCA, a rare honour among umpires. President Alan Davidson presented me with the life member's cuff links, and I wear them proudly at official cricket functions. In September 2000, I received another rare honour: the Australian Sports Medal.

Looking back, for what it's worth, the finest batsmen I saw from the middle was Greg Chappell, with his elegance and style, Viv Richards, for raw power and determination, and David Gower – the most graceful of them all.

Dennis Lillee was the best of all the fast bowlers – the only bowler incidentally to wish me good luck at the start of a Test – with Jeff Thomson the fastest of the lot. Michael Holding was fast and silent in his run-up (the 'Whispering Death' was a most fitting appellation), and Sir Richard Hadlee was the best all-round bowler of my time.

Rodney Marsh was a great wicketkeeper and competitor, and, as far as captains go, Mike Brearley left the rest for dead.

DICK FRENCH'S UMPIRING CV

70 first-class matches between February 1976 and December 1988

Official Test matches – 19 (Australia v. England 7, West Indies 2, India 4, Pakistan 4, New Zealand 2)

Internationals – 7 (NSW v. England 2, West Indies 2, Pakistan 1; SA v. England, 2)

Sheffield Shield matches – 44

One-day internationals – 58

Robin Bailhache

Blame Football

It's a strange job, umpiring. For a start, it's the only one where you have to start out perfect and get better every time, and umpiring is the only occupation in the world where the highest accolade is silence.

Cricket, to many, is an odd game, developed on the other side of the world but wholeheartedly embraced by the people of Australia. The umpire is an important and intricate part of the game. So important that it has been suggested, with acknowledgement to the unknown author, that the umpiring fraternity should have its own Coat of Arms, as befitting the grand English tradition. It might best be represented by two white sticks quartered, with a pair of spectacles and a hearing aid, supported by two guide dogs rampant over the motto: *Erectum digitatum ad nauseam*. Freely translated as 'Once you get your finger up, keep it up'.

A common belief is that the word umpire derives from the Latin *non pere*, which literally translates as 'the odd one'. So who would want to become an umpire? I did – but initially of Australian Rules football. I became involved with cricket umpiring later for the wrong reason and, certainly, some would have plenty to say about that statement.

In the 1960s, I was heavily involved in football and cricket in Adelaide. Over ten seasons with South Adelaide in the SANFL, I played sixteen league games and ninety-three seconds games. In fact, I'm a life member of the club's seconds.

I took to football umpiring in 1964 after suffering a knee injury. It was serious at the time but I recovered to the extent that I was able to umpire footy without restriction. During training, a chance remark from one of the umpiring coaches struck a chord: 'To improve your concentration levels in your football umpiring,' he said, 'take up cricket umpiring. There's nothing more demanding on concentration.'

So, to improve my football umpiring, I gave up playing cricket with Kensington District Cricket Club and attended cricket umpiring winter classes in preparation for the 1969–70 cricket season. Initially, I didn't feel attracted to the new task, but I persevered through that summer. My football fell away and I grew to love this new involvement in the great game of cricket.

Later, a transfer in employment as development manager for a fire and general insurance company took me from Adelaide to Melbourne in July 1977, and I continued umpiring cricket in Victoria until the end of the 1993–94 season.

But it all began with umpiring district fourths with the South Australian Cricket Association in October 1969. Before the start of the 1971–72 season, the retirement of one of SA's best and longest-serving umpires, Fred Godson, created a vacancy in first-class ranks. Who filled it was a toss-up between another new umpire, John Wilson, and me. To help in the selection, we were both appointed in November 1971 to a one-day Coca-Cola knockout match between SA and Tasmania at the Adelaide Oval. Most of the action happened from my end and, apparently, I got most of them right. My colleague had hardly a decision to make, except that he finished the match when scores were tied by calling a no-ball. Being in the thick of the action and handling it competently ensured my selection. It was slightly more democratic than a coin-toss, but in the end, the coin came down on my side. Them's the breaks.

This meant I walked out with fellow South Australian Max O'Connell for my first Sheffield Shield match, Victoria v. SA, at the same Adelaide Oval, on 26 November 1971. The match went well for me and I followed up with SA's match against the World XI, the team that replaced the planned, but banned, South African tour that summer.

Two more Shield matches completed a wonderful season for me. As a reasonably new chum, I felt honoured and somewhat terrified at times to be out there witnessing such fine cricket played at one of the world's most beautiful venues, the Adelaide Oval, on which, only a few years earlier, I'd played, then umpired, Australian Rules football. My use of the word 'terrified' relates to my obsession with umpiring to my maximum capacity, in concentration, decision-making and upholding the Laws of Cricket. I was fortunate in having the ability to concentrate (keeping your brain where your body is) for long periods of time. I'm convinced that while good eyesight, hearing and physical wellbeing are important, without this ability to concentrate long and hard amid all the distractions, any hopes of reaching the top in cricket umpiring are doomed.

The next two seasons, 1972–73 and 1973–74, brought me six more Shield matches, a SA v. New Zealand four-day match and two one-dayers between the same two teams. A single Shield match, SA v. WA, in 1974–75 was the calm before the storm. When SA took on the MCC at Adelaide Oval from 1–4 November 1974, the equally combative Ian Chappell and Tony Greig took an instant dislike to each other. A torrid match presented me again with more than my fair share of decision making, and I walked off at the end of the final day feeling well pleased with myself. Apparently the English camp felt the same way, leading to my surprise selection (to me and the cricket world) in my sixth season of umpiring, after just ten Shield matches, two four-day internationals, and three one-dayers.

The biggest shock of my life came when I took a phone call from cricket writer Mike Coward late on a Sunday night in November 1974, to congratulate me on my first Test appointment, the Australia v. England series opener in Brisbane starting the following Friday.

I had had no warning, and now I had four days to get organised and fly to Brisbane by the following Thursday. Needless to say I made it, but it was my first visit to the Gabba (I didn't even know where the ground was) and I was to officiate with Tom Brooks, whom I'd never met. But we got on fine; so well, in fact, that we umpired all six Tests, with Tom guiding the new chum along the straight and narrow.

Tom was a great helpmate in my career. Not only did he partner me in that first Test, we were together again when Tom stood in his last Test, the second Ashes Test in Perth in December 1978. Tom announced his retirement during that match and it was distressing to me to see such a fine umpire and gentleman leave the scene in the manner he did, surrounded by controversy. Tom set a great example for me, both on and off the field. He had a favourite saying: 'Whatever you think's a fair thing, young Robin,' which he threw at me whenever I was threatening to run off at a tangent.

He was a very religious man and, in any new town or city, I sometimes thought his first priority was to find out where the nearest Catholic church was, rather than the location of the cricket ground. Tom was also a very proud man – proud of his standing in the cricket world especially – and the abuse and criticism he received from some sections of the cricket establishment and media were as unfortunate as they were unwarranted. The Australian batsman who brought matters to a head was Graeme Wood. In the overall picture, Wood was a fairly ordinary player and when Tom gave him out, caught behind, in that final Perth Test, the petulant dissent and lack of respect shown to my colleague was worse than ordinary. To put it mildly, it was disgusting. To make matters worse, Wood was reported in *The Cricketer* of February 1979 as saying: 'I agree with his retirement. In this game he has been at fault. It's pretty hard to play cricket anyway without this.'

I certainly didn't 'agree with his retirement'. Cricket lost a great umpire at a time when the game could least afford it. Tom would probably take me to task about this comment, but it had to be said, because 'I think it's a fair thing'.

That 1974–75 Ashes series, my first, was a physical and mental challenge, to say the least. By then, television was exposing the umpire to ever-increasing scrutiny, and umpires became 'fair game', especially for some members of the print media. One of the most vocal media critics, a so-called expert, I am told, had to ask for a diagram showing the names of the fielding positions, just before the start of the first day's play. Some expert!

These were great times for Australian cricket, with Jeff Thomson and Dennis Lillee launched upon Mike Denness's unsuspecting Englishmen. Perth, the MCG, Sydney and Adelaide all followed, and apart from one occasion when

I told the press that I had had 'a gutful', ordered them out of our change rooms and advised them to obtain their information on the day's events from other sources, life was good. The ordering-out was, however, not a smart move, as Tom was quick to observe, because the reporting became even more critical.

In every capital city, we received invitations to Government House, to dinners for this and that, and Tom and I spent a fair portion of 1974–75 living out of a suitcase. It was a great experience, but the pressures both on and off the field eventually became a burden. Today, officialdom would not subject an umpire to six Test matches in a series. What with the occasional Shield match to umpire, the odd district match and finals, I was one relieved umpire when the end of that season finally arrived.

Still, of all the series I was involved in, this was undoubtedly the best. Why? Firstly, the high esteem in which cricket was held at that time; there were no scandals and it turned out to be a great series played before huge crowds.

It was a confident England side that arrived in 1974, and why shouldn't they have been? Dennis Lillee was recovering from a serious back injury, and Jeff Thomson (Thommo) was basically untried at Test level. His previous experience of Test cricket wasn't awe-inspiring. The Englishmen's confidence, however, was soon shattered.

The one dark cloud over the series, and thus Tom and me, was the matter of intimidatory bowling. It took a long time for the Laws of Cricket to be strengthened and clarified in order to eradicate this problem that was to figure so prominently in the 1974–75 series. I was a new chum, just five years old in cricket umpiring terms, and it was up to me to sink or swim. I learnt a lot, and very quickly. And I made mistakes, including those off the field, especially in my lack of patience with, or tolerance of, some sections of the media, but I like to think I learnt from those mistakes.

I have always felt a responsibility as an umpire not to let the side down. After all, you are representing Australian umpires. You don't want to let them down, you don't want to let your country down, and you certainly hope that you do yourself proud. The fear of not achieving these ideals was a great motivation for me. I learnt to keep very quiet on the field during play, concentrating on the game and trying to ignore the pressures, the crowd noise, the antics of the players and the state of the game. Players are not comfortable with umpires who appear flustered and uncertain. The object is to appear calm and totally in control. An umpire can be likened to a duck swimming upstream: calm and serene on the surface, while under the surface it's all hard work.

This quiet, 'leave me alone' attitude, while it was vital to me as an umpire, did not sit well with some of the players and gave me a reputation of being surly and unapproachable. I could, and did, become quite forthright when I believed actions on the field warranted it, as I was, and remain to this day a strong advocate for cricket to be played within very clear boundaries of conduct and fair play.

The 1974–75 Test program, dubbed by the marketing men as the 'Pace Like Fire' series, began in Brisbane where I arrived the day before the start: on a Thursday, just after the city's Chinese laundry atmosphere had erupted into a violent thunderstorm. The Gabba was also in the process of being renovated, and the umpires' change rooms were not finished. However, they were ready by the Friday, thanks to that great

Queensland character Alderman Clem Jones, curator and local councillor.

The storm had swept floodwater and silt all over the ground, including the wicket area. The silt had subsequently dried out and formed a solid crust over what was supposed to be tomorrow's Test wicket. It's not often one turns up at a ground twenty-four hours before the start of play to see the curator on all fours, belting the tripe out of tomorrow's wicket with a large mallet. Apparently it was impossible to sweep this silt and rubbish off the playing area, the only recourse being for Clem to break it up with a heavy object, namely a mallet, and sweep it off. Sure enough, it worked and the match began at the scheduled time. Quite a character was our Clem.

I turned up bright and early on the Friday only to be refused admission to the players' and umpires' area by the gate-keeper. I was too young to be an umpire, he said. 'You might be named Bailhache, but it must be your father who's umpiring.' While I took it as a compliment, it's not a great start to the biggest day of your umpiring career. However, some of the players vouched for me, and the game, and series, got under way with Ian Chappell winning the toss and choosing to bat.

I thought the Englishmen would be well pleased to contain Australia to 309, of which Chappell made 90, but they responded with 265, due mainly to the 110 of Tony Greig. Chappell declared his second innings at 5/288, leaving England to make 333. A resurgent Jeff Thomson was never going to allow that, and his 'sandshoe crusher', aimed at ferocious pace at the feet of Greig to skittle him for 2, was a beacon ball on the way to 6/46 off 17.5 overs. England was dismissed for 166, with Thommo well backed up by Lillee and the well-named 'Tangles' Walker.

I felt quite satisfied with my first Test match. In the excitement of being appointed for it, I had told my wife Josephine that if I ever got a second Test match, I'd take her and our three daughters, Catherine, Susanne and Belinda, with me so they could see their husband and dad at work. A few days after the Brisbane Test I got a call from a SACA official telling me I'd been appointed for the second Test in Perth, so true to my word, it was five of us who arrived for a holiday in the West, sandwiched around a Test in which the wicket gave real meaning to 'Pace Like Fire'.

Australia made 481 and 1/23 after knocking over England for 208 and 293. This was the Test to which Colin Cowdrey was called up from the English winter, hopefully to combat the pace of Lillee and Thommo. One had to admire the gutsy innings played by the 41-year-old Cowdrey, summoned to fill in for the injured John Edrich and Dennis Amiss. He batted at No. 3 on the fastest and bounciest pitch in Australia and was not the worst performer by any means with his defiant knocks of 22 and 41. I saw very few better innings in my career than the one played by Doug Walters, and his 100 in the session between tea and stumps tore the English attack apart. Local hero Ross Edwards chipped in with a fine 115 as Australia built its crushing total towards a 9-wicket win and 2-nil series lead.

A big crowd, building eventually to 77 000, was at the MCG when Tom Brooks and I walked out to start the third Boxing Day Test in Melbourne. With the supremacy of his pace attack well established, Ian Chappell chose to insert the Englishmen when he won his third successive toss. Thomson again starred: 4/72, with good support from Lillee (2/70) and spinner Ashley Mallett (2/37) as England struggled to 242.

Australia, in reply, could manage only 241. Dennis Amiss's 90, a doughty innings interspersed with body blows from Australia's speed twins, carried England to 244 in its second dig. Set 246 to win, the Australians allied what was at times negative batting with the Englishmen's tight bowling to hand victory to the clock. The game ebbed and flowed, but ended in a disappointing draw.

Tom and I were getting a pasting from the media, at home and abroad. Lillee and Thommo, too, were getting plenty of attention for their so-called intimidatory bowling, and we were copping it for allegedly doing nothing about it. During the series we both, on several occasions, warned the bowlers on both sides about their over-use of short-pitched deliveries.

The pace of England bowlers Bob Willis, Derek Arnold, Chris Old, Tony Greig, Peter Lever and Mike Hendrick was about 40 per cent less than that unleashed by Lillee and Thomson, yet it was the English bowlers who started the 'bumper war', right from their first innings in Brisbane when the extremely combative Tony Greig dismissed Lillee with a bouncer that Dennis tried to hook but merely flicked on its way through to 'keeper Alan Knott. As he departed, Lillee's words to the gangly Englishman singed the eardrums of those who heard them. Lillee's physical response as the series played out was almost as vexing to Tom and me as it was to his quarry who had to fend off his missiles.

Australia continued its swathe through the Englishmen in the fourth Test in Sydney, winning by 171 runs. Chappell won his fourth toss and Australia batted all the way to 405, to which England replied with 295 (Thomson 4 wickets). Ian Redpath made a fine 105 before Chappell declared at 4/289, setting England an impossible 400-run target. It managed 228 and so went to three down with two to play.

Naturally, Tom Brooks and I had numerous discussions during the series about short-pitched deliveries bowled by both sides. We felt we handled the issue evenly and adequately. However, whenever we did ask a fast bowler to ease up on intimidatory bowling, the request was not well received. A press photo in the Melbourne *Age* showing me addressing the back of Dennis Lillee is headed: 'The umpire warns – and Lillee stumps off'. The item explained: 'Lillee shows signs of frustration and distress as he gets another warning in the fourth Test in Sydney yesterday'. A Lillee bean ball to tail-ender Bob Willis in the same Test didn't go down well with the Englishmen either, especially when Willis dropped his bat, staggered out of his crease as though dazed, and Rod Marsh threw his stumps down. The first man to appeal was the same Dennis Lillee. The verdict: not out. Lillee's language (blue!) was also an issue at times, and in the third Test in Melbourne I had to ask Ian Chappell to try to calm him down after a verbal salvo unleashed on opening batsman Amiss. After that incident, England captain Mike Denness, when asked if there had been some swearing out on the ground, was quoted as saying: 'I asked my two opening batsmen, Amiss and David Lloyd, what was going on. Both informed me that there had been some swearing from Lillee and after one face-to-face confrontation, Lillee had said something to Amiss, who had asked him to repeat it because "I can't understand a word"'. Denness also said he thought the umpires had handled the situation 'very well', and Amiss, asked if he had heard swearing when he was batting, answered diplomatically: 'No, I'm afraid not. I'm never out there long enough.'

The really fast bowlers often suffer some sort of white-line fever, and one has to speak slowly and in short syllables to ensure that the message gets through. I never had any problem with the definition of gross stupidity: 144 fast bowlers.

It was during this Test in Sydney that my wife received a threatening phone call at our home in Adelaide. The caller threatened to harm our daughters, and of course this distressed her greatly. At the time she elected to keep this occurrence from me. Instead, she phoned the local police, who maintained a vigil around our home for the next few days. There really are some cranks out there, and it's a sad state of affairs when umpires and, indeed, officials of any sort can be subjected to such harassment.

On my journeys around Australia I was also receiving my share of abusive mail, most of which went immediately into the bin, especially if I saw it bore a United Kingdom postmark. My forebears hail from the island of Jersey, in the Channel Islands, and quite a few families of our name still live on that lovely island. One of the letters I did receive was from Jersey and mentioned that all my possible relations there had unanimously disowned me! Without exception, every letter from that part of the world got stuck into my ability as an umpire and questioned my parentage.

Australia got the staggers in the fifth Test in Adelaide, but from being 5/84 made its way to a very respectable 304, thanks to the efforts of bowlers Terry Jenner, Walker, Lillee and Mallett. Striking a wicket that for the first time in the series suited his bowling, Derek Underwood took 7/113. Some rain had penetrated the covers overnight and one end of the wicket was quite damp. With his pace and accuracy, Underwood's spin proved a real problem. So, too, were Lillee (4/49) and

Thommo (3/58) when England batted, and their 172 was nowhere near good enough. Chappell declared at 5/272 and England, chasing 404, was bundled out for 241, a tally now equating with their optimum range. Lillee was again principal wrecker, with 4/69, but Underwood had even better match figures: 11/215, the best by an England bowler in Australia since another left-armer, 'Farmer' Jack White, captured 13/256 on the same ground in 1928–29.

What a turnaround in the final, sixth Test in Melbourne. Chappell won his fifth toss (he called wrongly only in Adelaide) and decided to bat even though water had spilled from the covers on to a section of the pitch. Australia was skittled for 152. To make matters worse, Jeff Thomson was out with an injury, and Lillee was sidelined after bowling six overs (1/17) with a bruised right foot; he didn't bowl again in the match. Freed from the shackles of extreme pace, the much-maligned Denness showed he could bat with 188 and was ably assisted by Keith Fletcher, who was good at flailing county attacks at home, and now found his touch with 146. So England compiled a huge 529, then knocked over the weary Aussies for 373, saving some face for their trip back home with a win by an innings and 4 runs.

It had been a fascinating series, and the 'Pace Like Fire' brand name was well chosen. Lillee and Thomson did instil fear and trepidation in the English camp; Lillee with his fire, aggression and immaculate control; Thommo with his fire, aggression and lack of control. Lillee was accurate and always at the batsman, whereas Thommo, who only ever wanted to bowl as quickly as possible, really had everyone guessing as to where the next ball would pitch. Whether it was at his own feet or at the batsman's (the sandshoe crusher) made no difference to Jeff and, of course, if he had no idea where the next ball was going to pitch, you can be damn sure the batsman had even less idea. Lillee and Thomson were backed up by astonishing catching from all the Australians, by a wonderful team spirit and astute, aggressive captaincy by Ian Chappell. Six Test matches in the series, and we witnessed some great performances in batting and bowling from both sides.

It was a great experience for me, a newcomer to Test cricket, and one I shall cherish forever. The public lapped it up, too – 62 079 people came to the Gabba; 75 948 to the Perth Test; 250 721 to the Boxing Day Test in Melbourne; 178 027 to the SCG; 99 323 to Adelaide Oval; and 111 421 to the sixth Test back in Melbourne.

The captains' attitude has a major bearing on the ease or otherwise of umpiring any match and, despite the billing of 'Pace Like Fire' and the combative nature of many of the key players, Tom and I had few complaints in that series with Chappell or Denness.

The captains have their own share of responsibility and burdens. They have to make the correct bowling changes; field placements; be able to correctly call every toss of the coin and read the conditions when deciding to bat or bowl; and they, not the umpires, are responsible for the conduct of their players (Law 42, Section 1). Last, but not least, at the end of the match they have to, in a fair, calm manner, complete a report on the umpires' performance. The report is, of course, vital to us. A good report can mean promotion, and a bad one produce no promotion or, worse, demotion.

Of course, consistency of appraisal from different captains is never achieved, just as consistency of interpretation eludes umpires; but then, we are all different. What concerns me is just what constitutes a 'bad' umpiring performance. Is two perceived umpiring errors acceptable, or three? Perhaps there were errors 'when doubt favoured the batsman'. In this case, if there was reasonable doubt and the umpire had weighed up all the facts in that second or so at his disposal, is this an error? Of course, if the batsman receives an alleged let-off at zero and then proceeds to make a century, that does rather compound the original 'error'. That one decision then assumes much more importance to the captain completing the report, especially if his team has lost the match.

Umpires are the sole judges of playing conditions in relation to ground, weather and light, and in many cases their decision on whether to play will disadvantage one of the teams. However, these decisions have to be made and an umpire should not be marked down solely because of his determination to apply an impartial and considered judgement of the ground, weather and light. Of course, all umpires have made, and will continue to make, mistakes. The odd bad positioning, lapse of concentration, pressure-related mistakes . . . they're the same types of errors committed by the players themselves.

Following the advent of TV and slow-motion replays, umpires now have pressure as never before. This pressure extends down through the ranks to all grades, especially in regards to lbws. Some captains are now criticising umpires, not for the obviously wrong lbw decisions where the batsman has been given out, but for favouring the batsman in decisions where real doubt exists – just as the Laws require.

Good umpiring is a very integral and necessary part of cricket, but without constructive and accurate captains' reports, it becomes much more difficult to ensure that deserving umpires achieve their goals. Hopefully, captains realise their responsibility does not end at the call of 'time'. One responsibility remains: a rational and detailed report of the umpires' performance.

But let's reverse the roles! In the years I experienced first-class cricket behind and square of the wickets, Ian Chappell impressed me most. It has to be said that under his aggressive leadership, 'sledging' was developed to an art form, but mostly it was within bounds and by players with the ability to back it up. 'Chappelli' never gave an inch, and if I had to ask a batsman under any conditions to make a hundred to save my life, he would be the one I'd choose. Chappelli always made things happen, as distinct from his younger brother Greg, who gave me the impression he was waiting for things to happen. You always knew where you stood with Ian, and if he thought you had made a mess of things, he would really let you know. But he bore no grudges. I remember commiserating with Ian at the conclusion of a Shield match that South Australia had lost. Casually, I said to him, 'Hard luck – you can't win them all.' Ian's response was: 'Bullshit, who said you f—ing can't!' After that, I kept my mouth shut.

It was Chappelli who dropped his pants in an Adelaide Test match and exposed his bare backside to the Members' stand. There were those who argued that he did this so people could hear more clearly what he had to say. I wasn't one of them.

Let's take a look at some of Ian's contemporary Test match captains – a disparate bunch indeed:

MIKE BREARLEY

Great captain, very astute, but unfortunately was not really up to scratch as a player. A product of the English tradition of selecting their best team and then selecting a captain, not necessarily on playing ability.

VIV RICHARDS

The best batsman during my time. Whenever he came to the wicket, I would move back a pace or two from my normal position, so hard would he hit the ball. Viv, who took over the West Indies' captaincy from Clive Lloyd, always appeared to have a chip on his shoulder, and I did not consider him a great tactical captain.

Vic possessed a frightening persona and really put pressure on umpires. During the Perth Test match in 1988–89, I had occasion to continually no-ball the Windies' speedster Patrick Patterson for over-stepping. Patrick was bowling quick – real quick – and despite my continually telling him when he was getting close, he kept transgressing. It came to a head when Australian batsman Tim May who really, I felt, didn't want to be out there, ducked under a bouncer and gloved the ball to the 'keeper.

I had, however, called, 'no-ball', and Tim had to stay. Of course, Patrick, from his great height, gave me heaps, but worse was to come. Viv, fielding in his customary position in slips, ambled towards the pitch and yelled across to Malcolm Marshall: 'Hey, Malcolm, you move around in line with the crease and make sure this Mother's getting 'em right.'

Malcolm looked slightly embarrassed, but moved into position to 'umpire the umpire'. I found this terribly insulting and demeaning and, somewhat peeved, I walked towards Viv and said, 'Viv, let's get one thing straight. I'll umpire this bloody game; you play it.'

Viv glared at me but, to his credit, backed off and told

Malcolm to return to his normal position. Merv Hughes, who was the batsman at my end, made a point of coming to see me after the game and complimenting me on my stand. Thanks, Merv! Keith Stackpole also gave me credit. Writing a retrospective 'Best of the season' in a Sunday paper of 19 February 1989, Keith gave a nod to me: 'Robin Bailhache – best umpiring performance when he stood up to players from both sides in a tough game. He paid the price for his firmness by not being selected for another Test.' As I said, the captains' reports carry weight.

IMRAN KHAN

A marvellous all-rounder, but as a skipper he always seemed to me to be aloof from his team-mates, some of whom appeared to treat him with godlike reverence. Still, I guess that in Pakistan where cricket is a religion and when you are as good a player as Imran, this is not so surprising.

The captain and I came to grips in a one-day international in Perth. While bowling from my end, he swung one down leg side, which I promptly called wide, as befits the one-day rule. Imran mouthed off about the call and went back to his mark. The same thing happened later in the over and this time he gave me heaps, saying what he thought of Australian umpires and me in particular. I tried to laugh at the situation and with a smile on my face and using the Aussie vernacular, said, 'Come on, Imran, just piss off back there and bowl.'

It was the wrong approach, as Imran made quite clear, and the immediate reaction from the Pakistanis close to the wicket was one of amazement! They stared at me as though expecting me to be struck dead. I wasn't, and the game went on, but for the rest of the innings I had to put up with Imran calling out to me across the ground: 'And you can't even speak good English!' Perhaps not, but I can speak good Australian.

CLIVE LLOYD

I have a tremendous regard for this man. He suffered badly as part of the West Indies team that was humbled by the Australians of 1975–76, and I am sure his burning desire for revenge was instrumental in turning the tables. He managed to unite the West Indians' various factions and took his team to the top of the cricketing world where it remained, secured there by four-pronged pace attacks, for almost two decades.

Some of my most memorable and exciting matches involved the West Indies during Clive's reign, even though one had to work hard to keep them under control. I felt I had finally been accepted by them when at the conclusion of the Adelaide Test of 1981–82 (won by the Windies by 5 wickets), I went into their rooms to hand over the stumps, whereupon Gordon Greenidge, one of the quietest and least demonstrative players I ever met, approached me with half a glass of beer in his hand and a smile on his face, saying, 'Thank you, Robin.' He then proceeded to pour the glass of beer over my head!

GREG CHAPPELL

After a promising start, my relationship with Greg turned sour. Perhaps he thought Australia didn't receive a 'fair go' from me. Perhaps I was too hard? We had a couple of spats; one was in Sydney where overnight rain delayed the start of play on the first day of the second Ashes Test of 1979–80. The day dawned bright and clear, but any play still looked extremely doubtful. However, the groundsmen worked like beavers and the sun continued to shine. Me and my co-umpire, Bill Copeland, from Melbourne, conducted frequent inspections throughout the day. Just before tea, and another inspection, we told the respective captains (Brearley for England) that we would consider a start after the scheduled tea break. Greg made it loud and clear to us, and to me as the senior umpire in particular, that if we did make that start, he would ensure, by way of his captain's report, that it would be the last Test match I would officiate at for a while. Nevertheless, we started after tea and, on winning the toss, Greg put England in to bat. The match was eventually won by Australia late on the last day with the wicket, apart from one or two deliveries, playing truly.

I later incurred Greg's wrath when I adjudged him lbw (without playing a shot) in the 1981–82 Test against the West Indies in Adelaide. The great Michael Holding, nicknamed 'Whispering Death' because of his silent, gliding approach to the wicket, was the bowler and there was no doubt about the decision. During subsequent discussions with an Australian Cricket Board official before the start of the next season, it was suggested that Greg, who was having trouble batting because of a damaged hand as a result of being hit by some Windies' short stuff which he deemed to be excessive, thought I could have taken this difficulty into account. Sorry – if you're out there, if you're plumb, that's it!

I did, on one occasion, see one of my Test match reports from Greg. It read: 'No mistakes, but a pain in the arse – two out of ten'. I laughed when I read it. 'No mistakes' in a five-day Test match, with all its pressures and demands . . . whatever the comments, I will take that any day.

In December 1982, I retired from Test match cricket after yet another conflict with Greg over my no-balling of Jeff Thomson for intimidatory bowling against England at the

Gabba. I felt that I was receiving no support from cricket officials in my approach to, and policing of, Law 42 (fair and unfair play). And I felt I had lost the confidence of the players, which was a situation foreign to me and something I could not accept.

Having said all that, I have great admiration for Greg as a player. In full flight, there has never been a more elegant batsman. One must also remember the players, especially captains, are under extreme pressure, and clashes with other players, umpires and officials are inevitable. What I did I would do again, but that does not stop me wishing these confrontations hadn't occurred. Cricket umpiring is there to be enjoyed.

ALLAN BORDER

The little Aussie battler, or Captain Grumpy as he was called, took over the reins when Australian cricket was still wallowing in defeat and dispiritedness following the World Series Cricket upheaval and the retirement of such great players as Lillee, Marsh and Greg Chappell. He put his hand up in January 1985 for a job that virtually everyone else thought too hot to handle.

Certainly, Allan was not frightened to put pressure on umpires, wanting to know, for example, why Australia wasn't getting more lbws, making offhand but very audible comments to the bowler from his midwicket position. When a caught-behind appeal was rejected, he said: 'Watch out for the splinters when the ball comes back.'

For the umpires, it's all in a day's work.

Unapologetic 'Mankad' instigator Alan Hurst in full menace for Victoria during an MCG Sheffield Shield match in January 1977. The umpire is Bill Copeland.

The catch Richie didn't see! Cowdrey, caught Benaud, bowled Mackay for 23 in the second Test against England at Lord's in 1956.

Ian Redpath's habit of backing up too far costs him his wicket in the fourth Test at Adelaide Oval in January 1969. He's just been 'Mankaded' by the West Indies' Charlie Griffith, who sent Redpath on his way for 9.

Mark Taylor's dramatic all-points catch during the second Test v. the West Indies at the SCG in December 1996 – from Carl Hooper's bat to Ian Healy's leg, the catcher's ribs, hands, hat, then, as he fell on to his back, his foot and finally into his hands.

The Australian team watches the replay of Taylor's catch. From left: Blewett (obscured), Warne, Taylor, Healy, Kasprowicz (obscured), Ponting, Gillespie, Mark Waugh, Steve Waugh (obscured), Bevan and McGrath.

A nomination for 'Catch of the Century': John Dyson's goalkeeper leap to dismiss the West Indies' Sylvester Clarke off Bruce Yardley in the second Test at the SCG, January 1982.

The cricketing Rose family of Inglewood in central Victoria. Back row (from left): David, Ben and Wendy. Front row (from left): Lynette, Michael and Melanie.

John Gascoigne on a visit to his native New Zealand in 1972 (top); and (below) a more recent portrait.

Mel Johnson (left) and Dick French at the third Ashes Test in Adelaide, December 1982. It was a memorable match for Greg Chappell, who guided his team to an eight-wicket win after scoring his first Test century in his home city, his twenty-second for Australia.

French (left) and Johnson splash out during the rain-ruined Australia v. Pakistan second Test at the Gabba in November 1983. Torrential rain flooded the ground on the fourth day to secure Pakistan a draw after it appeared headed for an innings defeat.

Rex Whitehead (right) and co-umpire Tony Crafter during a break in play in the second Australia v. India Test match, Adelaide Oval, January 1981.

Rex Whitehead (behind wicket, far right) officiating in his second Test match, the Australia v. India Test in 1980–81 at Adelaide Oval. It is one of the few Test match grounds in the world to post the umpires' names on the scoreboard.

At the Gabba in December 2000, Mel Johnson (far right, second row from front) joined Indian Test match umpire Venkataraghavan (with spectacles, third row from front) to umpire a testimonial match for wicketkeeper Ian Healy. Pictured are (from left, back row): Stuart Law, Mark Waugh, Merv Hughes, Craig McDermott, Andy Bichel, Mark Taylor. Second row: umpire Venkat, David Boon, Allan Border, tennis ace Pat Rafter, Shane Warne, Healy, Michael Slater. Third row: Andy Symonds, Sir Richard Hadlee, Courtney Walsh, Brian McMillan, Graham Gooch, Kepler Wessels, umpire Johnson. Front row: Jeff Dujon, Abdul Qadir, Viv Richards, Adam Dale, Desmond Haynes, Alfie Langer (NRL).

Robin Bailhache (left) and Tom Brooks take time out during the fifth Ashes Test in Adelaide in January 1975. Both umpires were physically and mentally stretched by the unique demands of standing in all six Tests of the 1974–75 series.

Judging bowlers' complaints about the shape of cricket balls is part of an umpire's unhappy lot. Robin Bailhache (left) and Dick French confer during the fourth Ashes Test at the SCG in January 1979.

An easy one for Robin Bailhache as Kim Hughes catches Geoffrey Boycott for 49 off Alan Hurst in the second innings of the fifth Test in Adelaide, 1978–79. England won the match by 205 runs.

Robin Bailhache shakes the royal hand during a Crusaders tour of England in 1987. Making the introductions, at right, is Bob ('Swan') Richards, a co-founder of the Crusaders. The team played a Royal Household XI at Windsor Castle.

Jack Collins checks the Melbourne *Herald*'s reviews of his final official Test match – the Australia v. West Indies Boxing Day encounter at the MCG in 1975. Clive Lloyd's trenchant criticism of his umpiring led indirectly to Collins's resignation and a new appointment with Packer's World Series.

Seeing the light . . . Jack Collins shared a small piece of SCG history on 28 November 1978 when he umpired the ground's first day/night match, a WSC 'Supertest' between Australia and the West Indies before a 50000-plus sell-out crowd.

Passiveness and power: Steve Dunne watches the progress of a Shaun Pollock thunderbolt in Port Elizabeth where, in March 1998, South Africa was on the way to beating Pakistan by 259 runs in the third Test.

Daryl Harper (left) and Steve Dunne during the first Test, in Adelaide, of the 1999–2000 Australia v. India series. Steve Waugh's Australians won all three Tests by big margins.

A day in cricket infamy (from left): Darrell Hair, Steve Dunne and match referee Graham Dowling before the start of the Boxing Day Test match at the MCG in 1995. Hair no-balled Sri Lankan spinner Muralitharan seven times for throwing, an event with international repercussions that overshadowed all else, including Australian's 10-wicket win.

A more relaxed day for Dunne in Sharjah, October 2000. Steve (far right) is pictured with (second from left) English umpire George Sharp, flanked by his son and wife; Daryl Harper (centre); and match referee Denis Lindsay, of South Africa.

No wonder they called him 'Big Bird'. In 1982, West Indian giant Joel Garner, then playing for South Australia, dwarfs Terry Prue as he reaches skyward in delivery stride. Facing up is WA's Rodney Marsh.

It used to take just two to control a first-class match; now four share the workload. In Adelaide for the Sheffield Shield final in March 1998 are (from left) Terry Prue (as third umpire), Darrell Hair, Daryl Harper and referee Ric Evans.

Dad's got the job! Terry Prue at breakfast with his children (from left), Travis, Natalie and Jarrad, on the day in November 1988 when he was notified of his first Test match appointment.

Steve Davis (left) and Terry Prue get into their 'pyjama' uniforms to umpire a Pakistan v. West Indies one-dayer in Adelaide, December 1992.

In his first Test match, Terry Prue watches the result of a Merv Hughes delivery at the WACA during an Australia v. West Indies clash in December 1988. At the start of the Windies' second innings, Prue's raised finger to an lbw appeal gave Hughes a hat-trick.

KIM HUGHES

A great bloke, and perhaps too nice to be captain of Australia. Kim was a real goer as a batsman, but it seemed he didn't have the total, unqualified support of some of his team-mates, notably those mostly older and tougher characters who had been through the two years of WSC cricket, which he had chosen to avoid.

Kim featured in one of the most extraordinary decisions I had to make. In the Pakistan Test at the MCG in 1981–82, Kim was facing up to Pakistani spinner Iqbal Qasim and played a defensive shot into the ground. Or so he thought. I had seen the ball bounce from the wicketkeeper's foot and then into the hands of slip Majid Khan and was surprised when neither the wicketkeeper nor the slip appealed. It was left to Javed Miandad, a Pakistani the Australians loved to hate because he gave as good as he got, to acknowledge what had happened. With arms waving, Javed yelled out something, which I took to be an appeal. I signalled 'out' to a perplexed Hughes who clearly thought he'd hit the ball into the ground. Which just proved that you should never assume and never take your eye off the ball, even when to all intents and purposes play has come to a halt. But as an umpire you worry about these types of decisions. 'Did I get it right – did I see it as it happened?' So I glanced across at my colleague, Dick French, who was laughing his head off, clapping his hands and stamping his leg – the leg that used to go to sleep due to an old sporting injury. I took this to be an affirmation that he agreed with me. This communication and understanding between umpires is vital as we work as a team, and Dick French was one of the best team players around.

GRAHAM YALLOP

I found Graham (universally known as Wally) to be a complex character, as well as one of the best players of slow bowling I have seen. Graham was given the task of leading Australia around the World Series era of upheaval, and really had trouble forging a strong unit.

He was also the only captain I know of to put umpires on a charge, as distinct from the standard end-of-match report, citing Angelo Nicosia and me with failing to adequately control the time taken for drinks by the Sri Lankans in a one-day match against Victoria in 1982–83. The committee hearing the case decided to take no action, because the Code of Behaviour applying to the Australian players did not apply to visiting international teams. In other words, the umpires had no power to act – an anomaly that prompted the Victorian Cricket Association to explore the possibility of these visiting teams being bound by the requirements of the same code.

One vexed part of the game in which I stayed out of a lot of trouble concerns the lbw Law. I developed a reputation for being disinclined to uphold bowlers' appeals unless even the batsman could see he was out. Let me explain why that was. The Law conveys that the finger should be raised if the ball – failing to make contact with the bat and instead hitting some part of the batsman – would, in the opinion of the umpire, have gone on to hit the wicket. In recent times it would appear 'the umpire's opinion' has, in some cases, been relaxed to the extent that the fundamental Law of cricket in relation to 'doubt' favouring the batsman has been unaccountably ignored. The new Law 36 (under the 2000 code) says:

1. Out LBW

   The striker is out LBW in these circumstances:

   (a) the bowler delivers a ball, not being a No Ball, and

   (b) the ball, if it is not intercepted full-pitch, pitches in line between wicket and wicket or on the off side of the striker's wicket, and

   (c) the ball not having previously touched his bat, the striker intercepts the ball, either full-pitch or after pitching, with any part of his person, and

   (d) the point of impact, even if above the level of the bails either (i) is between wicket and wicket or (ii) is either between wicket and wicket or outside the line of the off stump if the striker has made no genuine attempt to play the ball with his bat, and

   (e) but for the interception, the ball would have hit the wicket.

2. Interception of the ball

   (a) In assessing points (c), (d) and (e) in 1 above, only the first interception is to be considered.

   (b) In assessing point (e) in 1 above, it is to be assumed that the path of the ball before interception would have continued after interception, irrespective of whether the ball might have pitched subsequently or not.

3. Off side of wicket

   The off side of the striker's wicket shall be determined by the striker's stance at the moment the ball comes into play for that delivery.

The lbw Law had been subject to controversy, animated and often heated discussion and, of course, player dissent long before its overhaul by MCC for the start of England's 1935 county championship. Before that year, the lbw Law had permitted unbridled use of pads to any ball that pitched a fraction wide. At last, after much consultation, MCC took the plunge and allowed the trial of a new rule, under which the batsman could be out if hit on part of his body on an imaginary line between wicket and wicket, even if the ball pitched outside off stump.

Under the Laws of Cricket, any doubt in the umpire's mind should favour the batsman, but I am convinced that in recent times, a 'close enough is good enough' mentality has crept into our game. Players are appearing to accept this – even demand this – as the norm. There are cases of fielding captains now questioning umpires on their failure to award lbw decisions, especially front-foot decisions, and castigating them for their firm, and quite correct, decisions.

Let's consider the facts. The wicket is nine inches wide. The batting (popping) crease is four feet from the wicket, and this is where the batsman normally stands. If he plays forward, say, extending his front foot two feet forward, this places him six feet from the bowler's nine-inch-wide target. If there is any deviation at all by the ball, and there usually is, you don't have to be Einstein to conclude that it would only be an educated guess, at best, as to the certainty of the ball hitting the stumps. And bear in mind that if the batsman plays a legitimate shot at the ball, then contact by the ball with the pad must be made in line between wicket and wicket. This virtually means that any sideways movement of the ball must be practically non-existent to ensure without doubt that the ball would hit the stumps.

Wherever the batsman is standing, quite sharp sideways movement of the ball makes it more difficult for the umpire to adjudicate with certainty as to the likelihood of the ball striking the nine-inch target.

The wicket is 28.5 inches high, and Australia's wickets are acknowledged as being the bounciest in the world. Often, batsmen are hit on or above the knee roll of the pad with the ball still on the rise, with the resultant lbw appeal being granted. With slow bowlers and the batsman playing back or from the crease, we may well have a candidate, but with any pace and resultant bounce, any umpire should be very loath to answer these appeals in the affirmative.

We have heard in recent times of bowlers getting more wickets lbw because they bowl 'close to the stumps' during their delivery. Well, bowlers have been bowling close to the stumps for 100 years, so nothing is new.

While I am normally suspicious of 'third umpire' technology, such has been the relaxed attitude of umpires in relation to the granting of lbw decisions that I think the use of such technology in this area is inevitable. In some senior quarters of Australian cricket administration, there is the belief that we should encourage, or at least consider, 'third umpire' technology in lbw decisions because more batsmen would be dismissed this way than is the current situation. One result of which could be, conceivably, matches not going the distance. Yet it's my belief that the opposite would apply; that is, there would be fewer lbw dismissals as the all-seeing eye of the 'third umpire' would establish precisely how difficult it is to judge that the ball would hit its intended target. This technology would also pick up what is often being overlooked now: the delivery that pitches outside leg stump or which makes contact with the pad when not in line between wicket and wicket. In past years umpires granted very few lbws. I'm sure they were nearer the mark.

Invariably, people talking to me about cricket want to know whom I considered 'the best'. It's a difficult question because I saw many great players, all at different stages of their careers. For example, Derek Underwood, Alan Knott, Lance Gibbs, Freddy Titmus and many others were nearing the end of their careers when I entered the Test scene.

Let's consider some of the quick bowlers. It has been my pleasure to watch from the 'best seat in the house': Graham McKenzie, Dennis Lillee, Jeff Thomson, Len Pascoe, Rodney Hogg, Geoff Lawson, Craig McDermott, Merv Hughes and Glenn McGrath (Australia); Malcolm Marshall, Courtney Walsh, Patrick Patterson, Colin Croft, Andy Roberts, Joel Garner, Michael Holding and Curtly Ambrose (West Indies); Wasim Akram and Imran Khan (Pakistan); Bob Willis (England); and Richard Hadlee (New Zealand). To me, the best were Lillee and Holding. Both had great actions, and their records speak for themselves. Lillee was full of menace and aggression, while Holding simply glided to the crease with so little effort, but was deceptively fast. The first time Michael bowled from my end, I turned around to see what was causing the delay, just as he glided past. 'Whispering Death' was an apt nickname.

As for the spinners, Bishen Bedi, Venkataraghavan, Prasanna and Chandrasekhar (India); Titmus and Underwood (England); Jenner, Mallett, Warne and May (Australia); and Mushtaq Ahmed (Pakistan) were the best of the bunch.

However, fast bowling dominated cricket during my first-class career, which spanned the years 1971 to 1992. Shane

Warne's arrival was instrumental in turning people's attention, once again, to spin bowling. Without detracting from Warne's great ability, I believe his arrival coincided with the considerable relaxing of umpiring attitudes towards batsmen receiving the 'benefit of the doubt', especially in relation to lbw decisions. This relates both to the Law governing balls pitched outside the leg stump and, I believe, some significant guesswork when considering the amount of turn and bounce that this bowler generates. Still, in the words of the immortal bard, 'He just asks 'em, he don't give 'em.'

When we talk of the best batsmen, when he was in full flight, it's hard to go past Viv Richards. I say that with some reservation, however, and my opinion of Ian Chappell's fighting qualities in tight situations has been stated elsewhere. Ian prized his wicket very highly and never gave it up easily. I couldn't say that about Viv, who hated being curtailed, which sometimes led to his downfall.

My 'best innings award' belongs to Doug Walters whose century between tea and stumps at the WACA in 1974–75 was a classic. Doug needed a four from Bob Willis's last ball of the day to reach his 100, but a six if he were to achieve 100 in a session. Willis dropped his last ball short, and Doug promptly hooked it hard and high over square leg whereupon, before the ball had even landed, what seemed to be every kid from metropolitan Perth charged on to the playing arena.

The boundary for that match was not the fence but a white line protected by a small hessian, or similar, barricade. The kids, overjoyed at Doug's rare feat, made short work of the fence, the upshot being I had no idea where the ball had landed. My co-umpire, Tom Brooks, had no idea either, and was heading off in a desperate attempt to retrieve the ball for the next day's play. Problem! If I signal four runs, which I should do if unsure, Doug gets his 100 but not his larger slice of history, because he had opened his account just before the tea break. Something caused me in desperation to look towards fine leg where stood England pace bowler Chris Old, who had also received a fair caning from Doug, with his arms in the air signalling either six or surrender. As he was in a good position to see, I took it as the former and did likewise. In the meantime, the said kids had pinched the stumps!

It was July 1979, and the England team had departed our shores when I received through the mail, wrapped in plain brown paper and tied with string, a most peculiar-looking package. I unwrapped it to discover one sweat-stained, much used and abused, batting pad. Attached to the pad was a note which read: 'From me to you – guess who?' I had no idea, and it was only by chance that I found out that it had been sent to me by a person reputedly with no sense of humour and certainly no expertise in poetry. A dour, Yorkshire-born batsman. You guessed it: Geoffrey Boycott. The other pad had been forwarded to Dick French. We both had occasion to give him out lbw during the season and he figured that as we were so attracted to his pads, we might as well have them!

The worst incident in my umpiring career was undoubtedly the Pakistani walk-off from the MCG on Australia Day, 26 January 1990, during its game against Victoria. After three unofficial cautions and two of the 'fair dinkum' variety, including advising the acting captain Ramiz Raja, all of which were ignored, I had no course other than to banish spin bowler Mushtaq Ahmed from the attack for running on the wicket. Suddenly, from taking no notice of me, all the Pakistanis wished to become involved, even the team manager, Intikhab Alam, who suddenly materialised on the scene. What I then heard was a load of tripe. Intikhab vigorously argued that Raja did not know his bowler was wearing rubber-soled shoes. Yes, I replied, but his twisting action on landing had burnt a patch the size of a dinner plate in the centre of the wicket, on a good length. Then, I was told I was 'too rigid', and so on.

Intikhab refused to leave the field, and refused to allow play to continue 'under the conditions', as he put it. We left the field and, as far as I was concerned, the match was over. Some heavy lobbying by the VCA officials and a convincing plea to resume play by the Victorian captain, Simon O'Donnell, led to our restarting the match. But as far as I'm concerned, and in hindsight, that decision to return was wrong. Later, I learned that the Adelaide Oval curator had complained at the end of a prior match about damage done to his playing surface apparently very similar to that at the MCG. The umpires, on that occasion, failed to act.

In the past decade, I have travelled to New Zealand a number of times and been well treated, for which I'm truly grateful, as I was the 'culprit' of the Cairns/Higgs incident which lit up the MCG Test match in 1980–81. The problem stemmed from the fact that the Kiwis' tour conditions stipulated that 'at no time' were bouncers to be bowled to tail-end batsmen. With all due respect to Jim Higgs, he well and truly fell into the category of a tail-end batsman. The furore erupted when Richard Hadlee's new ball partner, the fine all-rounder Lance Cairns, dropped a really quick one short to Jim, who admittedly had made a nuisance of himself by hanging around, but who had no idea how to play the delivery and nearly fell backwards on to the pitch. At the same time, he flung up his arm holding the bat and the ball appeared to come off his wrist and go through to the 'keeper. I had meanwhile called 'no-ball', which upset the New Zealanders on the ground and those listening and watching in their homeland.

NZ skipper Geoff Howarth queried the call, wanting to know whether it was for intimidatory bowling. I replied in the affirmative. Both camps had agreed to this condition of the tour, so I thought it a bit rough to make me the villain as the incident continued to be played out in the media for the next few days and weeks. One thing continued to trouble me about the incident. What would have happened if I had not made that call? I refer to my previous mention of 'appeared to come off the wrist', because being caught off the wrist under the Laws then applying constituted not out. Interesting!

The cricket umpire's role in 1969, when I started my career, bore no resemblance to that in 2002. Cricket, and umpiring included, has undergone huge changes. To remove any perception of home-team bias, Test umpires now officiate internationally as members of an independent world panel, and that's a concept that troubles me. This is because I believe the system fails to recognise umpires in those countries with stronger umpiring panels. I have no doubt the top umpires in one or two of the participating countries could be inferior to lower ranked umpires in the stronger umpiring countries. Until we have a system that will produce, say, the top ten umpires in the world, irrespective of where they reside, then we must stick with the system we now have. And the 'third umpire', with the technology he commands, frankly doesn't impress me.

Cricket, I believe, was never meant to be that precise. However, now that we have started using technology, unfortunately there can be no turning back. With the prize money and career incentives now available, with players' futures resting on a single decision, the third-umpire technology is there to be used, and I argue its use could extend beyond what we have now. In run-outs and stumpings, umpires are leaving it more and more to the third umpire, in many cases not even bothering to make position to facilitate their own decision. Calling the close ones in run-out decisions will soon be a lost skill, as will most aspects of umpiring.

The ICC has decided recently on a limited trial using the third umpire to assist in lbw decisions. Normally, I would strongly regret the perceived need for this further intrusion into the umpire's responsibility. However, the granting of lbw appeals has reached alarming proportions and, I repeat, the use of appropriate sophisticated technology will show just how few of these appeals should be upheld. Importantly, it must not be left solely to a third umpire, denied the benefit of advanced technology, because that umpire's interpretation and judgement may be no better, or indeed, inferior, to that of the umpire in the middle. We cannot be half-hearted about the use of technology, though. If we feel that this is the way to go, if we feel that the central umpire is virtually redundant, if we feel the need to intrude further into, interrupt and sanitise the game beyond its spirit, character and tradition, then perhaps we had best get on with it!

In addition, cricket can well do without its recently exposed betting and match-fixing scandals. Let's hope this cancer is now removed so that we can return to the heady days when the saying 'It isn't cricket' was synonymous with fair play and good behaviour. The young generation growing up amid all this highly publicised corruption dross will hopefully live to see cricket return to its former status.

One of my favourite 'takes' on umpiring is captured in the words of a man whose name you almost certainly won't know. Donald Jensen, an umpire, was struck on the head by a bat thrown in a Little League baseball game in Indiana, USA. Jensen shook off the blow and finished umpiring the game, but that night he went to hospital with head pains. While being kept in overnight for observation, Jensen wrote the following open letter to the parents of Little Leaguers everywhere:

> I'm an umpire. I don't do it for a living, but only on weekends for fun. I've played baseball, coached it and watched it, but somehow nothing takes the place of umpiring. Maybe I feel deep down that I'm providing a fair chance for all kids to play the game without disagreement and arguments. But there is one things that bothers me about my job – some of you folk don't understand why I'm there. Some of you feel I'm there to exert authority over your son. For that reason you often yell at me, or encourage your son to yell when I make a mistake. How many of you really understand that I try to be perfect? That I try not to make a mistake?
>
> I don't want your son to feel he got a bad deal from an umpire. Yet no matter how hard I try, I can't be perfect. I counted the number of calls I made in a six-innings game today – the total number of decisions on balls and strikes or safes and outs was 146. I tried my best to get them all right. But I'm sure I missed some. I could have missed eight calls today and still got about 96 per cent right. In most occupations that percentage would be considered excellent.

Let me tell you more about my game today. There was one close call that ended the game – a runner for the home team was trying to steal the plate on a passed ball. The catcher chased the ball down and threw to the pitcher covering the plate. The pitcher made the tag call and I called the runner out.

As I was getting my equipment to leave, I overheard one of the parents comment: 'It's too bad the kids have to lose games because of rotten umpires. That was one of the lousiest calls I have ever seen.' Later, at a nearby store, a couple of kids were telling their friends: 'Boy, the umpires were lousy today. They lost the game for us.' Well, I heard that and felt terrible. Those kids had made a lot of mistakes that cost them runs.

A parent or adult leader who lets a child blame his failures on an umpire is doing the worst kind of injustice to that youngster. That irresponsibility is bound to carry over into his future life.

As I sit here writing this letter, I am no longer as upset as I was this afternoon. At one point I wanted to quit umpiring behind the plate because of the pitcher who pantomimed his displeasure at any close call. One could sense he wanted the crowd to realise that he was a talented player who was doing his best to get along and I was the black-hearted villain who was working against him. This kid continued for two innings, at the same time yelling at his own players' mistakes. For two innings the manager watched this. When the kid returned to bat at the top of the third, the manager called him aside. In a voice that I was able to overhear, he said, 'Listen, son, it's time you made a decision. You can be an umpire, an actor or a pitcher, but you can only be one at a time when you're playing for me. Right now it's your job to pitch and basically you are doing a lousy job. Leave the acting to an actor, the umpiring to the umpire, or you won't do any pitching here.'

Needless to say, the kid chose the pitching route and went on to win the game. When the game was over the kid followed me to the car. Fighting back the tears, he apologised for his actions during the game. He said he had learnt a lesson he would never forget. I can't help but wonder how many young men are missing their chance to develop into outstanding ball players because their parents encourage them to spend their time umpiring the game rather than working harder to play the game.

The following morning, Donald Jensen, part-time umpire, died of a brain concussion resulting from the blow from the thrown bat.

Postscript: In September 2001, a three-man panel chose a Victorian team of the twentieth century and the State's best two umpires. The elite fourteen (including a 12th man) were named at the annual Bill Smyth award dinner. Robin Bailhache and Bob Crockett were adjudged best umpires from a 'final umpiring eight', who included the aforementioned Bill Smyth and Jack Collins.

ROBIN BAILHACHE'S UMPIRING CV

94 first-class matches between November 1971 and January 1992

Official Test matches – 27 (Australia v. England 12, West Indies 6, India 2, Pakistan 3, New Zealand 3, Sri Lanka 1)

SA and Victoria v. internationals – 15 (SA v. World XI 1, England 2, West Indies 2, New Zealand 1; Victoria v. England 2, West Indies 2, India 1, Pakistan 3, New Zealand 1).

Sheffield Shield matches – 52

One-day internationals – 22

Jack Collins
Cloud-gazing for Packer

So that's how you make your first million! It was an insight into the thinking of Australia's richest man. A small insight, because it was a small gesture, but a revealing one.

Kerry Packer and I were on a big adventure: Packer's World Series Cricket. Working at a modestly paid job as a boilermaker for the Australian Army at Maribyrnong in Melbourne's west, and with a wife and six children to care for, the offer of considerable funds to umpire in the new competition proved irresistible. The payment for my first three months with WSC would have taken me twenty months to earn in my army job.

So here I was at notoriously rainy Waverley Park, in Melbourne's outer eastern suburbs two weeks before Christmas in 1977, for what the marketing people packaged as a 'Supertest'. After lunch on the third day, I was walking on to the ground with my colleague from Perth, Bruce Duperouzel, to start play. As practised by umpires around the world, Bruce dropped the ball on the turf about midway to the wicket (for the captain, usually, to pick up and toss around amongst the players). Then we placed the bails on the stumps and waited for the players.

They didn't arrive, but the rain did. As AFL football followers who made the trip out to the rain belt to follow the fortunes of home teams Hawthorn and St Kilda or their opponents will tell you, when it rains at Waverley, it fairly buckets down. So Bruce and I removed the bails and pursued the players who had only just crossed the boundary before high-tailing it back to the rooms.

By the time we got inside, we were thoroughly drenched. I was removing my hat and coat when there was a loud knocking on the door. I opened it and there was the boss, Kerry Packer, absolutely drowned, with a cricket ball in his hand.

'Who left this ball out on the ground?' he barked. 'I'm not paying you guys good money to ruin property.'

I can't recall what incoherent gibberish I came out with, but it certainly wasn't English. I was dumbfounded. Some time later, I realised Kerry would have been watching proceedings with numerous guests in the VIP area, and he could have sent anyone out to retrieve the ball. But from his soggy state, it was obvious he had gone out himself.

Bruce and I apologised for our 'forgetfulness', and I suppose my respect for Packer grew from that moment. I could see why he was so successful in business, being clearly a convert to the principle that 'if you look after the pennies, the pounds will take care of themselves'.

Kerry came into the umpires' room the next morning to wish us well, and said no more about the previous day's incident, which had taught us at least one lesson: that although Packer had spent many millions of dollars in this gamble to lure the under-paid cricketers from the miserly establishment and ultimately to take over the television rights from the ABC, he still cared about the little things. Including a 156-gram cricket ball.

In the two years I knew Packer – the seasons of 1977–78 and 1978–79, which were the duration of World Series Cricket that so revolutionised the game – I found him to be a man of whom I could only speak highly. Apart from changing the game forever and sprucing up its television coverage on his Nine Network, it should be remembered the results of the millions he spent are with us still. How many people know, for example, that for WSC's second season he reportedly spent $4.5 million installing lights at the Sydney Cricket Ground?

Packer never failed to say hello and stop for a chat. He regularly attended the matches and often called into the umpires' rooms to wish us 'Good umpiring' or, after play, to say 'Well done, boys'. He was also a lover of cricket and, probably, a 'cricket tragic' as Mark Taylor's boys labelled Prime Minister John Howard. No doubt he was a fan of the players, whom he rewarded so richly, raising their payments to a level that had to be matched by the establishment (in Australia, the Australian Cricket Board) when a rapprochement was reached after the two-year schism.

On one occasion Packer provided a Lear jet and pilot to take Dennis Lillee and Rod Marsh back to Perth for some R and R during an airline strike, then picked them up to return. And there were many other such undisclosed favours.

WSC was a wonderful, unforgettable experience; two years about which I have no regrets, despite being 'cold-shouldered' by a couple of establishment leaders when I was invited back to the Melbourne Cricket Ground in the aftermath of the great experiment.

Four umpires took up the Packer offer: Duperouzel, Douglas Sang Hue (the West Indies' leading umpire), Peter Enright and me. In January 1979, Colin Hoy took over from Enright so that Peter could return to his 'real job'. All of us travelled with the players, officials and staff on planes, parlour coaches, train (from Perth to Kalgoorlie), hire cars or buses. We, the umpires, lived with the players in motels or hotels, attended civic receptions, dinners, sports nights and coaching clinics with the players, and were made to feel an integral part of the scene.

As for umpiring . . . because the Marylebone Laws of Cricket are copyright, the Laws, under Packer, could not be used in their entirety. So an addendum was added to the front-foot no-ball Law, which said: ' . . . however, the umpire may disregard the fact that the bowler's front foot has gone over the line, as long as he deems that the bowler has not taken an unfair advantage'. This meant that he could be a fraction over the rear of the line of the popping crease with his front foot, as long as it was not done frequently or to too great an advantage. I found that with so many world-class quicks around, this addendum worked extremely well.

However, WSC was also hard work as there were no reserve umpires on the panel, and with two matches generally going on at the same time – one in the capital city, one in the country – I could not afford to be unfit.

On one occasion I umpired eleven days straight across Victoria, NSW and South Australia. More than once I was in three States in one day. For example, I umpired at Adelaide's Football Park in a one-day game, got back to my motel, was up at 4 a.m., made it to the airport, umpired in a one-day match at Orange, NSW, went straight to the airport and slept that night at the Old Melbourne Motor Inn. Phew! A lot of time was spent travelling, and jet-lag was a big part of the deal. Fortunately, the four of us stayed fit and well, and not once was there need for a replacement.

After starting my umpiring with the Footscray Cricket Association in Melbourne in 1951 and managing one match a week at weekends, then later, five or six first-class matches a season, the WSC experience confirmed my long-held belief that Australian umpires don't get enough cricket to hone their skills to the level of the English county and Test men. Usually, that comparable standard is reached only when they're fairly advanced in age. Many of the English umpires are former county players, and they can umpire six days a week; seven if they want to.

Initially, I found umpiring similar to learning to drive a manual car. There's just so much to learn, but after a few years it becomes second nature. So with WSC, one became more professional more quickly. And World Series Cricket, with its far greater remuneration carrying over into the establishment sphere after 1980, enabled in its flow-on effect both umpires and players to remain in the game longer. That meant players of the calibre of Paul Sheahan and Bob Cowper, whom many believe left the game too early, were, post-Packer, able to stay five or more years longer than in the 'shamateur' and amateur days. Now, of course, the star players are a lot closer in earnings capacity to the top golfers, tennis players and footballers.

It's unarguable that Packer's Nine Network led the world in its innovations in telecasting the game. And in its promotion of the one-day game – a re-emphasis on fielding skills, 'pyjamas', night games, etc – WSC helped crank up the percentage of women involved in cricket, either as spectators or players. Following the 'pyjama game' is far easier, and more exciting, for cricket ingenues – men or women – than the Test match or four-day, first-class version. And that has contributed to the great strength of women's cricket worldwide.

My offer to join WSC came at a good time. I had worked for fifteen years with the army after an exasperating few years spent with a Melbourne-based employer for a large, national manufacturer. In fact, the Melbourne boss sacked me when I left for a few days, as we'd agreed, verbally, to umpire my first 'big' match, a Victoria v. NSW colts fixture at the MCG in November 1964. That sacking came as quite a shock as, at the job interview, I'd explained that I'd require time off to umpire first-class matches, then had agreed to take the lesser of the two jobs on offer to enable this to happen. Some days later, an article appeared in the *Truth* newspaper saying that a promising cricket umpire had been sacked by Australia's leading rubber/sporting goods company after a verbal agreement had been broken. How the paper found out remains a mystery to me.

In all, I lost my job three times due to umpiring and employers' broken promises. Even in the more stable army days, the umpiring life was hard on my family as I used up all my annual leave, and even took leave without pay, to officiate at Shield and Test matches. The result was that my family and I went for fifteen years without a holiday.

As with most kids, cricket for me started in the backyard. At first it was matches with a tennis ball against my brothers, Peter and Leo. Later, we'd be joined by all the kids in the neighbourhood, enough for two full-sized teams to compete in one of the adjoining paddocks. One of those kids was unbeatable. George Thoms, who later played for Victoria and Australia, would bat for weeks on end until he'd run out of partners.

I played school cricket and junior matches for Footscray United Socials and West Footscray YCW on Sundays. In 1951, aged nineteen, a knee injury turned my thoughts to umpiring and I began in the Footscray Cricket Association, feeling at that age rather like a football club mascot in the rough-and-tumble competition that was the FCA.

After five years, my opinion of my own ability seemed not to be shared, as I had not once qualified to umpire a final. So I decided to take myself and my unrewarded talents along to the Victorian Cricket Association pre-season lectures and sit the exams for appointment to the VCA panel. My sudden uptake in understanding the Laws had the side-effect of explaining my lack of success back at Footscray.

After a valuable season (1956–57) in sub-district where a number of ex-Shield players were engaged, I made it on to the VCA panel, spending three seasons in the thirds and one in the seconds before fronting up to the firsts in season 1961. Along the way I had been given invaluable advice, most of it from George Hele, Ron Wright and Bill Smyth.

I, and many other Victorians, still consider Smyth to have been the best – the doyen – of umpires' advisers, and it was a travesty of justice that he umpired in only four Tests. Bill's knowledge of the Laws was unmatched. A day I spent in his company, downing a few ales at the Essendon Social Club after rain had washed out play in my second district firsts game, shot me further up the learning curve than could any twelve-month span on the paddock.

My first finals match, a semi-final between St Kilda and Essendon, was shared with Bill Smyth who was then in a supervisory position with the Taxation Department. As we walked out to start play, Bill said, 'Jack, you've umpired thirds and seconds finals before . . .', and I started thinking, here comes the advice about umpiring in the big-time. I said, 'Yes, Bill.'

His next comment wasn't quite what I expected. 'Jack, do you put your umpiring earnings into your taxation returns?'

Stunned, I replied, 'Well, no, Bill.'

He simply said, 'Do.'

Talk about good cricketing advice! I spent the next hour more worried about the Taxation Department than my umpiring.

I was umpring another match at St Kilda when Bill, at the end of an over and before moving to square leg, came up to me and said, 'Jack, I'm dying for a leak. After the third ball of the next over, call me in to straighten up the stumps.'

I said, 'Okay,' and called him in. After pushing them a little, he said, 'Jack, the middle stump is split. I'll go and get another.' He was heading off and just gaining speed when the St Kilda property steward met him about five metres inside the boundary, with another stump. At this stage, Bill was motoring at full bore and said in a loud voice: 'Not that one, it's the wrong bloody colour.' A minute later Bill came out of the rooms, ran straight past the bewildered steward still clutching the stump, and inserted the replacement for the 'split' wicket. When play ended, Bill explained to the steward that replacing a stump can really be just a case of nature calling.

My first Sheffield Shield match, in December 1965–66, was Victoria v. WA, and with the frequently appealing, rambunctious leg-spinner Tony Lock playing for the West, it was a tough initiation. It didn't help much that I, aged thirty-one, was making my first-class debut, while my umpiring partner, Keith Butler, thirty, was in his second Shield match. The papers reported that, collectively, we were the youngest pair to officiate in a Shield fixture.

My second Shield game was a plum appointment: to the Boxing Day match between the old adversaries Victoria and NSW. I must have performed reasonably well, because during the game I was told by NSW captain Bobby Simpson that I'd been appointed as reserve umpire for the New Year's Day Test between Australia and Mike Smith's Englishmen.

Simpson let me know he was impressed by my upholding an appeal for lbw against Victorian wicketkeeper Ray Jordan. The colourful 'Slug', as he was known, was given out before he had scored, after he charged down the wicket to try to smash a Peter Philpott flipper out of the ground. Philpott had a different action for this top-spinner, going from the usual vertical arm to almost horizontal, and the ball would really fizz off the track. On this occasion, the ball pitched a little short of halfway, kept low and struck Jordan nearer the boot than the kneeroll, dead in line with middle stump. My problem was that 'Slug' had charged about eight feet from the popping crease when he was struck.

Naturally, the further down the wicket the batsman has gone, the safer he generally is in the event of an appeal by the bowler. I duly dwelt on my decision a little longer than my usual deliberations. Raising my finger didn't actually please 'Slug', and anyone who knew him would be aware he had a rare ability to express himself, especially when riled. But that night Simpson came to the umpires' room and congratulated me on being the only umpire game enough to give a batsman out when he was that far down the track. The compliment, if that's what it was, certainly lifted my spirits as I'd just started getting used to the idea of a premature end to my involvement in first-class cricket.

It was after the third day's play that Simpson told me of my appointment to reserve umpire for the Melbourne Test. And this came after only my second Shield game. It was a great thrill to me, but I was equally amazed when, just before the Test started, Simpson gave an impassioned, football-type speech to his players, reminding them they were about to play the old enemy, England.

After several more years in Shield, I felt I had a chance of umpiring a Test match in 1971–72, when the great South African team was due. History shows that because of the apartheid ban, the series was cancelled, and a World XI toured Australia in its place.

Luckily, I was appointed to the Rest of the World unofficial 'Test' at the MCG, starting on New Year's Day 1972, so I was privileged to see the magnificent 254 by (the now Sir) Garfield Sobers in the RoW's second innings. It remains the best innings I have ever seen and reportedly was the best, in his estimation, seen by Sir Donald Bradman. It was as brilliant a knock as it was unexpected; in his first innings, Sobers was out first ball in what had to be the worst 'short innings' I'd seen. I'd no sooner given Sobers his guard than he hung his bat out to Dennis Lillee, nicked the ball to Keith Stackpole at first slip, and didn't bother looking up before walking off. In fact, he looked for all the world as though he didn't care.

On the Thursday before this Rest of the World 'Test', I attended a dinner to welcome the World XI at Melbourne's grand Windsor Hotel. In his speech, Sir Donald Bradman, who was then chairman of selectors, mentioned that he really enjoyed watching Sobers bat and had been fortunate to be present for many of his innings. He had enjoyed it so much, he had often personally asked him to make a century. Yes, even against the Australians. And Sobers had always obliged him. Clearly, the Australians were somewhat superstitious about the Don's influence on the Sobers form. I didn't see Sir Donald prior to Sobers' first innings, so that may explain somewhat his inauspicious first-ball duck. On the morning before the great all-rounder's second innings, I was seated in the Australian rooms next to Lillee when the fast bowler looked to his left and said, 'Oh, no, look who's coming down the aisle! [It was Sir Donald, heading towards the World XI rooms.] Quick, all out to block his path – don't let him pass.' But it didn't work. The Great Man said, 'Good morning, boys,' brushed past the players and entered the RoW rooms. That night Sobers was 119 not out.

The next morning the Australian players spotted Sir Donald approaching again, and once more he pushed his way through, after another 'Good morning, boys,' to enter the Rest's rooms; presumably, the Australians felt, to ask Sobers to make another hundred.

Although Lillee and his mates bowled well, Sobers batted better and, just after lunch, when he was past 219 (his century for that day), I noticed the weary Lillee's demeanour suddenly brighten. 'What's that big smile for?' I asked him.

'Jack, that little so-and-so can't come out here to ask Sobers to make another hundred – so we've got him!' He was right. Sobers was out soon after for his unforgettable 254.

Next season, at last, I hooked my first Test match: the Boxing Day Test, Australia v. Pakistan, at the MCG. Later, four more Tests were to be added to my CV, along with the RoW unofficial 'Test' and a 'Bushfire Challenge Test' at the MCG in 1967 between Australian 'first XI' and 'second' teams which had just toured, respectively, South Africa and New Zealand. Those five official Tests and Packer's six World Series 'Supertests' were the highlight of a career that spanned thirty years. In that time I was called on to make some tough decisions, and here are a few of the stand-outs.

My strangest decision

I was umpiring, with Bill Smyth, Victoria v. WA at the MCG in 1968–69 when Bill Lawry, who was batting at the Outer end (I was behind the stumps at the Members' end), played the ball through the covers, towards the players' rooms and almost to the boundary. Lawry and his frequent batting partner Keith Stackpole completed their third run and Lawry headed back to his Outer end for the fourth as the ball was hurled back to the 'keeper. Bill was always going to be struggling, and as he took the return, the 'keeper emulated a cat taunting a mouse,

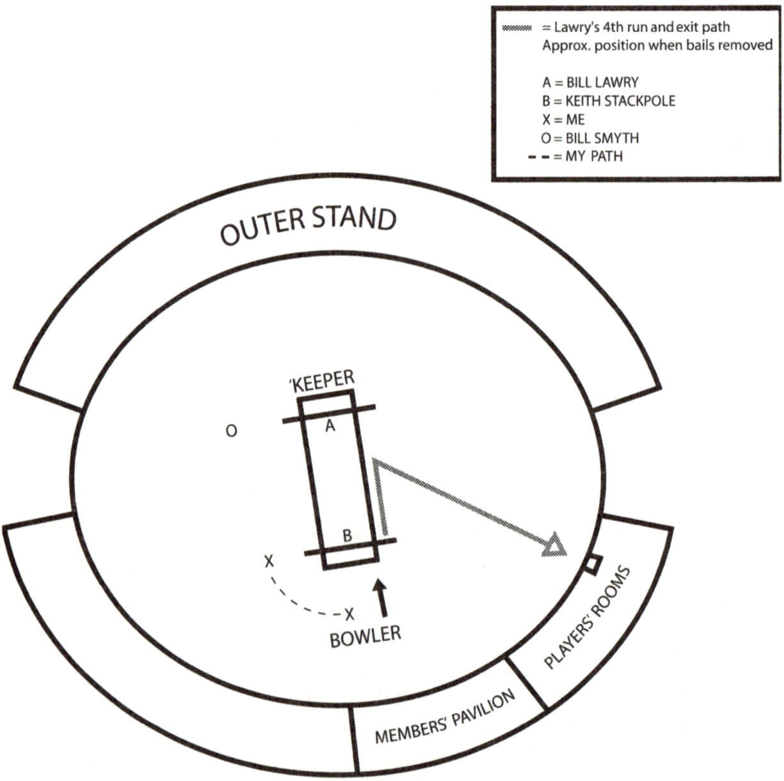

tossing the ball from glove to glove, with a big grin on his face. But he didn't remove the bails. Lawry, realising he was in no-man's land, turned about 130 degrees to walk off the ground. When the bails were finally removed and an appeal was made, Bill Smyth walked over to me before making a decision and said, 'Jack, I've got two questions for you. Firstly, where was Lawry when the bails were removed and an appeal was made? And, secondly, where was Stacky?'

I replied: 'Firstly, Lawry was about eight metres from the boundary and well past Stacky when the bails were removed. Secondly, Stacky had made good his ground, but while Lawry was walking off, he moved two feet out of his crease while he watched Lawry, and he was leaning on his bat, still well out of the crease, when the bails were removed.'

Bill Smyth walked back to his spot and said, 'Stacky, you're out, run-out.' This decision not only upset Stackpole, but also the WA players who had taken great delight in apparently removing the almost unremovable Lawry. Great umpiring, Bill, as the batsmen had crossed.

My most embarrassing decision

It was another Victoria v. WA match, again at the MCG, when Jack Potter was facing Tony Lock. The Surrey and England spinner, who normally gave the ball plenty of air, started bowling to Potter with a flat trajectory. I thought this rather strange, but after an over of darts he went back to his flighted stuff. One delivery forced Potter back on to his stumps and his left heel touched the bottom of the leg stump, without removing the bails.

I was thinking to myself, Jack, you're a genius. Watch Potter's back foot when he gives the ball a high trajectory –

Lock's trying to get Potter out 'hit-wicket'. But the next over or so were pushed through, so nothing to worry about. Then he was giving it air again and, sure enough, Jack stepped back to play the pull shot and his left foot hit the leg stump. This time, the leg bail dropped.

Up went my finger, and I was congratulating myself on a superb piece of anticipation and umpiring when I heard the 'keeper, Ross Edwards, say in a loud voice, 'Jack, I took it off with my gloves.'

I walked over to the stumps to find that the leg bail was behind them, while the off bail was well forward of the wicket. My problem now was that while I had been concentrating on watching Potter's feet and the stumps, I had completely overlooked Edwards's gloves. But Edwards owned up, which was not exactly commonplace in cricket, and I gave the cancellation signal, recalling Potter to the crease. It was extremely embarrassing, coming only moments after thinking how brilliant I'd been in my impersonation of Sherlock Holmes!

Talking of embarrassment, I encountered it early through my friendship with a neighbour of the Collins family in Footscray. Terry McKenna was involved in our neighbourhood matches, and when I was appointed to umpire my first game in VCA thirds, Terry, by chance, was in the Footscray team playing South Melbourne.

Now, Terry wasn't a very dashing batsman. All he could do was push and deflect, to the annoyance of opposition teams, and he was damnably difficult to dislodge. The whole South Melbourne team went up when its captain, an all-rounder, shouted for a caught behind off Terry from the second-last ball of an over. But I had seen or heard nothing to suggest contact with the bat, and, to the demonstrated annoyance of South,

I shook my head. The captain's stare was deadly, suggesting he would have the final say in his post-match report.

Off his final ball, Terry, in a moment of rashness, played a defensive prod down to third man and, unfortunately for me, ran a single. When he arrived at my end of the wicket, he had a big grin on his face. When he then put an arm around my shoulders, I thought he was going to kiss me. Instead, in a loud voice, he said, 'Thanks, mate.' Again, I noticed the filthy look on the face of the South captain, who must have thought there was something going on between us. With friends like that . . .

My mate Terry wasn't always an embarrassment, though I was grateful not to be so closely involved with him in another incident we shared. It was a second-eleven semifinal between Fitzroy and Footscray, at Fitzroy. Gary Hansen was batting for Footscray when he danced three steps down the track to a spinner, missed the ball and was stranded as the 'keeper took it and brought it forward to the stumps. At the critical moment, the ball slipped out of his gloves and landed at his feet. The 'keeper continued on with the motion to break the stumps, with Gary about eight feet out of his ground.

Now, in those days, the spectators at Fitzroy were the most volatile in the VCA. The packed grandstand was directly behind that end of the wicket, and the crowd was blocked by the 'keeper from seeing his fumble. I was at square leg with a clear view, so said, 'not out,' which bewildered not only those in the grandstand but also Gary Hansen and my colleague. After much booing, I said to the 'keeper, as I moved in to reset the stumps, 'Pick up the ball.' But he was enjoying my discomfort and, later, kicked it away. At the end of the next over, we came off for tea and, as I walked up the race to prolonged booing, I was spat on by a red-faced, screaming Fitzroy fan. I heard another voice say, 'Don't worry, Jack, I'll fix him.' I looked up to see Terry McKenna standing there. After the match, I asked him what had happened. He wasn't kidding when he said he'd taken the gentleman 'behind the grandstand and belted the shit out of him'. Which, I suppose, was a consolation for my embarrassment with him some years before.

My hardest decision

During the Rest of the World unofficial 'Test' in Melbourne, I had to give India's Sunil Gavaskar out, caught by Greg Chappell, in what was really a triple decision. Gavaskar had played defensively forward to a ball from Dennis Lillee with the bottom of his angled bat about three to four inches above and in front of his left instep. The ball, to me, appeared to nick the bottom edge of the bat, bounce off Gavaskar's left instep and carry towards Greg Chappell in slips, who dived forward, the bottom of his hand scraping the turf as he took the catch. But I had to decide: (a) did Gavaskar hit the ball? (b) did the ball hit his instep or the pitch? (c) was it a clean catch?

I said, 'Out, caught,' and instantly was embroiled in controversy. My decision didn't gain 100 per cent support, notably from Gavaskar. Next morning, coming into the ground, I was stopped by a member of the Australian Cricket Board, who said he'd like to talk to me about the Gavaskar affair. He and other board members, he said, had gone to the Channel Two studios last evening to see replays of the incident at normal speed, in slow motion and in freeze frame. The sequence was repeated five times before all agreed that my decision was correct. That day I walked on to the field ten feet tall!

My final Test was the 1975 Boxing Day fixture at the MCG when 86 000 people turned up on the opening day to see Australia play the West Indies. It was after this Test that I resigned from umpiring, due to scathing criticism by West Indies captain Clive Lloyd. Not only did I not agree with his assessment of my performance, but I felt that Clive handled the facts with remarkable carelessness. What made me decide to get out was my loss of faith with the ACB, as I believed it was a miscarriage of justice to allow Lloyd, after losing another Test, to write articles for newspapers blasting me when he had use of the correct channels to make his views known (the captain's report, for one), while the board refused me the right of reply through those same newspapers. All of this came after being told by the board's secretary, Alan Barnes: 'Don't worry, Jack, we're 100 per cent behind you'. What he meant was, 'one hundred miles behind you, running the other way.'

The problems with Lloyd started in that Melbourne Test of 1975 when I gave eight of the ten West Indies batsmen out in their first innings of 224. Jeff Thomson had a peculiar way of placing his front foot in line with, but just over, the popping crease in his delivery stride. Yet by the time he delivered the ball with his slinging action, that front foot had straightened with the heel shuffled back behind the line. This built-in self-correction to the over-stepping tended to happen when Thommo was warmed up and well into his spell, and it was not being fully seen by the backing-up batsman, Roy Fredericks. Roy saw the original 'misdemeanour', but, as he looked up to see his partner play his shot, missed the correcting movement as the 'offending' foot straightened and cut the line. Suddenly, Roy was complaining, 'Hey, he's bowling no-balls.' If only he'd held his gaze a fraction longer, Roy would have seen that in the moment of releasing the ball, Thommo was complying with the MCC Law 26, as it then stood: 'The umpire at the bowler's end wicket shall call and signal "no ball" if he is not satisfied that in the delivery stride some part of the front foot, whether grounded or raised, was behind the popping crease'. I felt that as part of Jeff's front foot was grounded behind the crease at the moment of delivery, he had fulfilled the law as it then stood. But when Fredericks was dismissed (caught off Thommo for the top score of 59), he obviously told Lloyd and his team-mates about what he had seen. One after the other, the Windies' batsmen made the same complaint. It certainly didn't put me in a good light with the captain and, added to the eight dismissals I gave in that innings, a persecution complex was built up, which carried over into World Series Cricket.

I believe the decision that most upset Lloyd was his own dismissal, after he had nicked Thommo to Greg Chappell at second slip. Chappell toppled backwards, apparently clutching the ball into his groin area. I knew Lloyd had made contact, but as his rival captain had both legs in the air, his knees at about his chin, I couldn't actually see the ball. So my decision took longer than usual and was given only after I'd requested, 'Show me the ball'. Greg reached into what seemed like the same groin area and held the ball up, to which I responded, 'That's out. Caught.'

I assume Lloyd thought that because my decision had taken longer than usual, I must have been guessing. In fact, I had wanted to ensure the catch had been completed before making what I still believe was the correct decision. I had covered every avenue, which is as it should be. When Australia batted, Bernard Julien, bowling left arm over the wicket, thundered one into Gary Cosier's pads and appealed for lbw. No doubt it would have hit the stumps; equally no doubt it had pitched outside the leg stump. It didn't help my standing with Mr Lloyd that Cosier turned this let-off into his maiden Test century.

It further irked Clive Lloyd, as he made clear in his newspaper column, that I had not given Jeff Thomson out lbw to Lance Gibbs. (The ball stood an extremely good chance of missing leg stump.) That decision didn't please Gibbs either. He nearly broke one of my fingers when he snatched his cap from my grasp at the end of the over. I decided not to hold his cap any more and spent some time planning a brilliant speech to be delivered before his next over. But Gibbs moved straight back to his bowling mark with the cap tucked into the waist band at his back. Round two to Gibbs. A few days after this third Test, I was a guest speaker at the Sandringham Football Club and, upon arrival, found that Lance Gibbs was also on the speaking panel. When his turn came, I found I was again in trouble, this time for allowing Dennis Lillee to bowl a bouncer at him, a tail-ender. I had to wait some time before I could speak, and made the point that I was not a mind-reader (as he had been in anticipating I wouldn't hold his cap) and that included the mind of D. K. Lillee! All I could do – and I had done – was to warn Lillee against repeating the dose.

I was particularly incensed by the passage in Lloyd's article which stated: 'We are not people who cheat [in appeals] and it got to the stage where our players were getting upset'. That, combined with allegations in the same article that I had made too many errors, seemed to imply that I was a cheat. This unwarranted criticism, coupled with the lack of promised support, played a large part in my resigning in disgust from the

ACB establishment. In hindsight, I suppose I could have handled it differently. But one good thing to come out of it was that it enabled me to begin another era of my umpiring career with World Series Cricket, for which I am forever thankful.

In 1977 I was appointed by WSC's umpires appointment board to stand in the first WSC 'Supertest' at Waverley, Australia v. West Indies. The establishment outfits of both nations had crossed to the new regime in bulk, and they were arguably the strongest sides of either country since Sir Donald and his Invincibles departed the scene in 1948.

All was going well in the first Supertest until Viv Richards, on 79 and in sight of the first WSC century, nicked a ball from David Hookes to Rod Marsh; straight into the gloves and out again, only to get caught in a flap of Rodney's pads.

With both gloves around the flap, Marshie took two paces backwards and on the third pace he sat down on the turf, enabling the ball to drop to the ground. Hookes appealed and as I considered that the ball had been in the 'keeper's control long enough, I said, 'That's out, caught.' But Rodney walked down the track and said, 'Jack, the ball fell out.' I answered, 'Yes, I know, thanks, Rod, but it's still out caught.' At this point, I looked at Viv, who was chewing his gum in typically nonchalant fashion, and not moving. So I said, 'You're out, caught,' with exactly the same result. No movement.

Phew! I looked at my watch for help. Luckily, it said two-minutes-to-lunch. I said, loudly, 'Time!', removed the bails and walked off for a snack. Soon after Sang Hue and I had entered the umpires' room there was a loud knock on the door and Clive Lloyd walked in. He got right down to business, asked me to cancel my decision and recall Richards. I replied that I couldn't do that, as such a reversal would have to be done prior to us leaving the playing arena, so it was too late and I considered the catch to have been well and truly completed. Then as we left the room, I heard some strange noises to my right, and there was the entire list of West Indies players wailing against the concrete wall. I started towards them, but was sent away by their manager, Rudi Webster. Bemused, we headed for the dining room for lunch. The first person I ran into was Kerry Packer, who said, 'Jack, what's that strange noise?' I replied that it was the West Indies players doing an imitation of Jews at the Wailing Wall. Kerry was more amazed than amused. After a hurried meal, we made ready to go out again, but before doing so went into the West Indies' rooms. Packer was already there, telling them in no uncertain terms they could either shape up or he would ship them out immediately! So after one session of Supertests, it was nearly the end of WSC. Fortunately, the Windies plumped for the former of the Packer options and sanity prevailed.

In our second, and final, season of WSC we toured the North Island of New Zealand, where I was told a story by a Kiwi umpire that stuck in my memory. It was during a grade game he had just umpired, and he had given a batsman out, caught by the 'keeper, when the captain of the fielding side demanded that he recall the batsman. After much pressure, he acceded to this request and allowed the man to resume his innings. The batsman then advanced his score from 3 to the 80s in very quick time and, with the game slipping away from the fielding side, the captain brought himself on to bowl. On the fifth ball of the over he struck the batsman on the pads and appealed vociferously from about three feet in the air. After the bowler had returned from orbit, the umpire declared, 'If you bloody well want to get him out, you can get him out your bloody self,' or adjectives to that effect. Which I felt, under the circumstances, was a classic reply.

Although its tight schedules made WSC demanding on mind and body, the experience wasn't lacking in lighter moments. While in Sydney I was called into headquarters and asked to go to Coffs Harbour. As the newspapers were suggesting rain, my assignment was to ascertain whether the weather would be fine for two rostered one-day fixtures matching the Cavaliers against Australia and the World XI. It was thought an accurately gloomy forecast from a 'man on the ground' (me) might save travel and accommodation expenses for three visiting teams and support staff.

I left early on a Saturday morning and reached Coffs Harbour before lunch. Obviously I had no idea of weather patterns or conditions in the banana-fringed NSW coastal city so, after booking into a motel, I walked to the nearest pub for lunch and noticed some old-timers at the bar. After my meal I went over and introduced myself to one of them. Soon enough our conversation turned to the weather (it was raining when I entered the city and still was), and I explained my task and my dilemma. 'Come outside, I'll show you,' the old chap said, then looking up through the mist, added, 'When you have difficulty seeing those hills, it will rain for a week.'

Now, I could barely see them, but as this was Saturday and the first match was not until next Friday, I felt that more research was needed. After all, I didn't have to report back to Sydney until 10 a.m. on Monday. So, clearly, I needed to talk to more locals. I don't know how many pubs there are in Coffs Harbour, but I inspected most, if not all of them, that afternoon and evening to conduct my 'weather research'. And all I heard was confirmation of that first prognostication.

Next day, Sunday, I hired a car to take in the wet scenery during the morning, then parked it to continue my research in the afternoon. On Monday morning I phoned the Sydney office to tell them it was extremely likely it would rain for a week, then began crossing my fingers. I was incredulous that here I was cancelling a match four days out from its coin-toss – surely some sort of arcane cricket record. The office thanked me for my report and said I'd done such a fine job I wouldn't be required in Sydney until next Thursday afternoon, which left me free to visit my new haunts and, as the rain tumbled down outside, to thank my research assistants. Back in Sydney I kept a check of the newspapers and, while I enjoyed some further R and R, was delighted that it rained in Coffs Harbour for ten whole days after my visit.

By the start of the 1979–80 home season, both WSC and I were ready to quit. It had been an honour and a privilege to umpire at the highest levels, both in Tests and WSC at a time of such sweeping changes in the game and when the standard was so high. Just look at the quality of players who made up the three WSC sides:

AUSTRALIA: Ian, Greg and Trevor Chappell, Ian Davis, Ross Edwards, Doug Walters, Ian Redpath, Kepler Wessels, David Hookes, Martin Kent, Bruce Laird, Rob Langer, Ric McCosker, Rod Marsh, Richie Robinson, Gary Gilmour, Dennis Lillee, Len Pascoe, Max Walker, Mick Malone, Wayne Prior, Kerry O'Keeffe and Ray Bright.

WORLD XI: Tony Greig, Alan Knott, Dennis Amiss, Derek Underwood; Barry Richards, Eddie Barlow, Garth Le Roux, Clive Rice, Mike Procter; Zaheer Abbas, Asif Iqbal, Imran Khan, Javed Miandad, Sarfraz Nawaz and Mushtaq Mohammed.

WEST INDIES: Clive Lloyd, Derek Murray, Roy Fredericks, Gordon Greenidge, Desmond Haynes, Viv Richards, Lawrence Rowe, Michael Holding, Andy Roberts, Joel Garner, Bernard Julien and Collis King.

Because there were two games being played at any one time, there was also a Cavaliers team, which enabled the spare team to play matches in the country. The Cavaliers were made up of players not selected in the No. 1 Australian team and also had the benefit of some late inclusions, not named on my list.

With such an array of talent, you can see why I say umpiring in WSC was a wonderful experience. In all, I stood in six Supertests, including both grand finals, in the first day/night games under lights at Waverley and the Sydney Cricket Ground, and was also one of the first umpires to don coloured clothing and adjudicate matches played with a white ball.

After WSC, I returned to umpiring in the VCA in 1979–80, but lasted only two seasons as I wasn't enjoying it as much as previously. In fact, I felt I wasn't accepted – no doubt due to the Packer era and my part in it. Approached to become president of the Sunshine Cricket Club in the Victorian Sub-District Association, I gladly took it on at the start of the 1982–83 season. In my second summer there, I invited my mate and mentor Bill Smyth to be guest speaker at our clubrooms, instructing the barman to 'look after him'. Everyone enjoyed his usual, extremely entertaining speech, but later it was obvious Bill had drunk heartily, and as he lived across the other side of town in Mentone, I told him not to drive home but to leave his car at the club and come back to my place where he could take a shower and sleep in our caravan. Early next morning, I went out to the van to wake him up for breakfast, but he had gone, leaving the caravan in a terrible mess, mattress and blankets piled on to the floor, the drawers open and contents strewn about. It looked as though the van had been hit by a hurricane, or had Bill wrestled a crocodile in his sleep? I drove to the club. His car was gone, which surprised me as I didn't think he'd be able to find it, let alone drive home. I was worried about him and phoned him repeatedly without an answer. Finally, in the late afternoon, he answered, sounding as fit as a fiddle and apologising to my tentative question about what had gone on in the van. He had woken up, he said, and couldn't find one of his socks. So he had to search for it – an understatement – but had given up and driven home, falling asleep on his couch before getting up to take a shower. Only then did he discover the awful truth – that he had both socks on his left foot. Perhaps it was just as well he'd stayed over.

I'm quite fond of the amber fluid myself, and admit frothy beverages crop up frequently in the list of forty-four different excuses compiled by my wife, Dorothy, allegedly tendered by her husband following late arrivals home after cricket matches and/or functions. Among the forty-four 'excuses' (actually, reasons) are:

1. Not enough people at the club so he had to stay to help drink the quota.
2. Umpires took each other's gear by mistake; had to retrieve same.
3. Took his brother Peter, who later became an umpire, to a match. Everyone wanted to shout him a drink and you can't walk out on people when they're being generous.
4. Players used up all the hot water in the showers; had to wait for water to heat up again.

5. Had to wait for angry crowd to leave ground.
6. Bob Figgis insisted on Jack staying back; Bob too big to argue with.
7. Ian Stewart, one of the few very non-drinking umpires, kept talking. 'Just too nice a guy to walk out on.'

The ultimate experience for Dorothy was when she took our six school-age sons to the MCG. At the close of play, she and the boys were asked to wait in the car a few minutes. At 9 p.m., three hours after stumps, Dorothy records, her husband arrived, offering the excuse: 'I couldn't come any sooner because the umpires paid for the beer and we had to make sure it was finished off'.

In September 2000, I was invited by the VCA Umpires' Association to the University of Melbourne for the annual Bill Smyth Award dinner at which recognition was to be given to the VCA's 'Game of the Century'. And that turned out to be the 1965–66 district final of Northcote against Essendon. The players of both sides were there, as were the umpires, Bill Smyth and me. That match was probably my own personal choice as well, being shared perhaps with the Rest of the World game in which I had had the best view in the stadium of Sobers's epic innings. But that 1965–66 final was an epic, too, and still the benchmark of memorable VCA finals. Essendon was odds-on, with a star-studded line-up including Ian Monks as captain, and Shield players John Grant (who was the best all-rounder in district cricket), John Swanson, Keith Kirby, Daryl Foster (later WA coach), and Essendon VFL footballers Greg Brown and Barry Davis. The team had lost just one game leading into the final. Northcote had Ken Walker, Frank Brew (who played Australian Rules football for South Melbourne) and, of course, the Test team's opening batsman, Bill Lawry.

Essendon won the toss and batted at the picturesque Albert Ground, beside the tree-lined boulevard of St Kilda Road. Ian Monks compiled an excellent 136 and all but one batsman contributed; there were two scores in the 60s, two in the 50s, three in the 30s, and a 20-odd, and Monks was able to declare at tea on the second day, at 9/514. Now, one would think that Northcote would have been down in the dumps with a target of 515 to chase. But when I went to their rooms I heard Lawry saying to his players, 'If there is someone out there with me at the finish, we will win this final.' Talk about confidence, but my first thought was, 'Bull'.

Soon after the start of the Northcote innings, Lawry was beaten by a Grant delivery that left him, and he was caught in the slips. Luckily for Bill, I had my arm out, signalling 'no-ball'. Northcote finished the day on 0/98, but still had an enormous task ahead.

Next day, before a formidable crowd packed into the pocket-handkerchief ground, Northcote lost 3 wickets and was on 219 when nineteen-year-old Tom Ryan came to the wicket. At this stage, Lawry's concentration seemed to desert him. In a fiery over from Grant, he gave a difficult chance to Ken Adams at slip, was caught behind off another no-ball, then slashed a four high over slips, before settling down again. I have read that Lawry never grinned. Well, he gave me a big, cheesy one after I'd signalled 'no-ball' to save him for the second time, and he said, 'Jack, it's not a bad game after all.' He guided Ryan, with plenty of conferences, to ultimately 82, and when bad light drove the players from the field on that third day, Northcote was 3/405 (Lawry on 236, Ryan 77).

As the match had gone for three days, arrangements had to be made for a fourth day, and I received a call from the VCA to see if it was okay to finish it on Thursday evening. I said I didn't mind, but when they contacted Lawry, I'm told he said, 'Thursday is for practice; Saturday is for playing.' So Saturday it was, even though it was the opening of the VFL football season. Tom Ryan was out early for his 82, but Frank Brew came to the crease and belted 47 off 56 balls to hasten Northcote to 5/516 and a remarkable victory.

Although the Essendon bowling didn't quite match the Test team's level, Lawry's 282 not out was, in some respects, close to being on a par with Sobers's 254. As the players were leaving the ground, the Essendon 'keeper, Tommy O'Neill, ran up to Lawry, tapped him on the shoulder and, when he turned around, said, 'So that's what you look like. All I've seen the last three days is your bloody arse.'

I used to drink in Footscray at the Albert Hotel where many happy times were spent discussing cricket and footy with the patrons, who included Rex Whitehead (Shield and Test umpire), Keith Butler (Shield umpire) and many leading cricketers, footballers and umpires in both codes. One of the patrons was a chap who was the social organiser for Pentridge Prison, and I was asked to officiate with my brother Peter, a VCA first-eleven umpire, at a match between a team from the Albert Hotel and the prison.

It was an extremely hot day, and when we arrived at Pentridge we were escorted through two huge, barred gates, searched and taken to the ground. Then the prisoners arrived. I couldn't believe my eyes. They were all in what must have been regulation dress: running shoes, shorts and tattoos. Now, in racing, you have some jockeys in the all-white colours of the club, but this was the all-blue colours of the prison. Some even appeared to have had their tattoos tattooed. The 'Federation blue' hair style Colin Miller wore in the Sydney Test against the West Indies had nothing on these guys. I had never seen so much blue skin and had to conclude that the richest man in Pentridge would be the tattoo artist.

The game was played on a Sunday, and it was obvious that some of the 'Albert' lads hadn't got over Saturday night. So they decided to play sixteen against the regulation eleven prisoners. After winning the toss, the pub side naturally batted, as you do in extreme heat. The captain of the prisoners looked to be well into his fifties, but was very fit. He opened the bowling from my end and was rather quick. His first ball hit the batsman over the heart, and he collapsed in a heap. He staggered to his feet, but was hit on his body with the next two deliveries, and it was obvious he wasn't seeing them too well. He was also breathing heavily and looked as though he'd had a late night. His next breath was a big sigh of relief when he hung his bat out to the fourth ball and was caught behind.

The other opening bowler was young, and even quicker and meaner. A real tearaway. I sensed the pub boys would rather be somewhere else – probably the pub – as their departure from the wicket, in rapid succession, was a lot more jaunty than their arrival. After about eight overs, I plucked up the courage to inquire of the Pentridge captain (who I found out was well into his sixties), 'Fred, you're a bit old for this caper, aren't you?'

With a big grin on his face, he replied: 'Jack, every time I get out of this place, they bring me back to captain the f—ing cricket side.'

When the wardens produced some sandwiches and drinks

for a tea break, the other opening bowler approached me and said, 'Jack, the pub doesn't seem to have many fit bowlers, so I'd like to bowl for them.' When I asked him why, he replied, 'Oh, I owe some of these bastards some return favours.' To which 100 per cent of the pub wholeheartedly agreed.

If I thought he'd had plenty of fire in the first innings, you should have seen the young quick in the prisoners' innings! It was a little like ten pin bowling. Unfortunately for the Albert, the bowling from the other end left a little to be desired, but it was interesting to watch the new 'contest' that was between the prisoner-batsmen trying to be at the non-facing end for the start of the tearaway's overs.

The ground was next to the maximum-security Jika-Jika section, with high stone walls and wire enclosure overhead. Every so often we could see a head and some fingers at the top of the wall. They were watching the game . . . until a loud voice ordered, 'Get down off the wall or we'll shoot.' No more heads appeared. The ground was close to one exterior wall of the prison, and the ball was hit over the wall several times. Not surprisingly, numerous prisoners volunteered to fetch it.

While one prisoner settled some old scores, the prisoners also won. At the end of the match, the prisoners were lined up with guards around them to be marched back to their cells. As they left us, one idiot from the pub yelled out to them, nearly causing a riot and inducing much work for the wardens: 'See you later, fellows. We're going back to the Footscray Cricket Club for a barbecue and two eighteens.'

We weren't invited back for a return match.

Like a lot of umpires who stood in the days before electronic aids came on the scene, I am not a big admirer of them. Before their arrival, umpires had to adjudicate on close run-outs. Normally, if the decision was by up to four to five inches (101–127 mm), at normal speed it could be called 'dead heat', so the umpire would be justified in saying 'not out'. However, with the aid of a camera for run-outs, stumpings and hit-wicket, it is evident that the umpires have become both lazy and frightened to make a decision, particularly when the distance is about 2 feet to 2 feet 6 inches (61–76 cm). They often call for the camera because they're frightened of making a mistake. This indecision can't do any good for the confidence of the umpires.

I was at the MCG for the Boxing Day Test in the 2000–01 Australia–West Indies series and noticed that the umpires now don't have to count the number of balls in the over, as it is all on the scoreboard – exactly as the scorers would tabulate, with dot balls, no-balls, wides and scores (1, 2, 3, 4, etc.) all laid out electronically. I would hate to see cricket become more and more like American football which, to me, is far too stop/start due to television, with the umpires having to speak into their microphones to explain their decisions to the audience. Cricket has enough stop/start moments: after each over; and even after each ball. So this indecision will only magnify if the mooted leg-before-wicket technology is introduced. I believe the electronics were introduced as aids to umpiring, not to replace umpires.

If the authorities are to continue with the use of cameras, they must ensure that every eventuality is covered. We don't want a repetition of the situation that occurred in the fifth Test in Sydney 2000, when Brian Lara claimed a catch off Justin Langer and the third umpire had to declare it 'not out', because there was no camera for the side-on view, or the view was blocked by players, or the cameras were not working at the time.

In my thirty years of umpiring, I had plenty of opportunities to evaluate the performance of captains, and I have no hesitation in saying that I couldn't envisage a better captain than Ian Chappell. He was head and shoulders above the rest.

'Chappelli' was able to inspire his team to great heights; he read the game superbly; and would never send others out to do the tough jobs – such as batting on a sticky wicket or coming in when his side was in trouble – when he could do them himself. Ian was a magnificent team man, who, through his ability to create a wonderful camaraderie between his team-mates, inspired individual players to reach their maximum potential.

Cricket has been very good to me. I achieved much more than I expected, but the greatest thrill it provided was in affording me the chance to meet so many people I wouldn't have met otherwise: the players, officials, parliamentarians, media and, of course, my fellow umpires. But if there's one person to whom I owe my umpiring success, it is Bill Smyth. In fact, I used to feel sorry for any umpire who missed out on the honour and privilege of officiating with him. In my mind, and many others', Bill was simply the best.

Of course, there were exceptions to the generally good times. On one occasion, I was relaxing in the MCG umpires' room after a Victoria–MCC match when a fellow umpire, Ken Collicoat, who wasn't officiating in this game, came up to me and said, 'Jack, I'd like you to meet Bob Hawke.' I turned around to shake hands with him, but when Bob saw my face he said, 'You – you bastard!' I thought he must have been addressing someone behind me so turned around. To see a concrete wall. I got the impression the future prime minister was referring to me.

So I said, 'What's your problem?'

Bob replied, 'I used to play for Melbourne thirds, and you gave me out lbw.'

Naturally, I countered with, 'If I gave you out lbw it must have been plumb,' and turned around to continue my conversation. Hawkie could be a prickly bugger.

The WSC's twentieth anniversary reunion and black-tie dinner at Channel Nine's headquarters in Willoughby, Sydney, on 12 December 1997, kicked off one of the most memorable weekends of my life. It was great to meet up with the players of seven nations, the officials and the media personalities who contributed to the WSC adventure, and it's probably the highest compliment you can pay any reunion to say, 'I hope we do it again'.

JACK COLLINS'S UMPIRING CV

37 first-class matches between December 1965 and December 1975

Finished in World Series Cricket in February 1979

Official Test matches – 5 (Australia v. Pakistan 2, New Zealand 2, West Indies 1)

Unofficial Test matches – 2 (Australia v. Gary Sobers's World XI 1)

Bushfire Challenge Test – 1

Victoria v. Internationals – 7

Sheffield Shield matches – 25

Packer's World Series Supertests – 6

Other World Series Cricket matches – 35

Steve Dunne
Kiwi Globe-trotter

Umpiring international cricket takes you to some strange places. Strange geographically, with matches bobbing up in the most unlikely locations; strange, too, in the situations you can be thrown into.

On my return from Nagpur, in India, at the end of November 2000, I had umpired in ninety-three one-day internationals and thirty-six Tests in nine of the ten Test-playing countries, but none of those matches quite prepared me for my trip to Toronto in September 1999, for one of those one-day series that have proliferated around the world and that have a shelf life in the collective cricket memory of not much longer than their one-day duration.

That year, Australia's Daryl Harper, South African David Orchard and I (from Dunedin, in New Zealand's deep south) had been selected to umpire matches between the competing nations, India, Pakistan and the West Indies, in, of all places, Toronto, the State capital of the province of Ontario, in Canada.

For chaps like me, and the players, these one-day hit-outs are the most relaxed form of international cricket. This was my second trip to Toronto, and I've also had five to Sharjah in the Persian Gulf for what may be the umpires' equivalent of the footballers' end-of-season trip. In both these places, there is no 'home' side, but each has a great many expat Indians, Pakistanis and Sri Lankans; and without the home-town pressure, the cricket tends to be played without the intensity of matches in the Test-playing countries.

In Toronto in 1999, the media, led by the television company doing the series, TWI, was keen to play a game of cricket against the tournament host, the Toronto Cricket, Skating and Curling Club. Keen as it was, the club was short on numbers, so Daryl Harper and I were roped in to play. Our side batted first and gave the media a good total to chase. A couple of decades had gone by since I'd done it, but I took the new ball with the wind behind me – and I wasn't even captain. It impressed me even more that I was taking the shine off the ball for former West Indian firebrand and now first change, Colin Croft. My first five balls were straight and quickish; I had warmed up well for my first competitive bowl in seventeen years, and I thought the umpire erred in turning down my two shouts for lbw, especially given that I'd told him before play started that I'd only appeal for the ones that were out. You just can't help some people! The setbacks must have fired me up, for in trying to bowl the sixth ball of this opening over, I tore a groin muscle and couldn't complete the over. In many years of playing cricket and rugby I had never experienced such an injury. Gee, it was sore!

About ten minutes later, the said Croft bowled a quicker one, the batsman edged it wide of slip. Daryl Harper, who was more third man than slip and, it must be said, dozing on his feet, turned sharply to chase it and promptly tore his hamstring. Next day, Daryl and I were the two men in the middle, and both the Pakistanis and Windies found it quite amusing that both umpires moved like men half-mummified in trying to carry out their duties.

I'd have to admit that cricket in the United Arab Emirates is a little different – often about two pullovers different – from the variety played in my home town of Dunedin. To illustrate: in 1988–89, on the first three days of my first Test match scheduled for my home turf of Carisbrook, Steve Woodward and I watched as rain fell steadily. It cleared overnight, making play possible, albeit with a late start, on day four. But the local officials, fearing there would be very few spectators to watch a match so severely truncated, and with the consent of New Zealand Cricket and the touring Pakistani management, cancelled the Test and opted for an ODI, my first one-day international. I had to wait until the following weekend to do my first Test, and what was supposed to be the second Test, became the series' first.

It doesn't rain but it pours! A decade later, I was rostered to umpire New Zealand's first Test against India, again in Dunedin, and the same thing happened, only this time it rained for the first four days. The Test was cancelled, and we made a bit of cricket history, playing an ODI on the fifth day using a red ball under lights. So my home town has given me the dubious honour of being the only umpire to officiate in more than one Test in which not a ball was bowled.

Just as I know there's life after cricket – and my umpiring career is almost at an end – there was life before. It began for me at the family home in Russell Street on 22 April 1943, and contrary to popular belief among some players, my parents were married at the time and this happy event had taken place in August 1938.

I was the middle one of their three sons, each of us four years apart and sharing an inner-city environment, a Catholic education and very few luxuries, being, as we were, at the poorer end of 'middle-class'. But we were always well fed and clothed by a mother who doted on her sons and made us her total life.

The name Dunne, with the 'e', is Irish. My lot left Dublin in 1854 for Melbourne, where my great-grandfather, James Dunne, became headmaster of St Francis school in the CBD's Elizabeth Street. He taught until 1883 when his employment was abruptly terminated. His record shows it was because he was found 'being drunk on a Sunday'. I ask you, what true Irishman won't have a drink on a Sunday? Anyway, great-grandad promptly left Melbourne and joined his family, some of whom had already moved to Dunedin across the Tasman. After arriving there, James Dunne did not go back to teaching, but bought a book shop in the city's George Street and spent the rest of his life as a bookseller.

After a primary education at St Joseph's, I moved next door in 1953 to Christian Brothers High School for my Standard 3 year. In the local patois, my initiate classmates and I were 'stinkers'. The education budget must have been stretched because I found myself in a class of sixty, and the only winter sport available was rugby. Playing it was compulsory. The only way out was to bring a note from a parent offering a valid medical or religious reason to be excused. Two of the sixty managed this and the rest of us, as kids are wont to do, considered the pair to be sissies and told them so in a continuing stream of ridicule. One of those boys with a medical reason was John McLeod, who many years later (around a decade ago) had a heart transplant. He's still doing well and I hope he feels thoroughly vindicated.

In Standard 4 the next year, no longer a 'stinker', I made the acquaintance of cricket. My older brother Michael and his friends would come round to our house after school and during the school holidays to play this game which I took to immediately. My father would join in quite often, as would I when allowed. Being four years younger, my value – and I'm sure it's the only reason I was allowed to play – was in being made to fetch the ball whenever it went over the fence into the neighbours' yard. They didn't have dogs, but had they done so, I'm sure they'd have set them on to me those numerous times I flattened their carefully tended flower beds.

Initially, I struggled against these older boys. But the more you play in older company, the more you learn, first to survive, then to compete; and I did. Our pitch at Russell Street was unique. Sixteen yards long, only three feet wide, with the house so close on one side there were no runs to be had on the on side for the right-hander, as I was. But there was a generous off side where you could cut and drive and edge. The edge, thick and thin, was my most productive shot.

Brother Michael bowled extremely fast, usually off about fourteen yards, always no-balling, and he swung the tennis ball both ways. It was hard to survive, let alone score off, but the success he had with that tennis ball made me determined to bowl fast. And so my way in cricket was determined.

As chance would have it, Sir Len Hutton's 1954–55 team had arrived in Australia and for the first time in New Zealand we were getting ball-by-ball commentaries of the Test series. I wanted the Aussies to win and my heroes were Ray Lindwall and Keith Miller with the ball, and Arthur Morris with the bat. Michael backed the Poms and especially their quicks, Frank Tyson and Brian Statham, and so, naturally, our backyard games became pretty spirited Ashes contests. The success of Tyson in that series is legendary and Michael and I decided if he could do it, so could we rip through sides by bowling fast. A few times, we did. Michael didn't stay in the game long after leaving school, mainly because of muscle problems in his legs, but I managed to kick on. No doubt the Russell Street 'Ashes' were the start of my great love of the game, and of bowling fast.

I played all through high school mainly as a fast bowler, but also wielding the bat with occasional good effect, and I was chosen for Otago, my province, in most of the age groups. No doubt my best showing was for Otago under-16s, which I captained against Canterbury, immediately to our north, in a two-day match. It was played on Dunedin's North Ground and the first day was rained out, but it cleared up enough to allow a single innings match on day two. I won the toss, and we batted. Leading from the front, or so I thought, I went in at No. 3, scored a single, then belted a big full toss down square leg's throat. It set a trend. We were all out for 76. Then we bowled. I took the wind (one of the advantages of being captain) and we dismissed Canterbury for 70. After this effort, my bowling career was bound to be downhill on the way to an anti-climax: I bowled unchanged that afternoon and took all 10 wickets for 11 runs. A week later, and unbeknown to me, someone decided to have the ball inscribed and presented to me at school. The school's staff and 700 boys duly assembled, and the presentation was to be made by the president of the local umpires' association, a Mr Beal, who just happened to have been the umpire at my end while I took the 10 wickets, which included four lbw's and two caught behinds.

Mr Beal had umpired without spectacles, and arrived to make the presentation, again without them. The headmaster told the full assembly of what was about to happen and then passed the inscribed ball to Mr Beal, asking him to read the inscription out and make the presentation. Mr Beal responded with: 'I can't see without my glasses.' As one, the whole school roared with laughter. As one, with the possible exception of me.

Leaving high school meant joining the North East Valley club in Dunedin. What a thrill! At the age of seventeen I went straight into the firsts and became a team-mate of the great Test match batsman Bert Sutcliffe. Although then getting on in years, Bert was still a prolific run scorer, both in first-class and club cricket. I very quickly learnt that our side had only one batsman, and if Bert got runs, we got runs. If Bert didn't get them, the scorers were in for an easy afternoon. My first match in first grade was against the top club, Albion YMCA.

We batted second and, thanks mainly to Bert, made around 240 after having bowled out Albion for 120. On the second day, Albion smartened up and were out for 210 right on the tea break. So we had to score 90-odd to win outright. We had plenty of time and weather wasn't a factor (yes, the sun does visit Dunedin). We sat down for afternoon tea and, to my amazement, Bert produced four half-gallon jars of the local beer, Speights, for the team to consume. We managed to do this without any trouble at all. Again thinking laterally, Bert announced the batting order was to be reversed since we needed only 90-odd. His inspired decision quickly had us at 5/25, then 7/35. Bert, now realising we had problems, promoted himself from ten to nine, but it was all too late. We were dismissed well short of the nugatory target and I went home that night wondering whether this was the norm for senior cricket. Fortunately, it wasn't and our captain never again fiddled with the batting order or primed us with ale at the tea break!

By the time the national under-23 tournament was played in Dunedin a few seasons later, I had learned that pace was not everything, especially on the slow, dampish tracks we usually played on in New Zealand's deep south. And the Dunedin tracks produced for this week-long tournament suited us admirably. Bowling a bit slower, seam up, our seam attack was too good for most and we comfortably won the tournament. My reward was a place in the national under-23 team that went on to play Wellington, who had just won NZ's main domestic competition for the Plunket Shield. It was my first first-class match, and a couple of seasons later I played my one and only full season of first-class cricket for Otago. Without distinction, I might add, in a team that was comfortably second-last in the first-class competition and really failed to compete against most sides.

I continued to play senior club cricket until the early 1980s, having led the club to its first premiership, until the continually worsening sore backs each Sunday after the previous day's bowling made me realise my time as a player was up. Over the previous four or five years I had had thoughts of umpiring, and now that I'd made the decision to stop bowling, it became a very easy decision to add the umpire's black trousers to the player's all-white ensemble.

The second half of the winter of 1983 was spent studying the Laws of Cricket and attending weekly meetings run by the local umpires for the purpose of learning the Laws and revising and learning the local playing conditions. And it was only now that I realised how little of either I really understood. I had played twenty consecutive years of senior cricket, captained many sides, debated many points with umpires at all levels of the game, but learnt remarkably little. In these few weeks I learnt more about the Laws of the game than I had since starting competitive cricket in 1954–55. Now I was an umpire, not a player any more, and in October 1983, I stepped out in the white coat for the first time.

In that first season, I umpired first-grade matches in Dunedin; likewise, in my second year when, at very short notice because of the withdrawal of an umpire, I was asked to stand in a 'B' provincial match between Canterbury and Otago. In my third year, I was appointed to the 'B' panel and did three of these second-eleven matches. The fourth season, I made it on to the 'A' panel and did one top-level domestic one-day game, three first-class three-day games and, towards the end of the season, umpired my first international match, West Indies against a Shell XI in Napier.

On day one, overnight rain had left the run-ups damp and the West Indies were not willing to risk injury to their fast bowlers so it was decided between captains Viv Richards and Martin Snedden that regardless of who won the toss, the West Indies would bat. Snedden won, duly declared, 'We'll bowl,' and the game got under way on time.

The track was very fast and bouncy, unusual for New Zealand, and more especially when you consider the quality of the fast bowlers playing in the West Indies team: Patrick Patterson, Joel Garner and Tony Gray.

Three memories remain from that game. The first was the ease and elegance with which Richards scored 117 not out; a brilliant innings. The second was the guts shown by one of the locals, the wicketkeeper Ervin McSweeney in also scoring 117 not out. The West Indies' bowlers pounded many bouncers into the hard and fast track at McSweeney and his colleagues, and McSweeney's only defence was to turn his back on them. From memory, he was hit on the back of the helmet eleven or twelve times. Each time he was hit, he shook his head and fronted up again to wait for one he could drive or cut. A gutsy innings.

The third memory was of a very young and largely unknown fast bowler playing for the Shell XI, Danny Morrison. Morrison opened from my end and generally bowled quite fast. The exception to this was his bouncer, which he bowled at express pace. The West Indies lost T. R. Payne and Larry Gomes very early and Richie Richardson joined Desmond Haynes. As was normal for him, Richardson was not wearing a helmet, just his large, floppy, maroon West Indian hat. Richie had been batting for about fifteen or twenty minutes when Morrison bowled one of his express bouncers. Richardson went for the hook but was too late and was pinned; he dropped like a log.

I called 'dead ball' and raced down the track to try to help and by the time I got there, several of the fielders were clustered around Richardson. The West Indian physio was a Queenslander, Dennis Waight, and he came racing out as quickly as his short, thickset legs would bring him. He arrived in the middle and had a quick look at Richie, who by this time was in a sitting position and looking more alive than I thought possible. To everyone's surprise, Dennis asked for a look at the ball. I gave it to him, he had a quick look at it and then said to Richardson, 'Richie, Richie, it's all right, you have nothing to worry about. You haven't damaged the ball at all, we can continue.' With that, Richie was helped to his feet and Dennis walked off the field laughing his head off. Needless to say Richie batted on and eventually made a very good century.

My fifth season, 1987–88, included an international match

in which Mike Gatting's England played a President's XI in Dunedin. The game, which the visitors won comfortably, was largely uneventful, with one exception. England's attack comprised mainly wicket-to-wicket bowlers Paul Jarvis, David Capel, Neal Radford and, to a lesser degree, Phillip DeFreitas. On a track that suited the medium pacers because it did a bit off the seam and kept low, the President's XI in its second innings declared seven down for 214, and five of the dismissals were lbw, all given by me. Not too often does an umpire give five lbw decisions in one innings. The visitors won comfortably by 8 wickets. As I said, rain somewhat marred my first Test appointment, against Pakistan in Dunedin in 1989, and my only other 'home' Test match, against India, in December 1998. Oddly enough, at the same time as the 1998 Test was to have been played, my Kiwi partner on the International Cricket Council panel, Doug Cowie, was officiating in a Pakistan v. South Africa Test in Faisalabad, where not a ball was bowled either. There, the squelcher was a thick, low fog, which made cricket impossible.

These wet days were not the rule in my career. I've tallied that in my one hundred ODIs and thirty-nine Tests I have witnessed more than 140 000 balls bowled. That means 70 000 were from my end. To look at it another way, since I began umpiring in October 1982, in all grades of cricket I've been in the middle for almost 1000 days, or about a total of two years and eight months. In 1993, the two top-rated umpires from each Test-playing nation (but four from England), making twenty in all, were sent to Coventry, England, to listen to what the ICC had in mind for an independent umpires' panel and to contribute to its formation.

The panel was duly formed, and sponsored by the National

Grid group of power companies. The panel came into being in February 1994, and the first Test played under the new system, between New Zealand and Pakistan at Auckland's Eden Park, brought me into contact for my first and only time with the legendary Harold ('Dickie') Bird. In some ways I had been looking forward to umpiring with Dickie. His greatness could not be disputed. But in other ways I wasn't looking forward to the Test. The word over the past three or four years from the English professionals who were playing in the New Zealand first-class competition was that Dickie was about five years past his best, was now difficult to work with and making a lot more mistakes than previously. Umpiring as a team makes the total job a lot easier, but the current word was that Dickie would expect help when he wanted it but would offer none in return. We would see.

Counting to six sounds simple, but try doing it ninety-plus times each day with everything else that's going on, especially in pressure times, and sometimes you get a little lost between one and six. I know I do. Before the Test started, I suggested to Dickie that we give each other a signal during each over after five balls, just to ensure that we got the count correct through the day. Dickie said he would, and he did: for one over.

During the first two days, without any help from my partner, I managed to get the count wrong in two or three overs and when I'd look over at Dickie after the fifth ball of each over, he would be looking everywhere except at me. I was on my own so I knew my counting would be far from perfect. The match spurts and judders along – the fast bowlers are dominant – and suddenly, late on day two, the umpires rise to an unwelcome prominence. Dickie is at the bowler's end; five balls have been bowled in his over. From square leg, I look at him to give him the signal, if he wants it, that five balls have gone. But he doesn't. He calls, 'Over,' and walks to square leg, oblivious to the fact he's just presided over a five-ball over. I delay walking in to the bowler's end and try to attract his attention to let him know there is still one to come; it's no use. Dickie is now at square leg and not interested in me. No great drama, but it will give one or two in the media something to talk about.

Sure enough, next morning at breakfast, Dickie is distraught. Overnight he's had a phone call at 4 a.m. from a journalist writing a social column back home for one of the big Yorkshire daily newspapers, and this chap wants to do an article on Dickie's five-ball over for his social column. Now, Dickie knows he has got one wrong and someone is wanting to tell the world. He couldn't handle it, and he was a mess. He went on and on and on, *ad infinitum,* about the five-ball over. Had he made a mistake? He couldn't have made a mistake! The cheek of the reporter ringing him! Were we sure it was five balls? Did the reporter not know he normally slept till 6:30 each morning? That journalist would not get any more interviews. Dickie would report him to the Press Council. Could the scorers have made the mistake? etc., etc. The diatribe went on all day, at every break, at every opportunity we had to converse.

It is worth pointing out that on day three, we checked every over with each other and got the count 100 per cent correct. It's amazing how a little teamwork can make our job so much easier. However, Dickie also managed to get a caught behind wrong on day one. Andrew Jones was given out caught off his pad off Mushtaq Ahmed, so this decision became our only topic of conversation on days one and two. With both sides seeming to play it more as two ODIs rather than a Test match, Pakistan won halfway through the afternoon session on day three. The expert fast bowling of Wasim Akram and Waqar Younis, who together took 15 of the 20 New Zealand wickets, greatly contributed to Pakistan's swift passage to a 5-wicket win.

By match end, my ears had taken a real battering. Mercifully, I managed to get the first flight out of Auckland the next morning; my ears could take no more.

Since this Test, I've been fortunate enough to umpire in all the Test-playing countries bar the most recently admitted, Bangladesh, as well as places such as Canada and the United Arab Emirates.

Test cricket is still the toughest form of the game and, in my opinion, it's the best form. But there are always light-hearted moments, no matter how tense the situation. I was at the bowler's end at Faisalabad in October 1997, for example, as Pakistan off-spinner Saqlain Mushtaq bowled to the Springboks' Pat Symcox. Saqlain bowled a straight one, Symcox played for the turn and missed. I heard a noise. Behind the stumps, Moin Khan came up with the ball and let out a huge appeal. 'Not out,' says I. Symcox is laughing and looking at his wicket. He had missed. In fact, the ball had hit the wicket very near the top, passed between the middle and off sticks, pushed the off one a few degrees further to the off, and gone through to Moin. Everyone thought it was a great joke, except for my partner, who came in from square leg, a little embarrassed, to remake the wicket, and Saqlain, who didn't get the wicket he had earned.

Probably the greatest thrill I have had in the eleven most enjoyable years of my cricketing life was umpiring the semi-final of the 1996 World Cup at Eden Gardens, in Calcutta.

Unfortunately, the Cup's opening ceremony, also at Eden Gardens, was a bit of a fizzer. A laser light show, meant to be the night's highlight, was ruined because high winds, which blew throughout, caused the screens to come unfastened and flap about. The result was that very little of the light show was actually seen. After the show was over that night and the crowds had gone, I walked around the ground with Australian umpire Steve Randell. It was the first time there for either of us, and we both thought it a magnificent place, able, as it is, to hold officially 110 000 fans; but add on the thousands who camp in the aisles and wherever they can find a toehold, and the capacity is 120 000. Steve and I agreed that if we could get a semifinal there we'd return home more than content. I was lucky enough to make it, sharing the match with Cyril Mitchley, of South Africa, and Ian Robinson, of Zimbabwe, who was third umpire. Former West Indies captain Clive Lloyd was referee. It was a nightmare getting to, and then into, the ground, and the fact that India was playing meant that every seat, every vantage point was going to be taken. With Sri Lanka as the opposition and plenty of their countrymen present, we were not going to be short on atmosphere.

The stadium was chocker when we started, the noise deafening. I have never heard anything like it, and when Srinath had both openers caught on the third-man fence off balls two and four of his first over, the atmosphere was at fever pitch. Shortly after, Gurusinha was also out cheaply and I'm sure the Indians thought it was over; the Sri Lankans certainly didn't. Aravinda De Silva played the innings of the tournament, stroking the ball to all corners, and he was very well supported by the captain Ranatunga, who nudged and deflected superbly as they achieved a weighty total of eight for 251 on a track that was showing increasing signs of turning square before the night was out. Sure enough, the Indians batted badly, sections of the crowd rioted, and we had to call the match off and award it to Sri Lanka. The crowd was so disappointed with India's inept batting performance, they fired anything and everything they could lay their hands on over the eight-foot-high security wire on to the field of play. They could not be controlled, and that was the game: awarded to Sri Lanka. It was an experience I will never forget; from a cricket point of view, for all the wrong reasons.

The southern 1995–96 season brought me to Melbourne where I stood with Darrell Hair in Melbourne's Boxing Day Test match against Ranatunga's Sri Lankans – the match in which Darrell called Muralitharan seven times for throwing. Yes, I stood at the opposite end to Darrell and did not call the bowler. The whole affair was huge news in all the cricket-playing nations, and continued to make headlines for months after the season had finished. However, time creates new problems, new interests and life moves on. Seldom now do I ever get questioned on the affair. The subject of throwing and/or illegal bowling actions is not one I am prepared to revisit at this point in time, but I would like to point out that at no stage, either then or now, have I received instructions as to what I could or could not say about the incident. The whole affair was done to death at the time and in the months that followed. Let it rest in peace.

Probably the biggest change to the game since I got involved with it is the use of the television camera and the third umpire. Initially, television only showed the game at the pace that we saw it out in the middle, and the directors would usually show a replay after each ball, but when the commentators thought they could fault the umpire, several replays would follow, all at normal speed. I have never had a problem with this; if TV can show that I got one wrong, then I have to wear it. The commentators and the world are privileged to have endless replays, and from eight or nine different angles, and if these can show that one of us has erred . . . then so be it. For all their vast experience, especially at international level, umpires are still fallible; we make mistakes, and if they are shown up, fine. The degree of difficulty in umpiring is immense. Compared to rugby, soccer or basketball, all of which I have umpired/refereed, the degree of difficulty with cricket, in my opinion, is many times greater. I don't say that controlling those other games is easy; it is not, but they are certainly not as difficult as cricket.

However, add in the slow-motion cameras and you have a totally new dimension. The whole world has access to this extra information; out in the middle, we don't. The world often knows more about the delivery than the umpire, yet we are charged with the responsibility of making the decision. This is wrong. If there is more information available, the decision-maker must have access to it before he or they make that crucial decision that will affect the immediate life of the batsman in question and could ultimately impact on the match result. Simply, if the world has access to slow-motion, so should the umpire/s prior to making their decision, if they want it.

This brings me to the point of who controls what the TV stations show. Should they be allowed to show never-ending repeats of something that is considered either wrong or, expressed in the favourite word of the media, 'controversial'? Let's face it, the TV media have their own agenda. Should we in the middle fire out one of the home country batsmen in 'controversial' circumstances, the replays are usually never-ending. Should we give out one of the visitors, again in 'controversial' circumstances, the replays are usually much fewer in number. About five years ago I was in Durban, South Africa, and gave the later-disgraced and banned, and now deceased, Hansie Cronje out caught behind off India's opening bowler, Venkatesh Prasad. Cronje played back to a ball that pitched middle and off, then moved away in the air. As it started to move, Cronje pushed at the ball, there was a nick and 'keeper Mongia behind the stumps did the rest. There was a huge appeal (when isn't the appeal huge when Mongia is involved?). I thought about it and was deliberately slow with the decision because the noise was not as 'sharp' as normal. I replayed the ball in my mind, decided it had to have hit the bat, then put my finger up. Cronje saw the finger and was momentarily slow to leave the crease. No other reaction from him. Obviously, I noticed his hesitation.

Fifteen minutes later we had the first drinks break of the day and ours were brought out by the fourth umpire, Wilf Diedricks. I said to him, 'Hansie was a bit slow going. What did the TV show?' Wilf replied, 'No doubt about it, he nicked it. Good decision'. An hour later we came off for lunch. Wilf walked over and asked me whether I wanted to know more about that decision. 'Yes,' I said. Wilf said it had taken fifteen replays to prove the ball had hit the thigh pad and not the bat. My decision was wrong. I have lived with that, and have no problem with it. In fact, if I had to adjudicate on the same appeal again, seeing and hearing the same things, I would go the same way. But how many replays should be allowed? This was the home-town batsman given out. If it had been a member of the opposition and especially a low-order batsman sent on his way, I wonder how many replays would have been put to air. Should cricket authorities limit the replays, or should the TV companies be free to do what they like? Should cricket decide its destiny, or should TV decide cricket's destiny?

A few years ago when in Toronto umpiring an India–Pakistan series, on one of our days off, I went with referee Peter Burge, of Queensland, and co-umpires Ian Robinson (Zimbabwe) and Peter Manuel (Sri Lanka) to the Toronto Skydome for a night baseball game between the New York Yankees and the Toronto Bluejays. We were lucky enough to be invited to watch it in the hospitality box of the authorities who were running the game, an exciting fixture won by the Yankees. Watching live rather than on the replay screen in our box, I saw the umpire signal that the batter was run out at first base. Far from convinced he was out, the batter was keenly debating with the umpire. I turned to the TV screen in our box to watch a replay, and especially a slow-motion one, to see whether the umpire was right.

But there was no replay, either at normal speed or in slow-motion. I turned to the CEO, who happened to be sitting beside me, and asked: 'Why no replay?' His answer: 'We aren't going to let TV ruin our game.' I hope I have made my point.

Incidentally, after the game was over, we tried to get down to the umpires' dressing room so we could meet the three guys who had officiated. We were told they weren't available. It would have been great to talk to them about the similarities between both games and how they handle the pressures of professional sport. I bet umpires in both codes have many things in common. Pity.

In this India–South Africa Test, the one with the tricky

Cronje decision, I saw the best three consecutive balls I have seen in Test cricket. The track was fast and bouncy, plenty of carry, and the South African 'keeper Dave Richardson was standing miles back to Allan Donald, who was bowling very fast indeed. Not too many of the Indians were interested in getting in behind the ball against the quicks, especially Donald. Dravid and Tendulkar were the exceptions to this, though even the great Tendulkar wasn't having much success.

Donald to Tendulkar: first ball pitches middle and off on a good length, swinging away a little. Tendulkar, playing mainly on the crease line, pushes forward. The swinging ball just beats the outside of the bat. Donald again. Same length as the previous ball, pitching on off and again swinging away a little. Tendulkar, again crease-bound, pushes forward and, remembering the previous ball, a little farther to the off. The ball beats the bat again on the way to Richardson. Third ball: same length, again on off stump, and Tendulkar, conscious he's almost nicked the previous two, pushes forward, even wider. This time the ball comes back off the seam, spearing between bat and pad to take the top off a stump that cartwheels before landing at the feet of Richardson. Brilliant bowling, and cricket at its best.

On 21 November 2000, I set off for Nagpur in India to do the second Test between India and Zimbabwe. Nagpur was not a place I was looking forward to visiting again. I had been there during the 1996 World Cup and found that, apart from the cricket, there was nothing to do. Nowhere to go, nothing to see, or so I thought, and I was not exactly looking forward to the return trip.

What had made it even worse for me was the fact that after

the World Cup match between Australia and Zimbabwe at Nagpur, my next venue was to be Colombo in Sri Lanka where, at the time, the Tamils were waging a bombing campaign. In the interests of my own safety, I decided against going to Colombo three days before my next game, as per my schedule. Rather, I'd go in the day before the match, arriving with the Zimbabwe team, who were to play the locals, and sharing their umbrella of tight security.

A day or two earlier, the Tamils had been reported in the newspapers as saying they wouldn't harm the cricketers. I hoped like heck this included umpires. Still, it seemed to me the safest option was to go in with the Zimbabwe team. Delaying my flight to Colombo meant that I spent eight days and nights in Nagpur with nothing to do or see, so I was not exactly looking forward to going back for twelve days. But I did.

In 1996 there was not a blade of grass on the track, but in 2000 there was plenty of it and the game was played out to a draw on what proved to be a very good wicket. India batted first and three of their order reached three figures: Tendulkar, an undefeated double century, Dravid 150, and a relatively new opening bat, S. S. Das, scored his maiden century. Zimbabwe had to follow on after a sub-standard first innings where Grant Flower's century stood out like a beacon. In their second innings, after being three down for 60 and evidently on the verge of collapse, Al Campbell batted well to score his first century in Test cricket and Andy Flower scored an undefeated double century, which was one of the best Test innings I'd seen in a very long time. Flower played the reverse sweep to perfection against the Indian spinners (their star leg-spinner, Anil Kumble, was out with a shoulder injury) and probably scored as many as ten boundaries with this one shot.

I enjoyed the Test and, much to my surprise, the visit to Nagpur as well. Having Barry Jarman as the referee and A. V. Jayaprakash from Bangalore, in India, as my partner, meant that there was always someone to have a beer and a laugh with, and we all enjoyed most of our time there.

However, there was one day I did not enjoy. I discovered there was some sightseeing to be done about sixty kilometres away where there were some very ancient temples. Being a keen sightseer and impatient with hotel rooms, I decided to pay them a visit. In making this decision, I knew that there were two minor problems to contend with: one, my driver could not speak my language other than four or five words, and I certainly couldn't speak his; and secondly, he had a compelling BO problem. To go sixty kilometres on Indian roads in the vicinity of Nagpur takes about ninety minutes. Could I stand ninety minutes with the car windows down and accept the heat and dust and miss the BO, or was it better to have the windows up and utilise the air-conditioning and accept the BO? I chose the latter, the lesser of two evils.

Before setting out, I asked the hotel staff to instruct the driver where I wanted to go. The staff told me there was a man-made lake/reservoir just beyond the temples. Did I want to go there as well? Yes, I said, and these instructions were relayed to the driver.

We set off. One-and-three-quarter hours later, with my smelling apparatus having been greatly overworked, the driver pointed to a hill in the near distance. 'Temple, temple,' he said and, sure enough, there were these magnificent structures up on the hill. But he didn't stop. He kept going. Perhaps we had to go round behind them to get up to the temples, I thought. Fifteen minutes later we were at the lake, a very ordinary lake if first impressions were correct. We got out and saw some paddle boats, some rather ordinary pleasure craft, and other very ordinary things. 'Boat, boat, ride, ride,' the driver said. He was obviously very proud of this place and wanted me to enjoy what he thought was a great pleasure park and lake. 'Temples,' I insisted. 'I want to see the temples.'

'Yes, yes,' he said. And half an hour later, after he had shown me everything there was to see at the lake, we started back. But by this time my fears about Indian roads were surfacing, especially as it was getting dark and a Test match was due to start the next day. I resigned myself to the fact that I wasn't going to see the temples and that I had wasted three quarters of a day. As we passed the graceful buildings in the gloom on the return journey, my driver reiterated, 'Temple, temple.' My reply was brief and to the point, something along the lines of 'You f—ing idiot, that's where I wanted to go in the first place!' The remainder of the journey passed in silence. Perhaps as well as *speaking* a couple of words of English, he *understood* a couple also. I will never know, but at least I got to the Test on time the next day.

Cricket umpiring as a career was never in prospect when I began my working life. After leaving school at the end of 1960, I went to Otago University and studied for my Medical Intermediate Certificate, a one-year course at the end of which the grades you earned determined whether you qualified for entry into the Medical School the following year. I wanted to be a doctor; a surgeon, in fact. Sadly, sport played a much greater part in my life in 1961 than did studies and my resulting grades were not good enough to gain entry to the Medical School. So medicine was not going to be my career path.

I then studied industrial management and accountancy; I had to, to get a job with McSkimming Industries, which manufactured building bricks and clay sewer pipes. I stayed with this firm for seven years, got sick of it, resigned, took a job as a clothing salesman in 1969 and discovered – and developed – a great interest in fashion. It lasted twenty-four years.

Believing strongly in my own abilities and fashion sense, I started my own clothing business in 1970, both retailing and manufacturing women's fashion clothing. In the mid-1970s, Lesley, my wife, gave up her teaching career, joined me in the business, and took control of the retail side while I controlled the manufacturing. At the height of our success, we employed about eighty people, had sixteen retail stores in the South Island and lower half of the North Island and three in Sydney, and owned our own factory in Dunedin where we designed and manufactured about 80 per cent of the merchandise that the stores sold. It was a large operation by New Zealand standards.

Ever-increasing imports of made-up clothing, mostly from Asia, in the latter half of the 1980s and early 1990s made things increasingly difficult until, in July 1994, we finally closed the doors for the last time, pleased to be finished after not having made a profit since 1992. The clothing trade is extremely volatile; there is only the quick and the dead, and had we not closed down in 1994, we might well have joined the latter.

Lesley went back to teaching and the advent of the ICC panel kept me off the street corners, and so, from July 1994 to the present day, teaching for Lesley and umpiring for me has given us a reasonable income.

My family – Lesley and our sons Michael and John – and

cricket have given me my greatest enjoyment in life. Michael is an account director for a marketing research company, living and working in Wellington, while John works in the security industry in Brisbane where he hopes to establish his own company in the near future.

I've had a marvellous time in cricket, seeing all the best of it from by far the best position to do so. I still cherish my involvement in the game, and am proud of the fact that I have now umpired 104 first-class matches, beating the New Zealand record held by Fred Goodall, who retired at the end of the 1988–89 season after a career that included twenty-four Tests.

To be able to meet and mix with the best cricketers in the world, travel to all the cricket-playing countries, see and officiate at all the famous grounds and, to top it off, to get paid well to do it, has made for a wonderful lifestyle. In fact, I can't understand why anyone with an interest in the game wouldn't want to umpire it.

STEVE DUNNE'S UMPIRING CV

111 first-class matches, from January 1987, and still going

Official Test matches – 39 (NZ v. Australia 3, England 5, West Indies 1, South Africa 2, India 2, Pakistan 7, Sri Lanka 1, Zimbabwe 2; England v. Australia 1, South Africa 3, Zimbabwe 1; Australia v. India 1, Sri Lanka 1; South Africa v. India 1, Pakistan 2, Sri Lanka 1, Zimbabwe 1; West Indies v. Sri Lanka 1; India v. West Indies 1, Pakistan 1, Zimbabwe 1)

International matches (NZ teams against touring sides) – 10

Shell Trophy matches – 62

One-day internationals – 100

Terry Prue
Out of the West

Eighteen years as a player, then just four seasons as an umpire . . . and now here I was, intimately involved with the game at interstate level, supervising the coin-toss for a McDonald's Cup match at the WACA with co-umpire Peter McConnell. So much a novice in December 1982, in fact, that no sooner had I been introduced to visiting captain David Hookes from Adelaide, than David did the reverse honour, introducing me to my 'home' captain Kim Hughes.

My rapid rise through the ranks to this point was extremely gratifying, though on that memorable day I was under no illusion that, most likely, this would be my personal umpiring zenith. How lucky, then, almost two decades later to be able to look back on seventy-five first-class matches, nine of them Tests, enjoyed from the centre of the nation's major grounds.

My rites of passage traversed the narrow confines of cricket (combined with a little summer tennis and swimming) and Australian Rules (in winter). That pretty much was the thin sporting menu on offer for a boy born in Perth in December 1948.

My first cricket coach, from age ten, was Charlie Bull, a man whose path I would cross many years later in his role as scorer for South Perth Cricket Club and the State team. A right-handed batsman with South Perth, I enjoyed strictly modest success, counting the greatest contribution as perhaps my captaincy, which, in 1964–65, helped us to the under-16s premiership in the Western Australian Cricket Association. South Perth guided me through junior and senior cricket, the younger group being coached by Keith Nordahl, who taught us well, long before coaches became 'accredited'. Keith nurtured two youngsters who went on to Test match cricket: opening batsman Bruce Laird, who played twenty-one Tests for Australia, averaging 35.29; and me, the umpire.

As a kid, every Saturday afternoon in summer was spent at Richardson Park, at first watching South Perth play, then joining in the action. Part of my job as third-grade captain entailed writing reports on the umpires, and having to at least know their names and assess their performance was the beginning of the journey to my cricketing fulfilment.

When, in August 1971, I married Robyn whom I'd met during our days at Applecross Senior High School, I missed one season while we established our new house in the southern Perth suburb of Willetton, and then joined the newly formed Western Australian Institute of Technology (WAIT) Cricket Club where I played six seasons, three of them as captain, in the WA Suburban Turf Cricket Association. Again, I sat in judgement of the umpires' performance, never suspecting the looming reversal of roles when judge would be judged. I still work, as a laboratory technician in the Chemistry Department at Curtin University of Technology (formerly WAIT), but it's a long time since I played.

I well remember going to the WACA in the 1950s and 1960s to watch Western Australia play Shield cricket, knowing I would find my grandmother Ethel Prue sitting at the western end of the Public Stand. Although time clouds the memory, I am sure there was a fascination in watching two blokes in black pants and funny hats marching out to do the same job that junior coaches did in my Saturday morning matches.

After six seasons playing for WAIT, now with two young children and a body that resisted active sport from old football injuries, I decided my playing days were over; the summers would change. Umpiring was a way of retaining contact with the game I loved, and having gotten to know some of the chaps who wore women's bowling hats as part of their uniform in the senior ranks, I decided to join them. Seasons 1978–79 and 1979–80 were spent working in that group, sometimes on my own. But in the second year, with the help of some great colleagues who imparted their knowledge and experience, I ended the season co-umpiring the grade-two final, and was well satisfied.

During the winter of 1980 I decided to 'move on' to WACA cricket, and answered an advertisement to attend a weekend training camp for umpires. On the Friday night I went to the camp site and was welcomed by WA Cricket Umpires' Association members, including the then president, Peter McConnell. Our paths continued to cross, with Peter becoming a Test umpire and mentor to his WA Test successors, Ric Evans and me.

Season 1980–81 was my first in WACA cricket and it was terrific to go to local grounds and see, on the adjacent ovals, State and Test stars under the custodianship of the State's best umpires, including Don Weser, who had umpired Test and one-day internationals. October 1981 brought me my first appointment to first-grade cricket, and I presumed this to be the ultimate. In my own mind, I had 'made it'. Here in my second year in the WACA, I was going to walk out with those who umpired at State, and even national, level. From that first match in 1981 until the grade-one final shared with Ross Emerson in March 2000, I was fortunate never to be 'dropped' from that level of cricket. By 1982–83, my third year in the WACA, I was really into the big time, experiencing the unique, and slightly embarrassing, introduction by David Hookes to my home-State and national captain, Kim Hughes.

In February 1983, I travelled with Colin Bezant by train from Perth to umpire a WA Country XI v. New Zealand match at Northam. Jeremy Coney and Warren Lees left the Kiwis' carriage at the Northam railway station fully kitted out to open the batting (the visitors always batted first in these up-country matches). After the 100-kilometre journey, the Kiwis marched over the road to the match venue, went straight out to the centre where they gave each other guard and were ready to play. It wasn't a match of any great account, and here were two international cricketers ready to enter into the spirit of the day.

In November that year, WA played Pakistan in a first-class fixture with McConnell and Prue again in charge. I relished the experience, absorbing and adopting Peter's philosophy: 'It's not a bad life – start at 11 a.m., finish at 6 p.m., have a couple of beers and go home'. These State matches against touring teams were an ideal introduction to first-class cricket. The basics were just that: play from 11 to 6, with no minimum over requirements. And our role was simple enough: count to six and get the 'ins and outs' right. How different it would be by the year 2000 when umpires had to be concerned with minimum over requirements; penalties for not meeting those requirements; overs to be bowled after a change of innings; the ability to make up lost time and to adjust to vision and concentration under lights; the use of an off-field (third) umpire to adjudicate some decisions using television replays; regular inspections of the match ball; responsibility for enforcing clothing regulations and a behaviour code for players . . . and to still count to six and get the 'ins and outs' right.

Later that summer I was invited to umpire, with Don Weser, my first Sheffield Shield match, Western Australia against Victoria at the WACA. WA was captained by the greatest player I ever 'stood' in a match, Dennis Lillee, and won a hard-fought game by 35 runs. WA, 184 and 284, defeated Victoria, 161 and 272. This was a match in which Victoria should have taken maximum points; the WA scores indicate that. But Lillee, leading by example, had other ideas and constantly reminded the WA players there was a game to be won. His match figures, 19.4–5–46–1 and 28.4–7–63–5, indicated his commitment to that cause.

On 2 January 1988, I was appointed to umpire my first one-day international (ODI) between Australia and Sri Lanka at the WACA, with Peter McConnell, by now an established Test umpire, as my partner. International sport, with the best seat in the house, watching the best players in the game and getting paid for it! I floated through the day well enough to be invited to Sydney for another opportunity at that level, with Australia again playing Sri Lanka. I flew to Sydney, stayed in a five-star hotel and, after meeting a whole host of Sydneysiders, umpired under lights with a partner I had only just met, Steve Randell. Allan Border captained Australia and Ranjan Madugalle led Sri Lanka. Some years later Ranjan returned to Australia as an International Cricket Council (ICC) match referee. Australia won the Perth match very comfortably (7/249 against Sri Lanka's 168), but the Sydney match was close, with Australia getting over the line with just three balls to spare. In my first visit away from the hard and bouncy

WACA, I wondered at fellow West Australian Mike Veletta's constant scratching at the pitch and asked him why he was continually taking guard from me. He told me to watch how the mark he made on the pitch was quickly lost on the dusty surface. No wonder the spinners love it.

By this stage the realisation had dawned on me that to operate at this level, a person needed to know and apply not only the Laws of Cricket, but also know the playing conditions, or rules, for each of the many competitions you were likely to umpire: club two-day and one-dayers, Sheffield Shield, one-day interstate, touring team matches, ODIs and Tests. While some operated under similar rules, none were identical!

In September 1988, I was mightily chuffed to be included by the Australian Cricket Board (ACB) on a nine-man panel to umpire internationals, and so joined Robin Bailhache and Len King (Vic.), Tony Crafter (SA), Ric Evans (WA), Dick French (NSW), Peter McConnell (WA), Steve Randell (Tas.) and Col Timmins (Qld). A few weeks after this promotion, Peter McConnell provided an interesting experience for both of us during the WA v. West Indies match. We went out after lunch on the fourth day and Peter indicated that he wasn't feeling well. The first over was bowled from my end and when it was completed, Peter decided he was unable to continue. Ross Emerson replaced him and for the next forty minutes I stood at the bowler's end, with Ross at square leg. After the drinks interval, it was agreed that Ross could take full responsibility as umpire. This event was frightening for Peter but interesting for me, and to this day I don't know what affected him.

My initiation to Test cricket came on 2 December 1988, when Australia took on the West Indies in the second Test at the WACA. The ACB sensibly chose as my partner Robin

Bailhache, who was standing in his twenty-seventh Test. While I survived the experience, Geoff Lawson used his jaw to stop a Curtly Ambrose delivery and took no further part in the match. In fact, Border declared the innings closed as Lawson was being stretchered from the field. Merv Hughes stepped up and removed Gordon Greenidge first ball in the second innings and then proceeded to bowl 37 overs, taking 8/87 with match figures of 13/217. My raised finger to Merv's roar for lbw against Greenidge at the start of that second innings completed the most convoluted hat-trick in Test history. Big Merv had ended the West Indies' first innings by having Ambrose caught behind with the last ball of his thirty-sixth over, then getting Patrick Patterson caught by Tony Dodemaide with the first ball of his thirty-seventh. In my first Test I'd helped bring about only the nineteenth hat-trick in 111 years of Test cricket, and, remarkably, it followed a hat-trick by Courtney Walsh in the previous Test. Merv was fired up for his hat-trick ball, snorting over the big Zapata moustache, and my memory is that Greenidge simply missed a fast, straight ball that didn't do a lot off the pitch. While the TV commentators were aware of the significance of my decision, the players at the time were blissfully ignorant that Merv had just completed a hat-trick. My wife and three children were sitting in the grandstand and the children were sent to watch the TV replays. The message came back to Robyn, 'Richie [Benaud] said it was out.' So the world was OK! Merv did nothing to acknowledge my decision, other than show Greenidge the direction of the change rooms. I truly didn't mind his ingratitude at my raised finger ensuring his place in hat-trick history, since he was given to kissing and ear-licking in those days. By the time I got to Adelaide for my next match, 'Hat-trick'

T-shirts were being flogged. Discretion precluded me from purchasing. Merv's heroics in Perth couldn't, however, prevent a West Indies win, by 169 runs, on the way to a 3–1 series win.

Robin Bailhache, who returned to Perth for his last ODI on 1 January 1989, was a great source of strength in my first Test and I've no doubt his vast experience and no-nonsense approach helped me then and subsequently. But, sadly, my first Test match was also his last. Five full days on the field and it was time to reflect on umpiring at that level. It had been an intense experience. These people were, after all, playing for their country, and while the injury to Lawson put a dampener on proceedings, I looked forward to more of it.

However, an ODI in Adelaide on 11 December was my next assignment and it was off with Ric Evans to another city for more adventure. Over the next several years I enjoyed travelling around Australia at the invitation of the ACB and was privileged to umpire Test cricket in every mainland State, ODI cricket in all States, and other first-class matches in Newcastle (NSW) and Devonport (Tasmania). Of course, a visit to Canberra for the Prime Minister's match in December 1996 rates very highly, with Mr and Mrs Howard greeting the PM's personal XI and the West Indies at The Lodge on the evening before the match. Allan Border was invited to captain the Australians, but ended up with a broken or damaged finger, while the West Indies' Patterson Thompson injured himself while fielding, dragged himself over the fence and wasn't seen again, not, at least, by the umpires who shared a most enjoyable lunch with the nation's leaders.

The early part of 1990 brought with it a remarkable episode in the serious business of first-class cricket. In February,

Queensland travelled to Perth and, under the captaincy of Greg Ritchie, made 273 in its first innings. This proved to be insufficient with Mark McPhee (113) and Michael Veletta (228) putting on 188 for the first wicket. As the score mounted, Ritchie encouraged Wayne Andrews to declare the WA innings closed and 'make a game of it'. Andrews declined and Ritchie resorted to an 8–1 field with his bowlers aiming wide of the off stump. This was the only time I saw such tactics. WA did declare, at 8/607, and Queensland crumbled to be all out for 157.

The following month WA played SA in the final of the interstate one-day competition in Perth. What a disaster! WA bowled SA out for 87 and made the required runs with about three hours to spare. It was in the days when two white balls were used in each innings, and the square-leg umpire held the ball not in use. As the match went towards its inevitable conclusion, I waited at square leg for David Hookes to throw the ball back to me. He did, eventually, and it landed – 'splat' – in my hands, completely covered in chewing gum. I thanked David and, in his usual laid-back manner, he continued his walk to first slip without a hint of acknowledgement.

The early 1990s was also eventful for another, more personal, reason. On 12 October 1992, Perth's Supreme Court was the scene of a remarkable event in Australian cricket history. It was the first day of a two-week trial in which umpire Peter McConnell and I sued a Sydney newspaper, the *Telegraph Mirror* (Nationwide News Pty Ltd), over an article that appeared on 4 January 1992. I assume we were the first (cricket) umpires to take such action. Len King and Steve Randell pursued the matter in Melbourne and Sydney Courts respectively. Under the headline of 'Aussie Cheats – Test legend hits out at our umpires', the paper accused Australian umpires of bias. The story referred to the views of former Indian captain Sunil Gavaskar and alleged that biased decisions were made in favour of Australian batsmen during the series against India. The opening text of the article read: 'Legendary Indian batsman Sunil Gavaskar has branded Australian umpires as cheats in an amazing outburst in an Indian paper. Gavaskar, who is working as a commentator for Channel Nine during the Indians' tour of Australia, wrote: "Hope readers back home are getting an idea what the India team is up against. Not 11, but 13 players"'. The article contained further quotes from Gavaskar including: 'But then, that is Australian umpiring for you', in relation to some incidents in the third Test which had begun in Sydney on 2 January 1992.

The only umpire named in the article was Tasmanian Steve Randell, but to this stage, Peter (first and third), Steve (first and third), Len (second) and I (second) were the four umpires who had stood in the series. Peter and I risked financial ruin pursuing the matter in the Supreme Court, but the jury found in our favour and we were awarded $25 000 each. However, legal costs consumed all of the award, and more. Peter announced his retirement from umpiring during the trial 'because of the distress caused by the report'. My friend who had been there the first time I walked out into both interstate and international cricket matches was now gone. Len and Steve later settled their actions out of court.

Those two weeks were, without doubt, the most harrowing of my life. My normal lifestyle was completely disrupted and my weekend recreation became non-existent. As a family, I'm glad to say we survived the experience and normal life resumed. I am extremely sad that such a difficult time was imposed on my loved ones, but after being labelled as I was, I felt something had to be done. That sport could extend to these extremes was also sad because I was just a normal person who tried to do his best. I occasionally wonder if the experience also had an effect on my career and, of course, there is no answer. My 'style' did not change and, as any sports official would do, I continued to give decisions as I saw them. What else could I do?

From December 1982 until March 2000, the players, my colleagues and certainly the way umpiring was treated all changed. For Australian cricket, the most significant change was that which arrived on 12 November 1993: the third (TV) umpire was used for the first time in an international match. The venue was the WACA and I was fortunate enough to be given the job of 'third man'. The on-field umpires, Darrell Hair and Tony McQuillan, could request help from me, glued to a TV screen, who would make the decision (on run-out, stumped and hit wicket) using television replays. The third umpire watches the match, *au naturel*, through a closed or open window, and in complete privacy. The room has a television monitor and phone access to the TV director. When called on to make a decision, the third umpire calls the director and the replays begin. After the initial replay, the third man might call for more 'angles'. In the case of close decisions, several replays and even a little rocking backwards and forwards in front of the critical area of action may be necessary. I'd attended a practice session with the then national manager of umpiring, Tony Crafter, the day before the WACA Test with footage from domestic matches earlier that season serving as preparatory 'homework', all of it homing in on the pressing of a green or red button. If the third umpire decides the batsman is out, the red light is displayed; the green light means not out. Should the third umpire be unable to respond, a white light is illuminated, indicating to the on-field umpires that the TV replay system cannot help on this one and they'll have to answer the appeal themselves. After Tony's tuition, I was more than ready for the real thing. And what happened? Five solitary days and not a single call for help from my two colleagues on the ground where New Zealand took a narrow first innings lead and secured an honourable draw.

The expectation of players in all sports is that the umpire will get it right, and cricket had moved to embrace technology to help achieve this. Australia's first innings of the fifth Ashes Test at the WACA in February 1995, ended with Steve Waugh stranded on 99 after a mid-pitch muddle between the twins. As third umpire, I had given 'Junior' (Mark, who was running for the injured Craig McDermott) out by virtue of a run-out after viewing the tape in slow-motion from three angles. The third umpire's room was at ground level at the eastern end of the Farley Stand, and getting to it meant a walk through spectators milling in front of two grandstands. Those people certainly let me know what they thought of my decision; a most unpleasant experience. The photograph in the next day's papers vindicating my call came all too late, but, even before then, there was no doubt in my mind Mark's bat was short of the crease and that use of this technology was thoroughly warranted. It was the only decision I was called on to make over the five days. Australia went on to win by a massive 329 runs, the biggest Ashes victory by a runs margin since 1948.

Over the next few years the scope of decisions for the third umpire increased, and when I retired in March 2000, the game was reaching the point where serious consideration was needed to decide if the limits had been reached. Some would say it has gone too far, some not far enough, and others would abandon it all together and 'allow the two umpires to umpire the game'. The quest to get the decision correct drove the use of technology, at least in international cricket. The philosophy of 'getting the decision correct' has always been there, but we were faced with a different way of doing it. Players accepted this process, and the desire to take the heat out of matches affected by 'crook' decisions has spread among the governing bodies of the ten Test-playing nations. Unfortunately, in recent times we have seen players standing their ground and almost demanding that the decision be referred to the third umpire. The problem is, of course, that the entire television audience, including those at the ground, can watch the slow-motion replays *ad nauseam* and decide whether the umpire is competent or otherwise.

The game's administrators must decide on how far the use of technology will go. At present, I think they have it right. Television will always show the adequacy, or otherwise, of umpires, but its use in decision making can defuse explosive situations.

The cricket community has to decide what is best for the game. At the highest level, technology's cost is not a great consideration, but at lower levels, at which the masses play, the use of technology in every game is most unlikely for the foreseeable future. The person who accepts the role of umpire in a park on a Saturday afternoon is going to have to rely on his or her own ability to make accurate decisions. And surely that is the enjoyment, the challenge, the source of satisfaction; otherwise the umpire becomes a coat hanger and hat stand.

For the 1994–95 season, the ACB experimented with day/night Shield matches. A world-first occurred at the WACA on 24 November when the historic Queensland–WA match began each day at 2.30 p.m. with the setting sun at the action's midpoint. Players and umpires wore traditional clothing, sight-screens were black and the ball yellow. Ric Evans and I were part of this history during which, on one day, play continued until 10.30 p.m., an hour past the scheduled time, to make up for time lost to rain. Playing under these unique conditions, Mike Veletta (95) and Allan Border (73 and 54 not out) were the outstanding performers. Great for them, but most people I spoke to during and after the experiment felt uncomfortable without really being able to say why. The playing of these matches continued for some seasons and was then abandoned.

Curtin University, my employer, was always generous in the help and encouragement it provided me as I pursued my 'other' career. I arrived at the then WAIT in 1970 and have worked as a laboratory technician in chemistry ever since. The university's schedule of examinations in October and November, with a new academic year starting at the end of February, gave me scope for taking various forms of leave to accommodate the two days, Fridays and Mondays, traditionally required for four-day fixtures. With the inevitable changes (a four-day fixture, sometimes in another State, being played from Tuesday to Friday) that were imposed on an umpire, particularly one engaged also in five-day Tests, an obliging employer was needed and the university certainly was that.

In March 1999, when I umpired my fiftieth Shield match, two players I had umpired in my first were there at the Gabba. Shaun Graf, who played for WA that season, was manager of the Victorian side, and Dean Jones sat in the television commentary box. To the best of my knowledge, I joined Steve Randell, Bob Crockett, Ted Wykes, Robin Bailhache, Col Timmins and Max O'Connell in a group who have umpired fifty Sheffield Shield/Pura Cup matches.

I would rather have hung up my Test match counter at a time of my own choosing, but the day arrived in May 1999 when I received a telephone call from the ACB. The national umpires' panel had been reduced from eight to five, and I hadn't made the cut. Since January 1988, I had been a small part of international sport and now it was almost certainly over. I was fifty and, in the jargon of the day, would be seeking 'new challenges'.

Throughout my time at interstate and international level the umpires were appointed, and remunerated, on a match-by-match basis. The ACB put the five members on contracts, not grand by any stretch of the imagination, but a step in a new direction. For some years (since 1994), the ACB had appointed two umpires to the ICC world panel and now it recognised their ability and commitment by putting those two, and three others, in a position, via a more attractive contract, to devote themselves full-time to the job. It had become a meaningful occupation for the elite.

I was fortunate to have been associated with thirty-two colleagues at first-class level and with probably more at club level. I learnt plenty from them; I hope some learnt a little from me. There was lots of fun, lots of pride and, on some days, a little sadness and frustration. The pride was not only in the personal achievements, but in those of my colleagues. In other words, I was always proud of the group I worked with and what the group achieved. The sadness, sometimes annoyance, arose from being human and making decisions that could, and should, have been shown to be incorrect. However, as I said many times to my Perth umpiring colleagues who might have questioned decisions they saw me make: 'The only difference between your decisions and mine is that you can watch mine on television'.

While various ancillaries are required for the game to take place – coaches, administrators, parents, spectators (optional) and umpires – cricket is a game for people to play and the focus should always be on the players and their achievements. I was fortunate to see some of the game's outstanding players. To compile a list of my World or Australian XIs would be to invite unkindness to so many. The West Indian side of November 1988, in batting order, read: Greenidge, Haynes, Richardson, Hooper, Richards, Logie, Dujon, Marshall, Ambrose, Walsh and Patterson. Not a bad line-up and, arguably, close to a World XI of its day. Apart from the outstanding feats of Merv Hughes against that side, as indicated, I was given the opportunity to see, almost at their elbow, Allan Border hit his 10 000th Test match run (against the West Indies in Sydney); Mark Waugh make his Test debut with 138 against England in Adelaide; eighteen-year-old Sachin Tendulkar score an 'effortless' 114 against Australia in Perth; David Boon score 149 against the West Indies in Sydney; Malcolm Marshall record 31–16–29–5 against Australia in Sydney; and Border, again, return match figures of 44.4–13–96–11 with his left-arm orthodox spin against the West Indies in Sydney. In December 1990, with Ric Evans, I watched Mark Waugh (229 not out) and Steve Waugh (216 not out) score a world-record fifth-wicket partnership of 464 for NSW against WA at the WACA. Steve is alleged to have expressed annoyance that they hadn't actually gone on with it! The comment, if true, served as a portent of the ruthless reign of Mark Taylor's successor.

But without doubt, the most remarkable event I witnessed occurred during the grade-one final of the WACA pennant competition in 1998–99. Matthew Garnaut (127 not out) and Brett Mulder (70 not out) shared a competition record tenth-wicket partnership of 177 to steer Bayswater–Morley to a most unlikely win over Midland–Guildford. The scoreline: Midland–Guildford, 329 and 194, lost to Bayswater–Morley, 196 and 331/9. Garnaut and Mulder came together thirty-five minutes before tea on the fourth day, and after the break I asked Mulder, 'What's the plan?' It was that they'd 'hang around for a while and make Midland–G. wait a little longer for the flag'. In mid-afternoon my eldest son, Travis, who was holidaying with our family at Mandurah, a seaside town an hour's drive south of Perth, turned on the radio to listen to the match broadcast and heard music playing. Naturally, he assumed the game was over. In fact, Travis had turned on in the tea break and Dad, whom they'd expected to see by 4 p.m., arrived after 7 p.m., still 'high' on the adrenaline of the 169-minute, last-wicket hijacking of a match seemingly well and truly lost.

Change is inevitable in life, but I think I saw more change in cricket over the twenty-year span of my involvement with the WACA and ACB than the game has undergone in any two consecutive decades of its centuries-old history. In the near future, Tests will be controlled by two visiting umpires chosen from a new elite group. I hope they are able to enjoy their umpiring as much as I did.

TERRY PRUE'S UMPIRING CV

75 first-class matches between November 1983 and March 2000

Also nine matches as third [TV] umpire

Official Test matches – 9 (Australia v. West Indies 4, England 1, India 2, South Africa 2)

Sheffield Shield / Pura Cup – 54 (plus three as third [TV] umpire)

Other first-class – 12 (WA v. Pakistan 3, West Indies 3, New Zealand 2, England 2; Tasmania v. South Africa; Victoria v. England)

One-day internationals – 39 (plus four involving Australia A in the quadrangular series of 1994–95, and six as third [TV] umpire)

Acknowledgements and Photographic Credits

The publisher is grateful to the following writers, agents, publishers and copyright holders for permission to reproduce their work in this book:

Dickie Bird, extract from *Dickie Bird: My Autobiography* (Hodder and Stoughton) 1997. Reprinted by permission of Hodder and Stoughton Limited.

Mike Coward, extract from *Calypso Summer* (ABC Books) 2000. Reprinted by permission of ABC Books.

Alan Hurst, extract from the *Bendigo Advertiser*, 2000. Reprinted by permission of the *Bendigo Advertiser*.

Mark Taylor, extract from *Mark Taylor: A Captain's Year* (Ironbark) 1997. Reprinted by permission of John Fordham, the Fordham Company Pty Ltd.

Photograph of Robin Bailhache watching a Kim Hughes catch reproduced by permission of News Limited.

Photograph of Robin Bailhache with Tom Brooks reproduced by permission of Moss Seigert

Photograph of Richie Benaud taken from *Benaud*, by A. G. Moyes (Angus & Robertson) 1962. Reproduced by permission of HarperCollins.

Photograph of Jack Collins reproduced by permission of the Herald & Weekly Times Photographic Collection.

Photograph of Steve Dunne with Daryl Harper reproduced by permission of Moss Seigert.

Photograph of John Dyson reproduced by permission of the Herald & Weekly Times Photographic Collection.

Photograph of Alan Hurst reproduced by permission of the Herald & Weekly Times Photographic Collection.

Photograph of Mel Johnson and Dick French reproduced by permission of Moss Seigert.

Photograph of Mel Johnson at the Ian Healy testimonial match reproduced by permission of Just Photography.

Photograph of Terry Prue watching Merv Hughes bowl reproduced by permission of Western Australia News Photographic Collection.

Photograph of Terry Prue with Darrell Hair, Daryl Harper and reproduced by permission of R. G. Hann & Associates.

Photograph of Terry Prue with Steve Davis reproduced by permission of Moss Seigert.

Photograph of Ian Redpath taken from *Always Reddy*, by Ian Redpath with Neill Phillipson (Garry Sparke & Associates) 1976. Reproduced by permission of Garry Sparke.

Photograph of Mark Taylor reproduced by permission of Getty Images.

Photograph of Mark Taylor and team-mates reproduced by permission of Getty Images.

Photograph of Rex Whitehead and Tony Crafter reproduced by permission of Moss Seigert.

Photograph of Rex Whitehead at Adelaide Oval reproduced by permission of Moss Seigert.